OSHUN'S
DAUGHTERS

OSHUN'S DAUGHTERS

The Search for

WOMANHOOD

in the

AMERICAS

VANESSA K. VALDÉS

Published by State University of New York Press, Albany
© 2014 State University of New York

For information, contact State University of New York Press, Albany, NY
www.sunypress.edu
Production by Ryan Morris
Marketing by Anne M. Valentine.

Library of Congress Cataloging-in-Publication Data

Valdés, Vanessa Kimberly.
  Oshun's daughters : the search for womanhood in the Americas / Vanessa
K. Valdés.
       pages   cm
  Includes bibliographical references and index.
  ISBN 978-1-4384-5042-1 (paperback : alk. paper)
  ISBN 978-1-4384-5043-8 (hardcover : alk. paper) 1. Women and literature—
America.   2. Yoruba (African people) in literature.   3. African diaspora.
4. Women in literature.   5. Cuban literature—Women authors—History and
criticism.   6. Brazilian literature—Women authors—History and criticism.
7. Yoruba (African people)—Cuba. 8. Yoruba (African people)—Brazil. I. Title.
  PN56.3.A45V35 2014
  809'.89287097--dc23

                                                           2013017499
                    10 9 8 7 6 5 4 3 2 1

This work is dedicated to
Robert Valdes Jr., con todo mi cariño,
and to Rose Donegan Bess (Miss Rose),
without whose generosity of protective space
and love this work would not have been produced

＞ ＊ ＜

Contents

Acknowledgments

First and foremost, I thank God for all of His blessings, for His angels and spirit guides. I thank my ancestors who accompany me on this journey, and the *orishas*, for providing me with their guidance, love, and support. I thank my parents, Robert Valdes Jr. and Iris Delia Colón Valdes, for their love and support. I thank my godmother, mi madrina, minha mãe-de-santo, my best friend Gina Bonilla, without whose love, generosity, and guidance this truly would not have been possible. I thank Leroy Martin Bess for his love and generosity; Mercedes Emilia Robles for her nourishment; and Marty, my godfather Martin Skolnick, for always being there. Thank you to the friends I've made over the years, for your kindness, laughter, and love.

I thank the staff of the State University of New York Press, especially my acquisitions editor, Beth Bouloukos, who gave unparalleled support for this project. I thank the anonymous readers whose comments prompted me to strengthen the manuscript by reconsidering the impact of the historical moment on all of these writers. Thank you to production editor Ryan Morris and copy editor Alan V. Hewat, for all of your work in making this book what it is. Thank you also to Philip Pascuzzo for a beautiful cover.

I have had the honor of spending seven years as an assistant professor at The City College of New York, the flagship school of the City University of New York system. I thank my students, past and present, who have allowed me to live my dream as an educator, and I thank my colleagues for their support throughout the years, especially Geraldine Murphy, Harriet Alonso, Richard Calichman, Silvia Burunat, Dulce García, Bettina Lerner, Corinna Messina-Kosciuba, and Regina Castro McGowan. Also, I would be remiss if I did not mention CUNY's Future Faculty Preparation Program, and my cohort of Spring 2010 specifically, led by Shelly Eversley: Maria Bellamy, Jason Frydman, Amy Moorman Robbins, Jody Rosen and Charity Scribner. Thank you for your insight.

The seeds of this book were planted long before I can remember: I would read poems and novels and recognize passing references to these religious traditions without any understanding or depth of knowledge. Years later, as a graduate student, Earl E. Fitz recommended that I read Helena Parente Cunha's *A Mulher no Espelho*: it is the only research that survives from my dissertation, as the rest was left behind to make room for this new project. I thank him for introducing me to this text, as well as for his initial words of encouragement oh so long ago. I thank his colleagues at Vanderbilt University's Department of Spanish and Portuguese, especially William Luis, Benigno Trigo, Cathy L. Jrade, Emanuelle Oliveira, and Marshall Eakin of the Department of History, for their faith in me. William deserves special mention for seeing the potential in me as an undergraduate at Yale and for encouraging me to pursue my studies on the graduate level at Vanderbilt.

I thank the community of scholars examining the representations of these religions in literature, some of whom include Henry Louis Gates Jr., Julia Cuervo Hewitt, LaVinia Delois Jennings, Robert Farris Thompson, Theresa Washington, and Donna Aza Weir-Soley. The publication of their work meant the creation of space for mine.

An earlier version of chapter 4 was originally published as "The Voice of Oxum: *Mulher no Espelho* (1983)," in *PALARA* 13 (Fall 2009): 102–12. In addition, support for this project was provided by a PSC-CUNY Award, jointly funded by The Professional Staff Congress and The City University of New York.

The Call

Hearing the Flow of the River

for we are all children of Eshu
god of chance and the unpredictable
and we each wear many changes
inside of our skin.
                    —Audre Lorde, "Between Ourselves"

Oshun's Daughters: The Search for Womanhood in the Americas examines the ways in which the inclusion of African diasporic religious practices serves as a transgressive tool in narrative discourses in the Americas. This study analyzes several representative novels and poems in an effort to understand contemporary representations of womanhood in the United States, Cuba, and Brazil. All of these works prominently feature protagonists who engage with variations of traditional Yoruba religion, an alternate religious system that survived the African slave trade and is often marginalized in the Americas. Blended with Catholicism in the New World, it is known as *Regla de Ocha, Lucumí,* or *Santería*[1] in the Spanish Caribbean and the United States, and *Candomblé Nagô* in Brazil.

There are a number of religions that were transported to the Western Hemisphere during the four centuries of the Middle Passage. These include, but are not limited to: *Vodou,* the religion of the Fon people of Dahomey, now Benin, transported to Haiti; *Regla de Palo Monte Mayombe,* an umbrella term for the Afro-Cuban religions that derive from the Kongo religion of the Bakongo people; *Obeah,* the creolized practices derived from the traditional religions of the Ashanti, practiced

1

in the British West Indies; *Quimbois*, the *Obeah*-related practice found in Martinique and Guadeloupe; and *Umbanda* and *Macumba*, creolized practices that combine *Candomblé* with Spiritism in Brazil. This study focuses on the representation of spiritual systems practiced by the largest group to arrive in the Spanish Caribbean and Brazil, the Yoruba (*los yoruba* in Spanish, *iorubá* or *nagô* in Brazilian Portuguese). This religious system, like many African spiritual practices, offers a different epistemology than that of what has been identified as European rationalism; this system of knowledge is more holistic in that it places importance on both the physical and metaphysical. There is no difference between the sacred and the secular within this system of thought, given that everything is imbued with the spirit of God. Binaries that dominate European thought (man/woman; mind/body; light/dark; good/evil) do not function in the same way within these religious systems, as the emphasis is not on extremes but on balancing these radical differences, on reconciling them.

Involvement with these African diasporic religions therefore provides alternative models of womanhood that differ substantially from those found in dominant Western patriarchal culture, namely, that of virgin, asexual wife/mother, and whore. Within traditional Yoruba religion and their syncretized variations found in the Western Hemisphere, we find images of the sexual woman, who enjoys her body without any sense of shame; the mother who nurtures her children without sacrificing herself; the warrior woman who actively resists demands that she conform to one-dimensional stereotypes of womanhood. In spite of differences in age, language, and nationality, all of the writers in this study are engaged in a project that spans the entirety of the Americas: they all turn to these diasporic religions as a source of inspiration for creating more full portraits of womanhood.

In her recent study *Yoruba Traditions and African American Religious Nationalism* (2012), Tracey Hucks notes: "The ways African Americans in North America and other global practitioners of Afro-Atlantic Yoruba religions create meaning is extremely diverse. Therefore, studies of the various groups (even intragroups) must always be historicized, contextualized, and localized" (4). There is no one single "correct" interpretation of these religious traditions, and no single one is more true than the other; instead, one understands that these spiritual systems have changed over the last centuries due to numerous circumstances, not the least of which include migration and persecution, both on the African continent itself as well as in the Americas. Hucks goes on to explain her inclusion of the term *diasporic* when referring to spiritual systems that have thrived in the Americas:

> From the standpoint of a religious historian, I use the categorical designator—*African diasporic* religious traditions—that speaks with greater precision to the historical processes of dispersed African communities and the diversity of innovative practices that attempted to localize and traditionalize throughout North America, South America, and the Caribbean without having to engage the labyrinthic conundrum of quantifying Africanity. *African diasporic* religions make the category of *African* much more fluid and receptive to flexible interpretations and point the reader to historical processes without the weighty conclusions and assertions of African-*derived*, African-*inspired*, and African-*based*. (5–6)

The use of the latter three terms privileges "Africa," communicating a sense of retention within these traditions à la anthropologist Melville J. Herskovits, as if this place was a homogenous zone with one single culture. As Cuban poet Nancy Morejón states: "The history of the African continent has been plagued by thousands of tribal conflicts. Only in America could Africa become a symbol of unity, due to the diaspora its descendants interwove in search of their liberation."[2] Recent studies about the representation of these religions in literature note that for many writers of the Americas who invoke Africa in their works, "Africa" is an imagined concept independent of the lived reality on the continent. In her 2009 study on the usage of the term in Spanish Caribbean literature, Julia Cuervo Hewitt writes: "[There is the] notion of an Africanness in the Caribbean that comes from Africa, but that no longer is African" (20). Instead, it is something different and new, a separate identity distinct from the original cultures.

The inclusion of these entities in cultural production across the Americas leads one to reconsider the definitions of diaspora identity. In his essay "Cultural Identity and Diaspora," Stuart Hall puts forth: "Diaspora identities are those which are constantly producing and reproducing themselves anew, through transformation and difference" (235). Writing along these lines is Emma Pérez, who notes: "The diasporic subject is not only here and there...but more, much more, is always re-creating the unimagined, the unknown, where mobile third space identities thrive, and where the decolonial imaginary gleans the diasporic's subjecthood" (79). She continues: "Diasporic subjectivity is always in movement, disrupting, re-creating, and mobile in its representation, converging the past, with the present for a new future." (79). These writers have revealed that within their own societies, the allegiance to a diaspora interrupts metanarratives of the founding of nations. There is a larger allegiance possible, one that harkens back to an epistemology often overlooked and ignored by writers and thinkers who have been educated in the tradition of the Enlightenment.

A Distinct Epistemology

A defining characteristic of postmodernism is fragmentation, the notion that there is no "knowable" integrated, unified self; instead, there is the splintered subject, each piece of the self coexisting, without any need to make these fragments come together in a cohesive sense. Though accepted by many literary scholars to be a "true" description of subject formation, the development of this train of thought must itself be understood as a product of its historical context: postmodernism arose in the first decades of the twentieth century in the aftermath of widespread destruction caused by wars that had transgressed national boundaries primarily on the European continent. Imperial powers that had deemed themselves to be the arbiters of civilization had revealed a penchant for annihilation, not only of the populations of supposedly savage territories they had conquered and rescued from such barbarity but indeed of each other. In the aftermath of these atrocities, it became conventional wisdom to believe that the attempt to make sense of one's self was futile: it was thought that one could never understand the unconscious motivations of the human subject and so it was useless to attempt to do so. One must recognize that this is the latest manifestation of thought whose roots are in the Cartesian division of the subject whereby thought was equated with being, thereby elevating thinking and the rational as the sole manner in which one can know and therefore assign meaning.

This study unequivocally rejects such a division because it is not the epistemology found in either traditional African religions or those spiritual systems that developed in the African Diaspora found in the

Americas. In fact, this train of thought goes against Yoruba philosophy. In her study on the modern construction of gender in Western Africa, Oyèrónké Oyěwùmí writes:

> More fundamentally, the distinction between Yorùbá and the West symbolized by the focus on different senses in the apprehension of reality involves more than perception—for the Yorùbá, and indeed many other African societies, it is about a "particular presence in the world—a world conceived of as a whole in which all things are linked together." It concerns the many worlds human beings inhabit; it does not privilege the physical world over the metaphysical. A concentration on vision as the primary mode of comprehending reality promotes what can be seen over that which is not apparent to the eye; it misses the other levels and the nuances of existence. (14)

The epistemology that informs the *Regla de Ocha* religion and *Candomblé Nagó* is one that acknowledges all life (plant, animal, human, physical, and metaphysical) to be interconnected. Both the physical and metaphysical realms of existence influence human beings. Postmodernist conceptions of fragmentation therefore have no place within this system of thought, where it is conceivable, indeed desirable, to make sense of oneself as an entire self. This is not to suggest that there are no conceptions of contradiction or incongruity within the human psyche; on the contrary, there is simply an acknowledgment and acceptance of human beings as whole beings possessing traits that may be deemed "good" and "bad." There is no castigation of those undesirable qualities, as under Christian thought, which urges practitioners to aspire to the ways of Jesus Christ, the Virgin Mary, and for Catholics, the saints, those paragons of virtue that seemingly have few faults or frailties. Instead, we learn through the parables of oral tradition that the entities that guide and assist human beings in their journeys through life also exhibit characteristics and traits that are both desirable and undesirable; as Dominique Zahan notes, "In traditional religions the believers and the Supreme Being in whom they believe share the same advantages and disadvantages, the same rights and the same duties."[3] Within Christianity, salvation exists outside of one's self; within traditional African religions and African diasporic religions, it is attainable in the present through the efforts one makes while alive: "the preoccupation of 'believers' consists here not in the handing over of their redemption to a transcendent being but in their taking upon themselves their own redemption by appropriate spiritual techniques."[4] The novels and poems under examination in this study are representative, therefore, of texts that reveal this spiritual consciousness.

In her essay, "Rootedness: The Ancestor as Foundation," Toni Morrison writes: "It is indicative of the cosmology, the way in which Black people looked at the world. We are very practical people, very down-to-earth, even shrewd people. But within that practicality we also accepted what I supposed could be called superstition and magic, which is another way of knowing things" (61). For Morrison, then, an indicator of Blackness for peoples of African descent in the United States is this legacy of balancing the natural and the supernatural. While the assignment of color to these values is problematic, it is indicative of U.S. society, where Blackness is equated with all that is African. Nevertheless, Morrison underscores the existence of a value system that is retained within the African American community and, I would add, to many populations of African descent throughout the diaspora, which is distinct from what has been identified as Western patriarchal thought, those discourses and ideologies that have their origins in the Age of Reason in Western Europe and have been subsequently codified. According to the cosmology found in Western Africa in particular, the aim of human life is to achieve a balance with all of these spheres while also understanding and realizing the destiny of each individual.

Gender as conceived within patriarchy, that is, female as derivative of, and subordinate to male, has no place in traditional Yorùbá thought. On the contrary, both sexes were valued in and of themselves; that is, each has both strengths and witnesses, and those qualities were not subject to the judgment of either good or bad. Oyeronke Olajubu writes: "Prominent in Yoruba philosophy and religion is the need for a balance between female and male principles, a notion informed by the assumption that the sexes are interdependent. Principles of oppression and domination were therefore not accommodated in the people's conception of reality" (21). The cosmology that informs these religious systems is one that has as a guiding principle the harmony of all elements of life: there is an acknowledgment of gender roles as well as a respect for the biological differences of men and women.[5] This is evident not only in the recorded histories of these peoples but also in their religious beliefs.

The novels and poems of these women writers reveal that fundamental in the subject formation of their protagonists is their spirituality. The sacred is ignored within a theoretical tradition that fragments the subject into opposing units such as mind/body, and that deems the spiritual as irrelevant because it is not something that can be proven to exist by logic or reason. Nevertheless, these literary works strongly suggest the need for its consideration when examining the subjectivity of men and women of African descent. Spiritual practice would therefore join other categories such as race, class, gender, and sexuality as the lens through which one understands the development of the subject in literature.

Select Tenets of African Diasporic Religions within the Yoruba Tradition

While this study is neither an interrogation of these religions nor an inquiry into the validity of the practices of these belief systems, it is important to provide a brief introduction to the principles with which the authors of these works are at least minimally conversant. Most African belief systems place emphasis on the presence of the ancestors, spirits who guide and protect living beings in the physical realm. (In Yoruba, they are referred to as *egungun*, in Spanish they are *egun*, and in Portuguese one will see both terms used.) This motif is found in literatures throughout the Americas: in Toni Morrison's estimation, an evaluation of black literature necessarily includes verifying the representation of an ancestor ("Rootedness" 61). She defines these presences as a: "sort of timeless people whose relationships to characters are benevolent, instructive, and protective, and they provide a certain kind of wisdom" (62). As presences closer to the Supreme Being, they have an access to knowledge that living beings, often limited by their capacities, do not, lending them an omniscience normally attributed solely to God in a Judeo-Christian context. Interaction with these presences (through prayer, for example) grants humans living in the natural world entrée to this knowledge; they can therefore gain understanding of past events that had previously been unrevealed to them.[6] In common parlance, they act as guardian angels, guiding their loved ones to make correct decisions. Contact with one's ancestors is also a means by which to pay homage to the family members who have come before the present grouping, and serves as recognition of the love and sacrifice made for the betterment of each subsequent generation. In many of the works in this study, protagonists interact with ancestral figures who are present in various forms: in the living memories of the characters, who recall conversations they had with relatives deceased in the present moment of the novel; as an older wise person who offers advice, the living ancestor; as deceased family members who communicate in spirit form.

In addition to an examination of the presentation of the ancestors, this analysis focuses on the presentation of the *orishas* (an approximation of the Yoruba word *orişa*, which in Spanish is represented as *oricha,* and in Portuguese *orixá*). Both the ancestors and the *orishas* serve as intercessors between Olodumare (Olorun in Brazil), who is God, the Creator, and humanity. The *orishas* are the spiritual entities endowed by God to be recipients of *aşe,* defined by Robert Farris Thompson in *Flash of the Spirit* (1984) as "spiritual command, the power-to-make-things-happen, God's own enabling light rendered accessible to men and women" (7). They are often associated with aspects of nature. Eshu-Elegbara (Elegba/Eleggua and Eshu in *Regla de Ocha,* Exu in *Candomblé Nagó*) is the first entity to be acknowledged in religious ceremony; analyses of these spiritual systems often follow suit and continue this practice. He is the guardian of the crossroads, the entity to whom practitioners dedicate every beginning and end of every ceremony. The crossroads is a reference to destiny itself, to the four cardinal directions of north, south, east, and west. In his seminal study *The Signifying Monkey: A Theory of African-American Literary Criticism* (1989), Henry Louis Gates writes:

> Each version of Esu is the sole messenger of the gods (in Yoruba, *iranse*), he who interprets the will of the gods to man; he who carries the desires of man to the gods. Esu is the guardian of the crossroads, master of style and of stylus, the phallic god of generation and fecundity, master of that elusive, mystical barrier that separates the divine world from the profane. (6)

He is the liminal figure between the heavens and earth, between humanity and Olodumare, the Supreme Power, and as such is the primary intercessor which practitioners consult when they are to make significant steps in their lives. Through interaction with him, one "cultivate[s] the art of recognizing significant communications, knowing what is truth and what is falsehood, or else the lessons of the crossroads—the point where doors open or close, where persons have to make decisions that may forever after affect their lives—will be lost" (Thompson 19). Communication with Eshu therefore signifies an attempt at learning to live according to one's destiny in the face of the uncertainty of life.

The title of this study refers to the Yoruba spiritual entity found throughout the Americas, in all of her permutations, as that which encompasses the female element, femininity, all that has to do with womanhood. In Yorubaland, she is known as Ọṣun; in Cuba, Ochún/Oshún; in Brazil, Oxum.[7] In their collection of essays about this entity, *Òsun across the Waters: A Yoruba Goddess in Africa and the Americas* (2001), Joseph M. Murphy and Mei-Mei Sanford reject unambiguously her demotion to the African equivalent of Venus or Aphrodite (1). They write: "These ethnocentric and reductive views fail to reflect the centrality and authority of Ọṣun in Yoruba religious thought and practice. Neither do they convey the multidimensionality of her power: political, economic, divinatory, maternal, natural, therapeutic" (1). They underscore not only the importance of this entity but also her critical significance in the entirety of Yoruba thought. Deidre Badejo dedicates a volume to the study of this entity; in *Òsun Sèègesi: The Elegant Deity of Wealth, Power, and Femininity* (1996) she describes her as

> a powerful woman, the owner of the beaded comb, Ṣèègèsí, which she uses to part the pathways to human and divine existence. . . . She is the giver of children, the leader of the àjé (powerful beings), a wealthy and beautiful woman, an herbalist and dyer. The symbolism and, therefore, the meaning of Ọṣun is complicated by her uncompromising femininity, for Ọṣun loves bathing in cool waters, pampering herself with fragrant soaps and oils, and wearing and changing her elegant clothing several times a day. . . . [W]e learn that her uncompromising femininity is an aspect of her innate, uncompromising powers, that she is a warrior-woman and protectress of the covenants by which the àjé ensnarl and release their victims, that she is a consummate being. (1)

Oshun is affiliated with sweet waters, specifically with rivers. Robert Farris Thompson relates the story found in divination literature of how she fell in love with Ṣàngó, lived in his brass palace, gave birth to twins, and accumulated a wealth of jewelry, which she took with her to the bottom of the river after her death (79). While her beauty and wealth make this figure enviable (and subject to comparisons with Aphrodite and Venus), she also has other characteristics: "her masculine prowess in war; her skill in the art of mixing deadly potions, of using knives as she flies through the night. . . . But Oshun's darker side is ultimately protective of her people" (80). Her love for her children, those who are consecrated to her and who have identified her as their primary guardian *orisha*, is incredibly protective and all-consuming. In each of these novels, the female protagonists and poetic voices all search for a definition of womanhood that corresponds with their own sensibilities rather than characterizations offered by the societies in which they live. It is for this reason that the title of the study proclaims that they are daughters of Oshun; indeed, all women, as per traditional Yoruba thought, are her daughters.

In addition to Oshun, there are *orishas* that are often mentioned in the novels and poems studied here; the first is Yemọja (Yemanyá in *Regla de Ocha*, Yemanjá/Iemanjá in *Candomblé Nagó*). The entity associated with salted waters (oceans) and with motherhood, Yemọja is the mother of all the *orishas*. She is identified with the Ogun River in West Africa, and represents reproduction as well as conception and growth. Oya (Oyá in *Regla de Ocha* and Iansã in *Candomblé Nagó*) is affiliated with lightning and the whirlwind. A consort of Ṣango, she is his female complement and his companion, a warrior in her own right who fights beside him. She guards the gates of the underworld, and is charged with assisting in the transition from life to death. She is the Mistress of Iku (Death), and has an intimate relationship with the *egungun*, the ancestors. The entity associated with the Niger River in Western Africa, Oya signifies transformation and change.

All of these female entities, in addition to their primary significations, are portrayed as warrior women in the *patakis* (short stories that offer lessons to the audience) of the religion. These three *orishas*, whom Thompson names the "riverain goddesses," all are fiercely protective of themselves and their children. He writes:

Imperially presiding in the palaces beneath the sands at the bottom of the river, the riverain goddesses are peculiarly close to Earth. In the positive breeze of their fans, the ripple of their water, there is coolness. In the darkness of their depths and in the flashing of their swords, there is witchcraft. And within the shell-strewn floor of their underwater province there is bounteous wealth. Yoruba riverain goddesses are therefore not only the arbiters of happiness of their people but militant witches. . . . But this is power used against the human arrogance of Western technocratic structures. The natural goodness within the evil of these water spirits is invoked by righteous devotion. (75)

This is a significant departure from the primary female images offered by Christianity, which consist mainly of Eve, the Virgin Mary, and Mary Magdalene: these images focus on sexuality and betrayal or the converse of self-sacrifice and obedience. Archetypes, they offer simple one-dimensional images of femininity, whereas the traditional religious system of the Yoruba is composed of rich and complex images of entities that are beautiful, wealthy, fierce, sexual, and all warriors.

The authors also make reference to male *orishas* in addition to Eshu, primary among them being Ṣàngó and Ọbàtálá. Ṣàngó (Shangó/Changó in *Regla de Ocha* and Xangô in *Candomblé Nagô*), the primary consort of Oshun and the embodiment of masculine energy, is affiliated with thunder, lightning, and storms. In the introduction to a collection of essays dedicated to this figure, *Ṣàngó in Africa and the African Diaspora* (2009), Joel E. Tishken, Tóyìn Fálọlá, and Akíntúndé Akínyẹmí write: "Ṣàngó is the most powerful and the most feared Yorùbá deity both in Africa and in the Diaspora" (2). They go on to explain that the most prominent image of this entity is that of an emperor of the Ọyọ Empire, a formidable warrior who at his death became an *orisha*. Ọbàtálá (Obatalá in *Regla de Ocha* and Oxalá in *Candomblé Nagô*) is the king of white cloth, the literal translation of his name. One of the oldest *orishas*, he represents clarity, lucidity, purity, and peace. He is the owner of all heads, the head being the site of one's destiny, one's *ori*. By including these figures into their works, the writers of this study all interrupt narrative discourse, infusing their novels and poems with meanings that are obscured by historical attempts to end these religious practices through years of persecution and marginalization of practitioners.[8]

Those unaware of Yoruba traditional religions and their syncretized forms of *Regla de Ocha* and *Candomblé Nagó* in the Americas have been unable to decipher these religious codes as they appear in literature.[9] All of these writers include representations of these spiritual entities in order to amplify the representations of womanhood in their works, revealing different possibilities of female identity.

Though outside the parameters of this study, male authors across the Americas also include these entities in their works. In his essay, "Religion and Art in Afro-Brazilian Cultural Experience" (1976), Abdias do Nascimento writes: "In *Candomblé* the paragons of white power and culture, which for four centuries have enriched themselves on the product of African sweat and blood, have no place and no validity" (155). Poet, actor, playwright, director, sculptor, painter, educator, and later, politician, Nascimento is the man largely responding for the raising of black consciousness in Brazil. For him, this specific religious system (not their more syncretized variants of *Macumba and Umbanda*) best preserves the spiritual values of the Afro-Brazilian community; this in spite of centuries of legal persecution and harassment by the Brazilian government. This system, then, is one that enriches the creation of art in all of its forms: "[A]rt has functioned as a spiritual force which sustains, to whatever extent possible, the identity and visibility of the African in Brazil, unalienated from his existential self and his original culture" (151).

Nascimento's assertion is shared by other male writers of African descent: his compatriot Antônio Olinto is the author of *Casa d'Agua* (1969), the story of a family of emancipated slaves who return to Nigeria from Brazil at the end of the nineteenth century. Based on historical fact,[10] the novel includes rituals from *Candomblé* and is written in a style that reproduces the *oriki*, a traditional Yoruba poetic form that conveys lore, traditional values, and history. He continues this novel with two others, *O Rei de Keto* (1980) and *Trono de Vidro* (1987), to complete his trilogy. Jorge Amado features allusions to this religious tradition in a number of his works, including his most famous novel, *Gabriela, cravo e canela* (1959). Colombian writer Manuel Zapata Olivella's magnum opus, *Changó el gran putas* (1983), a translation of which, *Changó, the Biggest Badass*, was published in 2010 in the United States, retells the history of the Americas using as a protagonist the entity associated with justice and whose symbols are thunder and lightning. Alejo Carpentier began his career with examinations of African contributions to Cuban culture; inspired by the events of the Haitian Revolution, he wrote *El reino de este mundo* (1949). U.S. author Ishmael Reed published his novel *Mumbo Jumbo* in 1972, a work that highlights Papa Legba, Vodou's entity that guards the crossroads (and the Fon equivalent of Eshu-Elegbara); Reed recounts historical moments of the African American experience from the perspective of the entity of crossroads. In at least two of the plays that are part of his Pittsburgh Cycle, *Joe Turner's Come and Gone* (1984) and *The Piano Lesson* (1990), U.S. playwright August Wilson included allusions to traditional African religious practices. Nobel Laureate Derek Walcott represents these religious traditions throughout his work, including his epic poem *Omeros* (1990). The protagonist of Ernesto Quiñonez's second novel, *Chango's Fire* (2005), struggles between his Pentecostal upbringing and his attraction for Regla de Ocha. Alex Espinoza sets his first novel, *Still Water Saints* (2007), in a Los Angeles botánica, positing this religious goods space as the center of the local community. In his Pulitzer Prize–winning novel, *The Brief and Wondrous Life of Oscar Wao* (2008), Junot Diaz includes allusions to these entities to describe specifically two of his female characters, the mother and sister of the protagonist, Oscar. Barbadian poet Kamau Brathwaite has published *Elegguas* (2010), a collection that calls on the entity of the crossroads and that also serves as an elegy to his dead wife, whose presence he calls upon in an act of homage that recalls the veneration of ancestors that is present throughout the African Diaspora.

Also outside the scope of this study is the representation of African diasporic religions, namely, *Vodou*, within the French and Creole-speaking world and its diasporas. Prominent in these novels, short stories, and poems is the figure of Erzulie, the entity associated with sweet waters, fertility, love, and abundance. Writers such as Toni Morrison, Edwidge Danticat, Paule Marshall, Gloria Naylor, and Gayl Jones all include her in their works. Other writers who incorporate *Vodou* are Léon-Gontran Damas, Lilas Desquiron, Wilson Harris, and Dany Laferrière, These entities some time also appear in works by Dominican and Dominican American authors, such as *El hombre del acordeón* (2003) by Marcio Veloz Maggiolo and *Erzulie's Skirt* (2006) by Ana-Maurine Lara; the latter is one of the few, if not the only, fictional work that presents lesbian protagonists and their relationship with Erzulie. These lists reveal the richness of the subject: men and women across the Americas and across cultural and linguistic traditions are invoking these entities, recalling epistemologies that allow for fuller definitions of both manhood and womanhood.

Advances in the Global Women's Movement

The novels and poems chosen for this study were produced in the last four decades of the twentieth century and the first of the twenty-first century, in the aftermath of significant gains made in the international Women's Rights Movement. Building upon the work of activists from the previous century who had pushed for the suffrage to be extended to women, as well as antiwar activists and civil rights activists, the 1960s and 1970s saw continued strides toward women's equality not only within the United States but throughout the Americas. In the United States, the decades subsequent to the extension of the vote to women in 1920 saw the first woman to serve in the presidential cabinet, Frances Perkins under President Franklin D. Roosevelt (followed by women in every succeeding administration with the exception of presidents Kennedy and Johnson); women working as leaders of the civil rights movement (1940s and 1950s); the legalization of birth control (1965); the founding of the National Organization of Women (1966); the election of Shirley Chisholm, the first black woman to Congress (1968); the declaration of no-fault divorce laws in 1969 in California; the Equal Opportunity Employment Act and Title IX (1972); the first black woman, Shirley Chisholm, to run for the U.S. presidency (1972); the legalization of abortion (1973), the establishment of the first shelter for victims of domestic violence (1973); the nomination of a woman to be the Vice President of the United States, Geraldine Ferraro (1980); the appointment of the first woman as U.S. ambassador to the United Nations, Jeane Kirkpatrick (1981), the appointment of the first woman on the Supreme Court, Sandra Day O'Connor (1981).

Cuban women gained the right to vote in 1933 and were consequently active in political life, serving in both houses of Congress, as mayors, judges, and as part of the Foreign Service. The Constitution of 1940 outlawed discrimination on the basis of gender and endorsed the notion of equal compensation based on equal work. Following the Cuban Revolution, women were mobilized to join efforts to establish social equality. Founded in 1960, the Federación de Mujeres Cubanas (the

Federation of Cuban Women) contributed greatly to literacy campaigns, dispatching thousands of women to teach throughout the country. The 1970s saw changes to the legal code that would address the material conditions in which women in the country lived. Nineteen seventy-four saw the passage of the Maternity Law, guaranteeing paid maternity leave and secure employment during leave; in the Family Code of 1975, full equality between partners in marriage was declared, in terms of both labor distribution and parenting. There was free health and dental care; divorce was easily attainable. Reproductive rights were demonstrated to be a priority of the Revolution, as contraception in all forms was made free.[11]

Brazilian women gained the right to vote in 1932, and have been politically active since then. The 1970s saw the beginning of *abertura* (opening) under the military dictatorship that had been established in 1964. Following the United Nations declaration of 1975 as International Women's Year, the Congresso de Mulheres Brasileiras (Brazilian Women's Congress) was held in Rio de Janeiro, in which Afro-Brazilian women drew attention to divisions of race and class within the women's movement. Following the meeting, the Centro de Mulheres Brasileiras (Brazilian Women's Center) was created in order to unify efforts for collective action; that same year the Movimento Feminino pela Anistia (the Feminist Movement for Amnesty) was created, denouncing the repression of the dictatorship. The following years saw a marked increase in the number of women's groups throughout the country (many of these early groups could be found in either Rio de Janeiro or São Paulo), as women continued to fight for reproductive freedom, gender equality in terms of compensation, and legislation recognizing gendered violence, among other issues.

In general, then, in each of the societies under consideration in this study, there was a notable push for gender equality in the 1960s and 1970s. The cultural production of those decades and the years that follow reflect those changes, as groups previously marginalized (men and women of African and indigenous descent, members of the working and lower classes, and homosexuals) all gained greater access to modes of cultural production. Each of the works under consideration here, then, is an acknowledgment of these gains as well as a supplication for further transformations on a local, national, and international level. These poems and novels reflect the myriad issues of identity that arose during these decades of change, in which women were challenged to define themselves, at times in new ways. *Oshun's Daughters* looks at how these writers, representative of their times, sought new images of womanhood in the spiritual systems originally found in Western Africa and transported to this hemisphere during the Middle Passage.

The first chapter, "Diasporic Revelation: Audre Lorde, Sandra María Esteves, and Ntozake Shange," examines several poems by Audre Lorde and Sandra María Esteves, as well as Ntozake Shange's novel *Sassafras, Cypress, and Indigo* (1982). These American writers (West Indian American, Puerto Rican American,[12] and African American) formulate a diasporic identity that is not confined to the experiences of the black woman just in the United States. Rather, they construct an identity that depends on the expansiveness of the African Diaspora; in order to better understand themselves, the dominant voices in these works look to these spiritual practices first practiced on the African continent and then introduced to the Americas. Key to the formulation of this sense of self is the support and assistance of the divine entities of traditional Yoruba religion and the *Regla de Ocha*. The inclusion of the spiritual entities of these religions in the texts provides the protagonists with the opportunity to reconcile seemingly disparate markers of identity such as race, sexuality, and gender.

The second chapter, "The Search for Home: Cristina García and Loida Maritza Pérez," looks at the redefining of home in these two novels. In contrast to the characters in the works of their counterparts studied in the previous chapter, who yearn for a consciousness associated with a mythic homeland, several characters in these novels by U.S. Latina writers initially long for their islands of origin, namely Cuba and the Dominican Republic, represented by the religions of these nations. They soon discover, however, that nation does not necessarily equate with home and so they come to understand that they carry this sensibility of love and nurture within themselves. Spirituality, therefore, is a means by which these female characters develop a sense of personal independence and self-care which they then associate with home.

The third chapter, "Love, Revolution, Survival: Nancy Morejón and Daína Chaviano," analyzes the representation of these spiritual systems in the cultural production of two women whose writings bookend the Cuban Revolution. In poems such as "Un patio de La Habana," "Los ojos de Eleggua," and "Amo a mi amo," Nancy Morejón highlights the omnipresence of the ancestors and the *orishas* in Cuba, underscoring a legacy of insurrection and revolt that predates 1959. For her, Cuban men and women of African descent are the true rebels who serve as the conscience of the Revolutionary project. The failure of this project is evident in the second novel of Daína Chaviano's *La Habana oculta* series. The protagonist, Gaia, has sexual encounters with two beings who she believes are personifications of two *orishas*, Oshún and Erinle. With this novel, Chaviano links sexual intimacy between men and women with the attainment of personal liberation; she puts it forth as the only legitimate tool for freedom under a tyrannical regime.

The fourth chapter, "Sacrifice and Salvation: Helena Parente Cunha, Sônia Fátima da Conceição, and Conceição Evaristo," studies the processes of psychic reintegration in the face of the corrosive elements of racism, sexism, and classism in Brazil. Parente Cunha's novel, *Mulher no Espelho* (1983), is a dialogue between the protagonist and her alter ego, *"a mulher que me escreve,"* who appears in her mirror. The woman's true self ("eu") rejects all that the *"woman who writes me"* has become: an upper-middle-class housewife whose husband and sons have no interest in her. The protagonist slowly reclaims her self by recovering the African elements of her culture that she was urged to leave behind. She increasingly interacts with the *orixás* of the waters, Iansã, Oxum, and Iemanja. Wholeness is readied by the development of a relationship with these entities. By the end of the novel the protagonist speaks in a single, rather than a multiple, voice. Her younger contemporaries, Sônia Fátima da Conceição and Conceição Evaristo, address the longing for such integration in their own works, which concern the Brazilian population of African descent. Whereas Parente Cunha's protagonist is concerned with the formation of her subjectivity, Conceição's poetic voice longs for clean water, health, and the ability to worship freely and fully; for her, the *orixás* are distant beings who are inaccessible to a person living in a Brazilian urban center but who, are nevertheless potent, as they signify insurrection in poetic discourse. Evaristo's protagonist rediscovers her voice after enduring racial discrimination and urban poverty, both of which cause muteness and catatonia. The emergence of her voice coincides with the recognition of an unwavering ancestral and *orixá* presence in her life, which she understands only after returning to the land of her birth.

The concluding chapter, "The Response: Reflections in the Mirror," reviews the examination of the interaction between these female protagonists and these African diasporic religions. All of the lead characters of these works reveal their discontent in idealized visions of womanhood that have been created by the Western patriarchal imaginary. Instead, they look to a religious system that allows for a more full sense of womanhood, one that celebrates both body and mind, both sacred and secular. These novelists are but a small sample of a number of women writers in the Americas who try to amplify the vision of the Female as they search for wholeness against a patriarchal imaginary.

Diasporic Revelation

Audre Lorde, Sandra María Esteves, and Ntozake Shange

They feel the blood of their mothers still flowing in them, survivors of the diaspora.

—Ntozake Shange, *Sassafras, Cypress & Indigo*

Throughout her first novel, Ntozake Shange makes numerous references to the history of the Middle Passage, the dispersal of enslaved men and women throughout the Americas, and their descendants. Her protagonists are in contact with these spirits through their artistic expression: they play music, dance, and weave. The spirits communicate with them in their dreams as well as in their chosen professions; they inform every decision these young women make in their lives, and serve as both guides and witnesses to all that they do. The protagonists in turn pay tribute to these spirits by listening to them, following their cues about how to live their lives as they attempt to find that which is in keeping with their destinies. In her novel, Shange creates an atmosphere in which humans live alongside the spirits of long-dead ancestors, who guide humanity as they try to survive the trials of life, presented here primarily as sexism, racism, homophobia, and discrimination, as well as a rupture between spirituality and quotidian existence.

Writing about related spiritual traditions, Audre Lorde, Sandra María Esteves, and Ntozake Shange reveal the depth of the spirituality of the African Diaspora, the strength of these beliefs in communities of African heritage in the United States, and their capacity to influence daily life on an ongoing basis. This chapter examines poems by Audre Lorde and Sandra María Esteves, as well as the first novel of Ntozake Shange, *Sassafrass, Cypress & Indigo* (1982). These writers formulate an identity that is not confined to the experiences of the black woman just in the United States. Rather, they construct a diasporic identity that recalls the expansiveness of the African Diaspora. The poetic voices and protagonists of these works are not provincial in their self-constructed identities: they do not self-identify as women solely of the United States, as American women or even hyphenated identities of African American or Caribbean American. Instead, looking to the history of the dispersal of Africans in the Western Hemisphere, they gain strength from those stories and allow those narratives to aid them in their journeys of self-realization. Key to the formulation of this sense of self is the support and assistance of the divine entities of traditional Yoruba religion and their American variants. Lorde, Shange, and Esteves allow their interactions with the *orishas* of Yoruba and *Regla de Ocha* to inform their sense of themselves as women in the New World. They find in these religions an effective strategy for both personal and communal liberation.

The 1960s and 1970s saw the development of nationalist movements in the United States within African American, Puerto Rican, and Chicano communities inspired by the civil rights movement of the preceding decades. One feature of the Black Power Movement and its cultural offshoot, the Black Arts Movement, was the resurgence of pride in all things African within African Diasporic communities across the United States. Both the Black Panther and Young Lord Parties advocated the study of their histories, which included an acknowledgment that enslaved Africans were brought to all of the Americas. The African Diasporic religions that had been uprooted and transplanted to the New World countries of Cuba and Brazil, among others, gained popularity in such U.S. cities as New York and Boston, as African Americans and Puerto Ricans reclaimed religious practices that had been conserved in some respects in the Caribbean and Brazil.[1] The *orishas*, the entities that serve as protectors and guides for humans, began to appear by name in African American and U.S. Latino/a literatures, underscoring the construction of a diasporic identity that supersedes nationalist affinities.[2]

The Call of Western Africa

Impatient legends speak through my flesh
changing this earths formation
spreading
I will become myself
—Audre Lorde, "Winds of Orisha"

Audre Lorde is a widely known and respected poet, essayist, and activist. Critics often focus on her autobiographical text *Zami: A New Spelling of My Name—A Biomythography* (1982) and on her essays, namely, those of *The Cancer Journals* (1980) and *Sister Outsider* (1984) such as "Poetry Is Not a Luxury," "The Transformation of Silence into Language and Action," "Uses of the Erotic: The Erotic as Power," and "The Master's Tools Will Never Dismantle the Master's House." When they concentrate on her poetry, they often do so using as their lens her self-proclaimed identity as a "Black, Lesbian, Feminist, warrior, poet, mother," as she stated in a 1990 interview with Charles H. Rowell, founder and longstanding editor of *Callaloo*, the journal devoted to literatures of the African Diaspora. During this conversation, Lorde explained why she had chosen not to include any poems published in *The Black Unicorn* (1978) in her subsequent reissue, *Chosen Poems, Old and New* (1982): "The poems in *The Black Unicorn* have always felt to me like a conversation between myself and an ancestor Audre" (58). Rowell quickly moves on to other subjects, leaving readers to ponder Lorde's assertion; with this claim, she clearly posits that the source of her poetic inspiration is not her own intellect or experiences, but rather an interaction, or series of interactions, with an ancestral presence guiding her. Rowell's apparent unwillingness to challenge his interview subject or at least to issue further questions about this topic conveys a nervousness experienced by her contemporaries as well.[3] Throughout this, her seventh collection, Lorde invokes West African spiritual entities from both Fon and Yoruba cosmologies, interacting with Yemanjá, Seboulisa, Mawu Lisa, Orishala, Shopona, and Eshu, among others. She continues her relationship with these spiritual entities in *Zami*, in which she encounters a woman named Afrekete. Widely considered her masterpiece, *Zami* is described on its cover as a "biomythography," which critics see as a reclaiming of an autobiographical narrative so as to, as M. Charlene Ball explains it, "create . . . myth from her own life" (61). Critics who have examined Lorde's interaction with these entities in her poetry often focus on how the inclusion of these figures allows her new feats with language in the creation of a woman-space. AnnLouise Keating notes that finding a West African spiritual heritage empowered Lorde: "By replacing her Judeo-Christian worldview with one which validates her African roots, she affirms her identity as a Black woman warrior poet. . . . By reclaiming figures from African mythology in these poems and others, Lorde simultaneously redefines herself and celebrates her access to language's transformative power" (28). Rooting herself in a spiritual system that provides images of female strength, beauty, and fierceness, Lorde writes herself into a narrative that is predominantly white, male, and heterosexual. Identifying traditions extant for thousands of years liberates her: no longer does she feel the pain and guilt of the self-mutilation that is living an untrue, unexamined life, but instead she is freed to explore the world from a position of wholeness. With these poems, then, Lorde posits the invocation of these spiritual systems as liberatory practice.

In her 1968 poem "When the Saints Come Marching In," Lorde writes:

> Plentiful sacrifice and believers in redemption
> are all that is needed
> so any day now I expect
> some new religion
> to rise up like tear gas
> from the streets of New York
> erupting like the rank pavement smell
> released by a garbage truck's
> baptismal drizzle.
> High priests are ready and waiting
> their incense pans full of fire.
> I do not know their rituals
> nor what name of the god
> the survivors will worship

I only know she will be terrible
and very busy
and very old.

1968 marked a year of crisis on an international level, as there were student protests around the globe leading to violent standoffs between soldiers and young people in the United States, Mexico, Brazil, France, and Czechoslovakia, among other places. The Padilla Affair in Cuba sparked a widespread disillusion with the Cuban Revolution for many, as the government imprisoned the poet Heberto Padilla for criticizing the regime.[4] In the midst of a U.S. economic crisis, New York City neared bankruptcy, as it faced union strikes and white flight to the suburbs. The failure of the Tet Offensive in Vietnam caused widespread disillusion within the population, as the optimism of the Kennedy administration gave way to the realities of war under the Johnson administration; it would be the deadliest year for U.S. soldiers during the war, leading to President Johnson's choice not to run for reelection. In the aftermath of the assassination of Martin Luther King Jr., significant parts of Washington, D.C., Baltimore, and Chicago were affected by riots, which had already destroyed sections of Newark and Los Angeles in the recent years; the Democratic National Convention saw rioting in Chicago, and later that summer, the assassination of Robert F. Kennedy. The nonviolent civil rights movement gave way to the militarism of the Black Panther Party, the members of which were explicit in their desire to protect members of black communities across the nation terrorized by police brutality, rampant unemployment, underfunded schooling, and the general disregard of the political system.

It is this environment that characterizes Lorde's "When the Saints Come Marching In." In the midst of widespread disenchantment with the institutions that undergird civil society, the poetic voice expresses the need for something else, for a new spirituality that can heal her broken city of New York. For her, it is a question of religion: "Plentiful sacrifice and believers in redemption / are all that is needed" (1–2). Rather than simply a question of faith ("believers in redemption"), healing will only come about through ample demonstrations of that faith ("plentiful sacrifice"). One detects a residing note of cynicism, irrespective of the assertion that opens the poem, as verses five through nine reveal the poetic voice's belief that this religion will emerge from the streets themselves, "erupting like the rank pavement smell / released by a garbage truck's / baptismal drizzle" (7–9). The analogy brings forth imagery of urination and the disposal of waste.

In the subsequent stanzas, the poetic voice again asserts the need for such a religion, one that has existed for millennia: "she will be terrible / and very busy / and very old" (15–17). With the use of the female pronoun, Lorde subtly rejects the patriarchal thought of Judeo-Christianity, searching instead for an alternate system, though she proclaims ignorance of its precise identification. Still, she asserts that this system will be characterized by the natural ("incense," "fire") rather than the trappings of the modern world, which have been reduced to the collection and clearance of refuse. Civilization has faltered under the religious systems of the Father; it is the moment instead to appeal to the Mother.

The first explicit mention of West African belief systems in Lorde's *oeuvre* is in 1970 with her poem, "The Winds of the Orishas."

> I
> This land will not always be foreign.
> How many of its women ache to bear their stories
> robust and screaming like the earth erupting grain
> or thrash in padded chains mute as bottles
> hands fluttering traces of resistance
> on the backs of once lovers
> half the truth
> knocking in the brain like an angry steampipe
> how many long to work or split open
> so bodies venting into silence
> can plan the next move?

The poetic voice opens with a strong declaration: "This land will not always be foreign." There is the intimation that the land has been familiar in the past, which indicates that something in the course of humankind has gone horribly wrong. In the eyes of numerous cultures, there has always existed a strong relationship between the land and human beings. Indeed, we as humans are of the earth; from dust we arose and to dust we shall return. With this opening verse, the poetic voice establishes that a rupture has occurred, and the employment of the demonstrative adjective "this" intimates that the poetic voice refers specifically to the United States.

For the next ten verses, she emphasizes the yearning, the necessity that women have to express themselves, to "bear their stories" (2). That desire for expression reveals itself in the physical, as an "ache" (2); "screaming" (3); "thrash" (4); "hands fluttering" (5). The poetic voice relates women to the earth, in one moment returning to a more mythic plane, in that women for millennia were, of course, associated with the earth for its fertility, for its ability to produce, to bring forth life. These figures toil to bring forth their stories and yet cannot, for they have gone "mute" (4). The poetic voice underscores another rupture, that which has divided the word, or the ability to formulate words, from the rest of the body. For while the verbs the poetic voice uses are ones that are violent ("screaming," "thrashing," "fluttering,") or at the very least indicate fierce movement, they remain without a voice. An additional disruption can be identified in the fifth and sixth verses, in which we find "hands fluttering traces of resistance / on the backs of once lovers." There is the implication that an intimate act has now become one of force, where two who may have once shared love, in some form or another, now are in the midst of a powerful struggle, one in which someone loses "traces of resistance." The act of lovers has now become one of brutality, and for at least one participant, one of futility. There is fracture and division all around.

In the second stanza of this first part of the poem, the poetic voice moves to the figure of the Greek prophet punished by the gods for insubordination with blindness. She writes:

> Tiresias took 500 years they say
> to progress into woman
> growing smaller and darker and more powerful
> until nut-like, she went to sleep in a bottle
> Tiresias took 500 years to grow into woman
> so do not despair of your sons.

In one account, Hera, goddess of women and marriage and wife of Zeus, changes the oracle from man to woman; the figure of Tiresias is, therefore, sexually ambiguous. Both man and woman, this personage may be considered the personification of balance between the male and female elements. Here, for the first time in the poem, we hear a tone of defiance: he spent five hundred years "growing small and darker and more powerful," says the poetic voice, concluding the stanza with the sardonic commentary, "so do not despair of your sons" (17). There is still hope if males choose to learn from females, if sons choose to learn from their mothers rather than view them as objects worthy of conquer, as in the Oedipal myth. By the poetic voice's summation, woman, or at least the woman Tiresias became, was "small," "dark," and "powerful." Here, of course, she defines "power" in a new way, refuting the thought that dictates power to be something characterized by great physical size as well as light in color; instead, she offers "power" as a synonym of strength that grows exponentially, as the nut is the seed from which the tree grows. The representation of woman has changed, from the first stanza to the second, from helpless, mute, and inarticulate to small, dark, and powerful. In an essay considering Lorde's relationship between her texts and her body, Margaret Kissam Morris offers the following: "She repositions marginal categories, placing them in the center of her discourse" (178). Chinosole makes a similar argument, stating that at the center of Lorde's project as a poet is an "affirmation of difference" (382); placing Lorde within a chronology of African American writing, she writes: "In the face of an oppressive culture bent on your obliteration, affirming difference as nonthreatening, a difference charged by change like the house of winds—a survival-oriented, self-defining change—is a current in slave narratives tapped and magnified in Lorde's own special vision of matrilineal diaspora" (382). Though "small," "dark," and "powerful" are signifiers of weakness in a white supremacist patriarchal culture, she infuses these words with new meaning, so that they are no longer peripheral. Lorde does so throughout her work in order to combat racism, sexism, and homophobia; by the conclusion of this first section, then, we have a formula for the healing of the fractures described in the first stanza, balance between the male and female elements must be reached.

It is in the second section of the poem that the poetic voice makes mention of the *orishas*.

> II
> Impatient legends speak through my flesh
> changing this earth's formation
> spreading

I become myself an incantation
dark raucous characters
leaping back and forth across bland pages
Mother Yemonja raises her breasts to begin my labor
near water
the beautiful Oshun and I lie down together
in the heat of her body's truth
my voice comes stronger
Shango will be my brother roaring out of the sea
earth shakes our darkness
swelling into each other
warning winds announce us living
as Oya, Oya my sister my daughter
destroys the crust of the tidy beaches
and Eshu's Black laughter
turns up the neat sleeping sand.

In this second section there is a shift from the third person ("its women," "they say") to the first person *I*. The poetic voice incorporates the myths of old: "impatient legends speak through my flesh." In this formulation the body now has the capacity to speak, to articulate mysteries. The voice goes on to juxtapose herself with the written word, as she becomes an "incantation," a chant, a prayer set to music. She then goes on to name five of the spiritual entities known to have survived the Middle Passage, as each continues to be worshipped by practitioners of the Yoruba religions on both sides of the Atlantic. These are the *orishas*, those "unique manifestations of *ashé*, the power-to-make-things-happen," as defined by Robert Farris Thompson in his seminal study *Flash of the Spirit* (1984). The poetic voice invokes all of these beings, calling their energies as a means by which to "change this earth's formation" (19). Again, her goal is one of fundamental restructuring: by calling on these beings, she hopes to reinstate balance. She calls on ancient spirits to remedy the fragmentation of the modern world, one in which a woman does not bear children but rather her angst, her pain, as she says in her first stanza. These are bodies that carry hurt and angst, and so must be "split open" (19), so as to release the grief and sorrow of progress, thereby bringing about healing and liberation.

This freedom may begin by interacting with Mother Yemanja, who "raises her breasts to begin" (24) the labor of the poetic voice. This gesture of raising the breasts is one of generosity—Yemonja, the deity widely identified with motherhood, offers to feed and nurture the "I" of the poem. Next she calls the "beautiful Oshun" (26), with whom she lives in order to make stronger her own voice. Here, the poetic voice, having turned from third person to first, has learned to rely on herself. Again, we see a reunification of the body and the voice: "in the heat of her body's truth / my voice becomes stronger" (27–28). While one might be tempted to read this as a physicalization of this spiritual entity, it is not so. Recalling again that the voice begins the first stanza by saying that these legends "speak through the flesh" (18), here she demonstrates that she carries all of them with her, in her blood. Each entity reveals a different aspect of the poetic voice's self to her self—here, with Oshun, it is her own body that strengthens her voice. The poetic voice moves on by calling on Shango, the entity that represents divine justice; he that will avenge slights for those he loves. Here, the poetic voice names Shango her brother (29), and so with him comes her defense, physical force in the form of the entity known to be the embodiment of masculine energy. She is also assisted by Oya, who she names her "sister, [her] daughter" (33). Oya is transformation. Symbolized by the tornado, she works alongside Shango, lovers and warriors both. The poetic voice states that she "destroys the crust of the tidy beaches"; indeed, Oya destroys so that new life may emerge.

She closes out this second part of the poem by invoking Eshu and his laughter (35). Widely characterized as the trickster figure, as in Henry Louis Gates's *The Signifying Monkey*, Eshu is invoked at the beginning and the end of religious ceremonies, as he is both the beginning and the end. He has historically been mischaracterized as the equivalent of a devil, malicious, playful, and roguish. Robert Farris Thompson writes: "Outwardly mischievous but inwardly full of overflowing creative grace, Eshu-Elegbara eludes the coarse nets of characterization. . . . [He is] the ultimate master of potentiality" (19). As the personification of possibility, he embodies all that could be; invoking Eshu, therefore, does not simply convey mischief but also restitution: in this cosmology, the most important characteristic of life is harmony and peace, qualities attained through balance. And so the poetic voice ends this section by calling on Eshu, he who indicates whether paths that may be opened or closed, and who in fact has the ability to open or close those roads. Here, we hear his "black laughter" (35), an indication, perhaps of success—the poetic voice has accomplished that which she set out to do in that she has become herself (21).

> III
> The heart of this country's tradition is its wheat men
> dying for money
> dying for water for markets for power
> over all people's children
> they sit in their chains on their dry earth
> before nightfall
> telling tales as they wait for their time
> of completion
> hoping the young ones can hear them
> earth-shaking fears wreath their blank weary faces
> most of them have spent their lives and their wives
> in labour
> most of them have never seen beaches
> but as Oya my sister moves out of the mouths
> of their sons and daughters against them
> I will swell up from the pages of their daily heralds
> leaping out of the almanacs
> instead of an answer to their search for rain
> they will read me
> the dark cloud
> meaning something entire
> and different.
>
> When the winds of Orisha blow
> even the roots of grass
> quicken.

Here in the third and final part, the poetic voice once again draws a stark contrast between the tradition of "this country" (37), and who she now is. Though she does not specify the name of "this country," we are led to believe it is the United States: the reference to wheat reminds the reader of the naming of grain in the first stanza (3), wheat being a staple crop in this country. Here, the poetic voice identifies capitalism as the malady that strikes its men who are dying: "money/ water . . . markets . . . power" (38–39). Unlike the first part of the poem, in which the poetic voice merely describes the desperation of the powerlessness, here, in this final section, she inserts herself, proposing herself as an alternative vision, something that will resolve their yearning for "completion" (43). With her last stanza, she implies that this change, this transformation, this healing, is inevitable. The only requirement is that one look inward, into his/her own flesh, as the poetic voice does, in order to find and rescue those ancient truths that one carries. It entails the recognition of one truth, an ancient veracity that is older than the beginning of time.

Lorde continues to invoke the spiritual entities of both the Yoruba and Fon[5] peoples in *The Black Unicorn* (1978). In her interview with Charles H. Rowell, Lorde reveals that this collection began after a visit to Dahomey (now Benin) in 1974 with her children (58). In the volume itself, she offers definitions of the entities she names in a glossary that concludes the collection, providing for her readers a foundation for understanding what she later calls the "archetypal experience" of black women.[6] Many critics focus on Lorde's utilization of these entities as an assertion of her blackness and her womanhood;[7] they have also drawn attention to the themes of motherhood and language.[8] For Lorde, admittedly, these entities and their accompanying mythologies (born in Western Africa) provide an underpinning for her own experiences as a Caribbean American woman. We see in this collection, as we did in the previous poem, an entreaty for healing from Africa, the birthplace of the diaspora; in the collection as a whole, she reveals her belief in the ability of these entities to bring about this cure.

These spiritual entities appear in the first of four sections of the volume; one of the first poems of the collection, "From the House of Yemanjá" (6–7), alerts the reader of a consistent theme, that of the mother. As stated previously, Yemanjá is the *orisha* most widely identified with motherhood. In the glossary that appears at the end of the text, Lorde defines this entity as follows:

Mother of the other *Orisha*, Yemanjá is also the goddess of oceans. Rivers are said to flow from her breasts. One legend has it that a son tried to rape her. She fled until she collapsed, and from her breasts, the rivers flowed. Another legend says that a husband insulted Yemanjá's long breasts, and when she fled with her pots he knocked her down. From her breasts flowed rivers, and from her body then sprang forth all the other *Orisha*. (121–22)

Lorde here emphasizes not only the violence, the hardships of these stories but more importantly, Yemanjá's ability to transcend that pain, transforming it into an act of creation. In calling out to her, then, Lorde implicitly seeks a similar goal for herself and indeed for all women. Her emphasis is therefore not on the tragic but instead on the sublime.

> My mother had two faces and a frying pot
> where she cooked up her daughters
> into girls
> before she fixed our dinner,
> My mother had two faces
> and a broken pot
> where she hid out a perfect daughter
> who was not me
> I am the sun and moon and forever hungry
> for her eyes.

Notable about this first stanza is the perspective of daughter that the poetic voice assumes: it is a daughter who is aggrieved by her mother's actions. The first deed that causes pain is that of socialization: in distinguishing between "daughters" (2) and "girls" (3), there is a suggestion of transformation from a claim of offspring to the detached biological status of being a young human female. The fourth verse indicates that the mother does this before the girls were either ready or prepared: they did not yet have the sustenance for this transition. In the next four lines, the poetic voice takes a more personal tone, as there is an implication of preferential treatment, of protection of a fellow girl-child. Taking into account the title of the poem, this voice resides in her mother's house, and yet there remains a constant yearning for this figure; the result is an attempt at self-consolation, as she attempts to convince herself of her own worth.

In the second stanza, there is a shift from a focus on the mother and her actions to a first-person voice. The girl has matured into a woman, it appears, one who carries both the well-known and that with which she is not yet comfortable. In an interview with Adrienne Rich, Lorde defines the black mother as the poet that each of us, male and female, carry within us (100). This figure is a metaphor for all that is feeling: "[It is] that back place, where we keep those unnamed, untamed longings for something different and beyond what is now called possible, and to which our understanding can only build roads" (101). Reviewing the second stanza of the poem, then, the reader understands that the pale mother is reason and logic, customs and behaviors that society has deemed acceptable. This mother brings a combination of sustenance and dread; this horror necessarily qualifies the kind of nourishment the poetic voice ingests. Also, she does so while the subject sleeps, which also qualifies the kind of rest the subject is able to enjoy. The pale mother, then, is one that ostensibly arrives with physical sustainment but who combines this with a psychological and spiritual means of control, that which takes advantage of worries and anxieties. Nevertheless, within that space is all that is inarticulate as of yet, natural, that which has not yet been disciplined by a society that has no use for its wildness. In her interview with Rich, Lorde resists simple characterization of the poem as an assignment of values based on racial identification, though the reader sees clearly how she has inverted values that assign all that is good to white and all that is bad to black. Notably, she does not use these colors, instead writing "pale" and "dark."

She continues to call out to the dark mother in the penultimate stanza:

> Mother I need
> mother I need
> mother I need your blackness now
> as the august earth needs rain.

In the repetition, the reader can see the urgency of the request: not only is this a daughter calling out to a mother but indeed a female voice calling out to the Source of all life. She pleads with that original foundation of life to save the rest. The "I" assumes more global resonances, as it is not one singular voice but instead numerous voices, asking for assistance, imploring the release of the undisciplined unchecked emotion, an original sensibility that has been hiding. The global consciousness needs to be saved from analytic thinking that tends to destroy rather than repair; instead, it needs thinking that dictates that all is possible, without limitation.

She concludes the poem:

> I am
> the sun and moon and forever hungry
> the sharpened edge
> where day and night shall meet
> and not be
> one.

Returning to the verses repeated in the first stanza, the poetic voice has now changed, as she is no longer hungry for the eyes of her mother (9–10); though she remains "forever hungry," she has developed a response to the interminable yearning, "the sharpened edge" (27). As Chinosole points out,

> the first and last stanzas, then, do not simply encapsulate duality, but are structured to represent progression from a tension-ridden difference to a non-threatening one. The power of unity is in that very separateness. Difference as a source of dread in the beginning, becomes the basis of self-acceptance still chanting its need and "ever hungry." (390)

The Mother has responded to the entreaties of the poetic voice; the earlier tone of despondency has been replaced with strength and willfulness.

Lorde continues to invoke this maternal presence in her poem "125th Street and Abomey" (12–13) where she identifies a woman as Seboulisa. She defines this entity at the conclusion of the volume as: "The goddess of Abomey [the capital of Dahomey]—'The Mother of us all'. A local representation of Mawulisa, she is sometimes known as Sogbo, creator of the world" (121). In her entry for Mawulisa, Lorde underscores the connection between these figures and Yemanjá, saying that as Mawulisa is the Mother of the other *Vodou*,[9] so too is Yemanja Mother of all of the *Orisha*. In seeing this figure on the streets of Manhattan, as indicated by the title, Lorde highlights how each person carries this legacy within him/herself, it is solely a question of accessing this consciousness. She writes:

> Head bent, walking through snow
> I see you Seboulisa
> printed inside the back of my head
> like marks of the newly wrapped akai
> that kept my sleep fruitful in Dahomey
> and I poured on the red earth in your honor
> those ancient parts of me
> most precious and least needed
> my well-guarded past
> the energy-eating secrets

The poetic voice immediately contrasts the wintry urban space referenced in the title and the first verse with the "red earth" of Dahomey (present-day Benin), creating a sense of discordance, in that tranquility evoked with "sleep" does not match the immediate surroundings. Nevertheless, as she trucks through the snow, she continues to carry her Mother within. In honor of this figure, she pours as a libation "my well-guarded past / the energy-eating secrets" (9–10); interaction with this figure empowers her so that she may discard those parts of her personality ("those ancient parts of me") that no longer contribute to her evolution as a person and as a woman. Carrying Seboulisa as she moves in the world, then, confirms that there is a concerted effort to mature and transform. In verses 11–14, the poetic voice reveals a renunciation of her self as she presently understands that self, an indication of a willingness to change, to assume qualities that may not come naturally to her but that will serve her in the future. She also cedes previous identities for which she no longer has any use. In her uncertainty, she looks to other paradigms of courage, after whom she models herself, her "warrior sisters" (18). These are the women of Dahomey, whom she identifies in her glossary as the Amazons of myth. She looks to alternate models of womanhood as a means of integrating those qualities she admires into the best version of herself. In the last two verses of the stanza, the poetic voice calls upon all of these entities to provide her with the "woman strength / of tongue" (21–22), which suggests language in both written and oral expression.

In the second stanza, she returns to the image of the Mother:

> . . . .
> Seboulisa mother goddess with one breast
> eaten away by worms of sorrow and loss
> see me now
> your severed daughter
> laughing our name into echo
> all the world shall remember

The poetic voice offers a vision of a decaying Seboulisa, implying that the virtues for which this entity stands are in decline. Again, for this poet, Seboulisa, like Yemanjá, is the Dark Mother, that version of being which she believes to be more available to women (though men can also reclaim this lost sensibility as well), intuitive understanding as opposed to knowledge. The act of calling these figures means to be decidedly un-ladylike, as per the definition offered by a patriarchal society invested in the majority of their citizens being silent, controlled, and domesticated. These entities are maternal in an aggressive way: warriors who defend not only their children but also their queen. In invoking these entities, Lorde amplifies the female imaginary; she is decidedly looking to other religious systems in order to find varied images of womanhood. The poetic voice recognizes that though she is severed, separated, from her mother, she will still laugh, recognizing both her maternal legacy and the contributions she makes to that legacy. The poem ends, then, with an optimistic tone, as she vows to remember her origins, and yet celebrating the new version of herself. Lorde implicitly asks her audience to do the same, amplify one's sense of self so that it may include that which is not quantifiable but nonetheless feels suitable to his / her values. Looking to West African spirituality for inspiration, she urges her audience to do the same; like her ancestors before her, she shares with a new audience these beliefs in the hopes that they too might be protected from the corrosion of values in the present age.

Keating notes a fundamental truth in Lorde's work, that is, the "acknowledgement of difference as an act of self-love" (31).

West African cosmologies focus on the balance of male and female principles, not on the domination of one over the other. With this spiritual heritage, Lorde found another source of permission to live her life fully, as a black lesbian mother warrior poet. In an essay describing her motivation for writing, she observes: "*I* feel not to be open about who I am in all respects places a certain kind of expectation on me I'm just not into meeting anymore. . . . I cannot simply be a Black person and not be a woman too, nor can I be a woman without being a lesbian" (262). Gloria T. Hull reminds readers that while one may be tempted to see Lorde's identities as static, in fact she wrestles with defining all of them at any given moment: "[These terms] represent her ceaseless negotiations of a positionality from which she can speak" (155). In writing, Lorde found a means by which to give voice to her multiple selves, and it is through writing that she creates a discursive space in which her readers can engage in similar exercises. The study of Yoruba and Fon philosophies allowed Lorde to reconcile seemingly disparate selves, not only in terms of personal identity but also ethnic affilia-tion: a black woman of Caribbean descent raised in an urban capital of African American life in the United States, she grew up learning to identify the West Indies as home, rather than the place in which she resided. Her poems suggest that the appeal to the *orisha* and *vodou* of West Africa bring her a sense of stability and permanence that she had not previously found. Acknowledging herself as a daughter of the diaspora and engaging the philosophies that were spread due to the enslavement of millions bring her peace. The inclusion of these entities is not a call to replace outright the "worship of rationality and that circular, academic, analytic thinking,"[10] but is instead an act of restoration of a sensibility that has been lost to popular and mainstream culture in the United States. Sandra María Esteves will engage in a similar project in her own poetry; in looking to Africa as a source of spiritual strength, both women reconceive of themselves not solely based on their Caribbean heritage but instead as a member of the diaspora. Neither rejects their traditions; they instead expand their under-standing of the foundations of these limiting identities by exploring to African and African diasporic spiritual systems and including them in their work.

The Griotte of the South Bronx

spiritual survivors reclaimed from a pilfered legacy
—Sandra María Esteves, "Bautizo"

Nuyorican poetry gained a foothold in the artistic circles of New York City in the 1960s and 1970s.[11] The idealism of the early 1960s had given way to the disenchantment of the latter part of the decade, what with the assassinations of John F. Kennedy, Malcolm X, Martin Luther King Jr., and Robert Kennedy and the ongoing conflict in Vietnam. Nevertheless, the influence of the nationalist movements at the time, particularly the black power movement, spawned the Black Panther Party and the Young Lords Party, groups promoting cultural pride, education and housing reform, and equal rights for all Third World peoples.[12]

The Young Lords Party in particular demanded an independent Puerto Rico, the establishment of a socialist society, control of all services that were benefiting their community (police, hospitals, firefighters, etc.), and an end to racism, sexism, and the imperialism of the United States government in the world.[13] William Luis notes that members of this group represented the larger Puerto Rican community living in the United States; many of them were born in Puerto Rico and moved to New York City as children or were born in New York City.[14] They were caught in an in-between space, belonging neither here nor there. He writes: "On the island, Puerto Ricans are subjected to a colonial status; on the mainland they do not escape a postcolonial condition, and they confront cultural and racial discrimination. Their double alienation, on the island and mainland, underscores Puerto Rican minority status and cultural identity" (xiv). Living in the United States, first- or second-generation Puerto Ricans often do not speak Spanish, and so face rejection when on the island. Dismissed as "American" on the island, they are often labeled "Hispanic" or "Latino" on the mainland. Much Nuyorican literature of the 1970s captures the confusion and anger felt by many who did not know how to be comfortable in this liminal space. Critics have noted that the predominant themes of this writing are a search for identity, the negotiation of dichotomized categories, as well as expressions of cultural pride in the face of such perceived ambivalence.[15] In her poetry, Sandra María Esteves posits a solution to this bind, putting forth a diasporic subjectivity that links her Puerto Rican heritage not to a Spanish Caribbean context but instead with a larger, more expansive diasporic consciousness.

Sandra María Esteves is the sole woman poet within the larger group of Nuyorican poets that include Miguel Algarín, Miguel Piñero, Tato Laviera, Pedro Pietri, and Víctor Hernández Cruz, among others. Nineteen seventy-five saw the publication of the collection that effectively identified these poets as a collective, *Nuyorican Poetry: An Anthology of Puerto Rican Words and Feelings*. Edited by Miguel Algarín and Miguel Piñero, it established the defining characteristics of the artistic expression of these poets. For the editors, the creation of poetry is a survival technique that carries the potential of rebirth: "Poetry is the full act of naming. Naming states of mind" (10). Through this medium of expression, then, this disenfranchised community gained the divine power of creation. Algarín expands upon the responsibilities of the poet: "He tells the tale of the streets to the streets. The people listen. They cry, they laugh, they dance as the troubadour opens up and tunes his voice and movies his pitch and rhythm to the high tension of 'bomba'[16] truth. Proclamations of hurt, of anger and hatred. Whirls of high-pitched singing" (11). For him, then, the poet serves a communal function, in that he (as the majority of the Nuyorican poets were men) gives voice to the frustrations, the pain, and the disappointment of living in the Northeast of the United States, the subject of racism and discrimination. The poet in this formulation is a priest in that he serves to exorcise the hurt, creating instead opportunities for celebration. Recalling Audre Lorde's comments about the recovery of the emotional, the dark and powerful, here Algarín reflects that the "tale of the streets" is felt not through analysis or rationale but with full bodies, as this community purges their sufferings and pains through dance and music.[17] Like many other traditional cultures, including the many that make up the African Diaspora, the Nuyorican community is one that comes together in times of grief and joy, sorrow and delight.

Algarín focuses on the traits of Nuyorican literature as a whole in an article of the same name, published several years later; there, he puts forth that the community of Puerto Ricans in New York is one created under false pretenses. Promises made about employment opportunities on the mainland result in urban poverty, prevalent discrimination, lack of economic stability, and a psychic disconnection from the families that remained on the island. Extolling the contributions made by Nuyoricans to the larger culture, he writes: "On the more positive side, we have maintained our music, we have put down in New York something called *salsa,* and we have carried forward into the 1980s, the Black man's religion, a mixture of Catholicism and African religions, and most importantly, we carry on the oral tradition" (90). In the poetry of Sandra María Esteves, we see all of these elements featured.

Esteves was born to a Dominican mother and Puerto Rican father in the Bronx, New York, and is the author of six collections of poetry: *Yerba Buena* (1980); *Tropical Rains: A Bilingual Downpour* (1984); *Bluestown Mockingbird Mambo* (1990); *Undelivered Love Poems* (1997); *Contrapunto in the Open Field* (1998); and *Portal* (2007). In each of the first three volumes, she posits herself as the griotte, the community's storyteller and preserver of history.[18] The tones of her poems reflect her shifting responsibilities as this figure: saddened and enraged by the economic conditions in which the impoverished in the urban North live; proud of her cultural heritage; mournful in eulogies of lost friends and victims of violence; hopeful that life will present new opportunities. Esteves is plainly joyful when she writes about art, which for her is the primary expression of freedom. As an epigraph to her first collection, she writes: "As artist, I project vision towards which to grow, for all who wish to learn, and then, we learn together." As a writer and visual artist, then, her work serves a communal function: her creations are not meant to serve an individual impulse but rather grow out of a desire to see not only herself but also her community as a whole continue to evolve. Also, she does not set herself apart as the instructor or the learned one; rather, learning is an ongoing process and each person is able to both impart and receive knowledge from their neighbor. Within this world of mutual responsibility and respect, she includes both entities of the African diasporic religion of *La Regla de Ocha* as well as mentions the religion itself. In the poems themselves, the religion stands as a legitimate alternate source of knowledge within her community of peoples of African descent. Indeed, while she places herself as a member of the Puerto Rican community, she is a politically engaged writer who also sees herself as part of the larger Third World[19] and so she takes up the predominant themes of the time. In her first two collections, *Yerba Buena* and *Tropical Rains: Bilingual Downpour,* the references to *La Regla de Ocha* serve as a cultural marker, something that distinguishes her

Spanish-inflected community from their surrounding environment. It is only in her third collection that she takes on the spiritual significance of this religious practice. As the manner in which she represents the religion takes on new connotations, we see a similarly new understanding of the poet herself.

She names the religion and/or spiritual entities of the religion in several of her poems in *Yerba Buena* (1980). In each, the religion appears as a marker of difference but also a referent that her audience easily recognizes as a part of their community and therefore of their identity. With "The ignorant laugh," she confronts an audience that looks down upon different ways of life.

> "The ignorant laugh"
> Don't they believe?
> in magic
> witchcraft
> brujería
> la religion
> santeria
> meditation
> chanting
> astrology
> caracoles
> spirits and other living beings
> even the rocks are alive
> there are other ways to live
> acupuncture
> shiatsu
> natural foods
> macrobiotics
> biorhythms
> metaphysics
> clairvoyance
> music
> the ocean . . .
> many colors. (38)

The poetic voice posits that there are many modes of existence, many ways of being. She conflates the different names of African diasporic religions in verses 2–6, including pejorative terms ("witchcraft" / "brujería") that have stigmatized these practices.[20] In doing so, she legitimizes religious traditions that have been largely marginalized even within the Puerto Rican community. Yet there is a distinction between that which has been more readily accepted by the larger U.S. society. Verses 11 and 12 reveal a central tenet of African diasporic religions, that is, that the spirit of the creator of the universe is to be found in all things: humans, animals, nature, etc. These verses demarcate the poem, separating esoteric knowledge that is mostly found within communities of peoples of African descent from that which has been accepted by a mainstream culture. Nevertheless, these practices all stem from the desire to live in conjunction with the surrounding environment as well as a recognition that all life on a global scale is connected.

Her tone shifts with "Oracion" ("Prayer") (61), where, after critiquing the colonialist history of Christianity, she offers her entreaties on behalf of the "third world, first world brothers and sisters" (20).

> Hail holy lord we are the sun
> today we are the tree of life
> the knowledge of our fathers

By beginning the poem with "Hail holy" (1), she reminds the audience of prayers directed to the Virgin Mary, yet the poetic voice immediately changes the recipient of the prayer, addressing instead a male god ("lord"). Instead of a request, she immediately issues a forceful declaration of identity, this communal "we" is light, strength, illumination. The phrase "tree of life" not only reminds the audience of Jesus Christ on the day of Crucifixion but also taps into an image found in numerous civilizations such as ancient Egypt, Mesoamerica, and those of Western Africa as well as religious systems including Judaism, Shintoism, Taoism, and paganism, among others. Using this image, then, underscores the notion that humanity is linked across geographical space and time; it also indicates that the present generation is the culmination of previous learning. The poem suggests that spirituality is therefore not something that remains external to the human experience, that is, it is not a series of rituals and ceremonies that have no connection to the lives of the practitioners. Instead, it is human beings who carry a series of traditions, all recognizing common universal truths found in each society across time.

In the next two stanzas, the poetic voice offers a strong denunciation of Christianity not as a religious system but instead as an ideological force that has destroyed countless lives in the name of fervor and righteousness.

> We are the crucified christians
> come claiming our piece of the pie
> and by the light of our white candles
> and silver blade knives
> we will survive

In these verses (4–8), Esteves recalls martyrs, those humans often killed for refusing to renounce their religious beliefs; for centuries, the lives of Christian martyrs ended in the same manner as did the life of their Messiah, in crucifixion. She also reminds the reader of the deaths of the enslaved indigenous of the Americas and their African counterparts, millions who died due to disease and brutal labor conditions, forced by civilizing Europeans to work while being saved from their primitive barbarism. Here, the poetic voice intimates that this collective "we" were unarmed and unprepared for the assault that they suffered. There is a sense that their end was unjust; in this, their return, they carry candles, symbols of light and knowledge, but also weaponry, thereby ensuring their survival.

> Hail blue virgin
> who gave birth through the scum of her lies
> we are the brown children
> mother earth nourished in her bosom
> inheritors of the blue sky
> Chango y Oshun
> Obatala y Ogun
> Yemaya, Eleque y Oya
> con fuego y espiritu, la luta continua

The poetic voice continues the assault on the Church as a political force by attacking the Virgin Mary, the mother of Christ and of the Church. In contrast to the Virgin who gave birth through her lies she presents Mother Earth, who is the true mother of "brown children"

(11). These verses recall Gloria Anzaldúa's recounting of the history of the Virgin de Guadalupe in her study *Borderlands / La frontera: The New Mestiza* (1986), in which she shows how the Church synthesized extant mythologies of the conquered peoples, incorporating their goddesses in the imagery of the Virgin. To Anzaldúa, the Virgin of Guadalupe is a figure used to dominate conquered peoples ideologically. These lines suggest that the same holds true for Esteves, as she calls on well-known entities of the *Regla de Ocha*. Naming seven *orishas* recalls the grouping known as the *Siete Potencias Africanas*, the Seven African Powers, who are Eleguá, Ogún, Changó, Yemayá, Obatalá, Oshún, and Orula.[21] Here, she makes the variation, substituting Oyá for Orula. Nevertheless, all of these figures are associated with nature, and so Esteves offers them as alternative to the institution of the church. This is the contrast that she draws then, the establishment versus nature, that which has gained conventional acceptance versus that which continues to be marginalized. Despite previous persecution, the poetic voice assures the audience that the struggle continues (17), both with weapons ("fuego," literally "fire") and with passion ("espiritu," literally spirit).

After establishing the historical context into which the collective "we" was born, the poetic voice offers a more traditional prayer:

> May our spirits ring true
> may we celebrate life for the living
> May we, the third world, first world brothers and sisters
> be delivered from democracy's prisons
>
> May our children be loved
> May our elders be respected
> May our workers be praised
> May our warriors be protected
>
> Fuego y espiritu
> may our spirits ring true.

In verse 20, she identifies the identity of the collective "we" she has been utilizing through the piece: men and women whose heritage is of the developing world but who live in the developed one. "Democracy's prisons" (21) is an allusion to the troubles that often face these communities: systemic racism, discrimination, political and economic disenfranchisement, all of which, the poem suggests, lead to a perennially unstable existence. Nevertheless, the poetic voice continues the request, blessing both the most vulnerable sectors of the population (children and elders) as well as those who provide for it (workers) and those who protect and defend it (warriors). One sees a repeated appeal to Spirit, to the eternal universal truth to which each person has access; this references not only that which each person carries within him/herself but also that which she acknowledges to be the Creator.

Esteves continues this religious imagery in her second collection, *Tropical Rains: A Bilingual Downpour* (1984). Miriam DeCosta-Willis notes that the inclusion of music and musical structures distinguish Esteves from her male Nuyorican peers, who write what Miguel Algarín characterizes as "outlaw" poetry (6). In the song "Yerba Buena" (8–9), written in Spanish, she writes of Puerto Rico, the land of "Albizu," (42) "Betances," (43) and "Burgos" (44).[22] After five verses and a chorus ("Yerba Buena[23] / Yerba Bruja / Bruja Buena[24] / Tierra tuya" / [Yerba buena, Yerba bruja, Good witch, Your land]), she ends the song with a rumba:[25]

Somos sol Martin, somos sol	[We are sun Martin, we are sun
Somos sol Albizu, somos sol	We are sun Albizu, we are sun
De Betances y de Burgos somos sol	Of Betances and Burgos we are sun
De la tierra Orocovis somos sol	Of the land of Orocovis we are sun
Somos sol Jesus Cristo, somos sol	We are sun Jesus Christ we are sun
Somos sol Divina, somos sol	We are sun Divine One we are sun
De la tierra noche y dia, somos sol	Of the land night and day we are sun
Blanco o negro hasta siempre, somos sol	Black or White forever we are sun
Somos sol de la vida tu y yo	We are sun of life you and I
Levantando Orishas, somos sol	Raising Orishas, we are sun
De Oya, Ochun y Yemaya	Of Oya, Ochun and Yemaya
De Elegua, Chango y Obatala	Of Elegua, Chango and Obatala
Somos sol desde mundo somos sol.	We are sun from the world we are sun.][26]

The repetition of "somos sol" creates a chant, as there is a reiteration of the unity of the humanity on the planet. The poetic voice is both culturally specific and at the same time calling out to a larger community. It is not solely that Puerto Rico or those who claim Puerto Rican heritage are the only ones "who are sun"; rather, everyone can claim this, regardless of religious affiliation, or ethnic background, everyone on the planet is joined in this claim.

In this last stanza, the poetic voice presents the *orishas* as guardian spirits: the collective we are *of* these entities. The use of the possessive pronoun is a nod to the belief that each person is born the child of a certain *orisha*; though all guide a person through life as one grows and changes, it is this particular entity that claims responsibility for that individual's destiny. A person discovers their guiding spirit through ritual, often one leading to initiation into the priesthood; this ceremony of initiation is the subject of "Bautizo," ("Baptism") (84) featured in Esteves's third collection, *Bluestown Mockingbird Mambo* (1990). In this publication, there's a notable shift, so that the religion no longer serves as a marker of Puerto Rican culture or even the cultures of the larger developing world; instead, the poetic voice emphasizes the import of the ceremony itself and the effect it has on those who enter this priesthood.[27]

> "Bautizo"
> Early Brooklyn morning
> Padrino counsels initiates,
> new children into his house,
> spiritual survivors reclaimed from a pilfered legacy.

The fourth verse of the first stanza is particularly striking in that irrespective of the ethnic background of the new initiates, they all are to undergo ceremony in this one specific religious tradition, traditionally practiced by the Yoruba peoples of West Africa. She notes that this spiritual heritage itself has endured attempts at ending its practice for centuries, and so both it and those who dedicate their lives to the tenets of their traditions continue to endure.

> Silent and anxious
> the iabos shed old clothes
> that hang on and grip like tight skins

of sold lead shackles. A burden
heavier than their ability to resist.
Acknowledging need to align
cumbersome physical being with Divine power,
diminishing the weight,
implementing knowledge of metaphysical chemistry,
the natural combustion of kinetic earth, composed
and refined in the transcendental laboratory of mind.

In this second stanza, the poet reveals the motivation for becoming an initiate in this religious system: it offers a new life, one that focuses on divine alignment (10–11). The practitioner thereafter lives his/her life in accordance with universal laws and all that surrounds him/her. The poetic voice offers insight into the emotions of these novices: they are caught between the creation of a new life (the desire of which needs to be articulated) and the comfort and routine of the old, which clings to them. Speaking and performing the desire for alignment with a divine element leavens the novice's existential burden. No longer does this person live as per his or her own rules but instead accepts the philosophy, the theology, and the practices of this new way of life.

Full of aché,
Babalorisha invokes the ancestors,
family of one-hundred-thousand names,
to join this rebirth,
sing and feast in prodigal victory,
reaffirming linkage
to bloodlines woven like luminous veils
over walls and windows of their souls,
opening to reveal the precious landscapes
and inherited panoramas of our connected intelligence.

For Esteves, undergoing initiation into the priesthood of traditional Yoruba religion is the key to freedom. In joining the religion, one immediately joins a lineage that extends beyond time and national boundaries. Priests and priestesses call upon the assistance and guidance not only of the *orishas* but also of those of the ancestors, those practitioners who have passed, the "one-hundred-thousand" (18) who have gone before. The ancestors, the *orishas*, the humans themselves: all are manifestations of Spirit, and while those who have been formally initiated into this religious tradition may have a greater access to these entities, they exist to help all of humankind. The poet puts forth this traditional religion as a great unifier, then, as it brings together worshippers of all backgrounds. No longer is her sense of self focused solely on Puerto Rico, as she states in "Here"; instead, Esteves posits traditional Yoruba religion as an important contributor to the continued vibrancy of the African Diaspora living in the Americas.

The Magic of Woman

It's so magic folks feel their own ancestors coming up out of the earth to be in the realms of their descendants; they feel the blood of their mothers still flowing in them survivors of the diaspora.
—Ntozake Shange, *Sassafrass, Cypress & Indigo*

Ntozake Shange is a writer best known for her choreopoem *for colored girls who have considered suicide / when the rainbow is enuf* (1976). Winner of the Obie Award and the Outer Critics Circle Award, it has garnered praise for its varied portraits of black womanhood. Shange has gone on to win numerous awards, including a Guggenheim Fellowship; Columbia University's Medal of Excellence; a Pushcart Prize; and the Lila Wallace-Reader's Digest Fund Award, among others. Less well known by the general reading public are her poems, essays, children's books, and novels, the first of which is *Sassafrass, Cypress & Indigo* (1982). It is the story of the three girls of the title and their mother, Hilda Effania, in Charleston, South Carolina, and later in Southern California, New York, and New Orleans. It is also a heterogeneous novel in form, as the author includes recipes, rituals, prayers, numbers to play (depending on the situation), letters, songs, and performance reviews; these objects serve as "authenticating documents," according to Arlene Elder, in that they serve to ground the narrative in the "female experience and/or Black tradition" (100). All are included in a narrative that also features poetry and drama. Shange associates each of her female protagonists with the spiritual entities of both the Yoruba and Dahomean traditions (like Audre Lorde), writing about Oshun, Shango, Damballah, Erzulie, and Yanvallou. She does so in order to reveal the depth and complexity of U.S. communities of descendants of enslaved Africans, which are often represented as homogeneous. With her three protagonists, Shange highlights different cultural influences, epistemologies, artistic expressions of this diverse population.

In addition to the *orishas* and the *lwa*, both the Yoruba and Dahomean traditions honor the existence of the ancestors; throughout the text, the narrative voice calls on those who have come before for their guidance and assistance. In these traditions, the ancestors may be represented by a talisman such as a doll: early in the novel, Indigo, the youngest daughter who at the outset is twelve years old (53), constructs her own dolls, who accompany her wherever she goes. The narrator reveals that Indigo has a living relationship with each doll; that is, they communicate with each other. In one instance, she hears a voice urging her to flee a situation of impending danger (29) and does so immediately. Because she attends to these spirits, first through her dolls, and later by playing the fiddle,[28] the narrator comments: "She had many tongues, many spirits who loved her, real and unreal" (28). She spends every moment with these dolls: dragging them through her neighborhood in Charleston, she speaks to them, has tea parties with them, and forces her mother to acknowledge them as real. The narrator notes: "Indigo had made every kind of friend she wanted. African dolls filled with cotton root bark, so they'd have no more slave children. Jamaican dolls in red turbans, bodies formed with comfrey leaves because they'd had to work on Caribbean and American plantations and their bodies must ache and be sore" (6). In insisting on naming what would become the different nationalities of the enslaved Africans in this hemisphere, Shange here reminds the reader of the diverse histories of enslavement in the Americas.[29] She also reminds her audience of the origins of many peoples of African descent in the Americas, including the following as a recurring chorus in Indigo's narrative, "And the slaves who were ourselves" (27, 28, 40, 45, 49, 224). Shange puts forth that these spirits live, then, so long as their descendants live; we, the audience, walk with these souls as our guides.

Indigo's gift is to feel intuitively the emotions of others, including those of the spirits who walk with her. As an adolescent, she begins to spend time in the Caverns, "a winding complex of underground rooms where gambling, cockfights, and a twenty-four-hour social room entertained the most adventurous of Charleston's colored subterraneans" (41). After a quick fight with the girlfriend of the owner of the Caverns, during which she defended herself and her fiddle, Indigo escapes through the halls, only to stop and take note of her surroundings. The narrator remarks:

> The slaves who were ourselves had known terror intimately, confused sunrise with pain, & accepted indifference as kindness. Now they sang out from the walls, pulling Indigo toward them. Indigo ran her hands along the walls, to get the song, getta hold to the voices. Rust covered her palms & fingers. She kept following the rings. . . . Indigo knew her calling. The Colored had hurt enough already. (49)[30]

Indigo is the healer: in listening to the plight of those who have passed generations before her existence, she alleviates their pain. For Teresa N. Washington, the Caverns recall other structures that housed human beings: "The Caverns are the North American equivalent of the Slave Castle and Slave Fort in Cape Coast and Elmina, Ghana. . . . The Caverns is the womb that gave birth to tragic lives destined for triumph and the wisdom, knowledge, understanding that are the keys to evolution" (163). The novelist suggests that the grief of those who have passed has gone ignored; the slave trade therefore leaves a fundamental rupture in how those who are presently living treat their dead. There has been little honoring the plight of those first Americans (inhabitants of the Americas): simply by saluting the agony, staying in it, rather than overlooking the anguish for the sake of her own comfort, Indigo gains the trust of these spirits, and with that trust, access to new sources of knowledge. With this scene, Shange strongly advocates that her audience honor their dead, and in doing so, they can not only restore the spirit guides that attend to each person, they will also initiate the healing of their own families and, by extension, the larger diasporic community.

At the end of the novel, the narrator implies that Indigo might be the direct descendant, if not the reincarnation, of an enslaved African woman who was owned by the Fitzhughs, the same family for whom the girls' mother works. Like Indigo, Blue Sunday "move[d] the sea" (222). Every time her master would attempt to approach her, the ocean would react violently: "[T]he sea would getta fuming, swinging whips of salt water round the house where the white folks lived" (222). Sea water would have negatively affected their crop, indigo, and so there was a financial effect for his attempted indiscretions.[31] He makes a fool of himself for this favorite of his, lavishing silks on her: she in turn leaves them for the hogs. In an attempt to tame her, he whips her in front of her fellow enslaved Africans, then gives her to two overseers to be raped: she nevertheless remains inviolate. When he himself penetrates her, she turns into a crocodile, biting his leg and disappearing (223). This is the spirit that walks with Indigo, she who "changed the nature of things . . . [who] colored & made richer what was blank & plain" (40). The audience learns more about Indigo's character when we learn of those who guide her.

Not only does Shange associate Indigo with spirits but also with *orishas*. Her name reminds the reader of blue, the primary color of Yemanja, whose primary element is salt water, that is, the oceans. As we have seen, Indigo has a relationship with the ocean that laps the shores of Charleston, South Carolina. Washington points out that the crocodile is the guardian of Yemanja (146). Finally, as an adult, she works as a midwife, bringing new people of color into the world (223); Yemanja is the entity identified with motherhood. In her capacity as midwife, Indigo may also be associated with Oshun, who is the spiritual entity affiliated with femininity, and to whom women who want to be mothers appeal.

Like Indigo, her sister Cypress also has an extensive interaction with both the spirits and the *orishas*. While Indigo appeals to her spirits through her music, Cypress does so when she dances. If Indigo is the healer, Cypress is definitively the dancer, who accesses the divine through the movement of her body. With Cypress, Shange provides a reflection on the relationship between a woman's body and her sense of self. In the details of her description, the reader notices that Shange affiliates Cypress with Oshun, not only because she is a dancer but also because she is inspired by mirrors, Oshun's primary implement (69); she lives in an apartment of amber and green, two colors associated with the entity of femininity (102); she compares her lovers to Shango, recalling the relationship between the two *orishas* (106); and with Cypress, Shange focuses on eroticism. As the entity that is most associated with the female element (as Shango is with the male), she is often misunderstood to encompass the sacred prostitute or whore. She is the full embodiment of womanhood, and one who celebrates the healthy sexuality of woman celebrates Oshun.

As a dancer, Cypress becomes jaded in her first professional dance troupe because there was a relentless exchange of partners amongst the men and women of the group, to the extent that sex no longer meant anything but a bartering of fluids. The narrator comments: "The lovemaking was so active and one-dimensional [Cypress] preferred pulling coats round her ears, and sleeping with her face in the corner" (138). This recalls Audre Lorde's definition of pornography in her landmark essay, "Uses of the Erotic: The Erotic as Power": "a direct denial of the power of the erotic, for it represents the suppression of true feeling. Pornography emphasizes sensation without feeling" (54). The narrator implies that for these dancers, sex has become another physical expression of their bodies rather than of themselves as whole beings. Cypress finds this emphasis on wholeness with her next company, an all-female group called Azure Bosom (the use of blue and the reference to breasts again recalling Yemanja). With them, she is able to revel in her womanhood: "They were regarded as the thrust of the future for women in dance, articulating what women had never acknowledged: our bodies are not our destiny, but all freeing-energy. Azure Bosom brought man women to tears, to joy . . . a sense of quiet easiness they had never known" (141). With their performances, this troupe creates a safe space for females in their audience, allowing them to celebrate themselves, without an attendant hyperconsciousness about who is looking at their bodies and an analysis of that gaze. They are simply free to be themselves.

The narrator states clearly that another routine recalls the Haitian *lwa* associated with the feminine. She writes: "'How Do She Do' is the coquette Erzulie, introduced to modern lovers unaccustomed to pure pleasure of flesh and spirit combined. . . . She . . . allowed women to linger in their own eroticism; to be happy with loving themselves" (144). In her seminal article on this figure, Joan Dayan writes: "[T]he presence of Erzulie in writerly re-enactments fixes an erotic impulse into image" (18). The *lwa* associated with love and femininity, she has three predominant incarnations: Erzulie-Fréda, she who embodies love, beauty, and luxury, she is often portrayed as a *mulâtresse*; Erzulie Dantor, a dark-skinned peasant often syncretized with Madonnas with children; and Erzulie-gé-rouge, the red-eyed woman of rage and retribution

(Dayan 6). Erzulie corresponds to Oshun of the Yoruba system; with the mention of Erzulie, Shange posits the erotic as an energy that empowers women, as natural to their being, something separate from an expression of sexuality, with either men or women. Audre Lorde's words about the power of the erotic come to mind: "When I speak of the erotic, then, I speak of it as an assertion of the lifeforce of women; of that creative energy empowered, the knowledge and the use of which we are now reclaiming in our language, our history, our dancing, our loving, our work, our lives" (55). For Cypress, she is able to discover this force among a group of women when they are in performance. Outside of their presentations however, she grows dissatisfied, comparing their interactions to a slave market (145). Only when she is in relationship with Leroy does she find fulfillment. After a night of lovemaking, Cypress comments: "She was warm; felt so good. She giggled, getting together where she was, who was this, why so good. Here she was herself again. She was her own mystery" (157). The act of lovemaking, then, brings Cypress back to herself: she is able to revel in her femininity in the face of the masculine element. In Leroy, a musician and an old friend, Cypress finds her complement, her balance. In achieving this, a sense of equilibrium, she feels free, a quality that reveals itself most clearly in her dance (161). In her relationship, she can accept herself as she is, recognizing those parts that remain unknown even to her. With Leroy by her side, she permits herself to celebrate herself as a whole being. Shange ends the part of the novel devoted to Cypress with a marriage proposal from Leroy, the culmination of their commitment to each other.

Cypress's oldest sister Sassafrass also searches for this sense of wholeness: for her, the clearest way to achieve it is by undergoing ceremony for the *Regla de Ocha* tradition to become a priestess. Prior to this moment, the narrator focuses on Sassafrass's relationship with her boyfriend, Mitch, a saxophonist who "thought of himself as a god" (78). He is a demanding lover, one who believes Sassafrass should conduct herself in a proper way, namely, demure, ladylike, and quiet. He believes, for example, that a sequin-and-feather hanging shaped like a vagina should be hidden: "[I]t wasn't proper for a new Afrikan woman to make things of such a sexual nature" (78).[32] In attempting to control her art, and by extension her, Mitch tries to separate that which comes naturally to Sassafrass. She creates her hanging in honor of Josephine Baker; far from being reductively essentialist, it is a celebration of a woman who celebrated her eroticism on the French stage.[33] Sassafrass is therefore paying tribute to a woman who expressed her whole integrated self, sexuality included. In her study of eroticism and black women's writing, Donna Aza Weir-Soley writes: "While Western epistemology locates the sacred and the secular in separate and even opposing realms, the African worldview recognizes no such separation" (1). This underscores the irony of Mitch's assertion that a "new Afrikan woman" would do no such thing as create a rendering of female genitalia; his vision of Afrika is a patriarchal one, in which he controls all surrounds him, including his lover.

Whereas it is wrong for Sassafrass to create art using an image of the vagina, according to Mitch, he and his friends can speak freely about the quality of Sassafrass's vagina. In a scene that can be read as a criticism of the misogyny within the Black Arts Movement, Otis (a friend of Mitch's) speaks about his new book, entitled *Ebony Cunt,* which he inscribes to Mitch: *"for sassafrass . . . I know yours is good"* (86; italics in the original). Mitch joins in on his friend's banter, declaring it to be "'the best pussy west of the Rockies'" (87). In isolating her genitalia and in speaking about it with such crassness, we are again reminded of Lorde's definition of pornography. There is no sense that they are talking about Sassafrass as a whole woman; instead, they minimize her to her sexual abilities.

For much of their storyline, in fact, Mitch abuses Sassafrass, belittling her, though she views his comments as encouragement. In a moment where she finds herself defending herself after Mitch has unleashed criticism, the narrator notes that she stops herself: "[S]he did want to be perfected for him, like he was perfected and creating all the time" (80). She has placed him on a pedestal, treating him as the god he believes himself to be, following his lead. In doing so, she minimizes herself, disregarding her goals for herself: "She didn't care about her dreams, if her truth—her real life—was hurting, and Mitch was real life, and needing from her was something she could give, and did" (129). In spite of his constant disdain for what she wants, and despite a beating that she suffers at his hands, she remains with him. Her subsequent possession by the *orisha* Oshun should be seen as an attempt to rectify this imbalance.

Shange writes: "Sassafrass has tried everything to be a decent Ibeji [*sic*], a Santera. She desperately wanted to make Ochá [*sic*]. To wear white with her élèkes [sic]. To keep the company of priests and priestesses" (213). During the first year of initiation, a practitioner of this religion, the iyawo, will wear all white: s/he is a newborn, and so must be swaddled in white. The elekes of which she makes mention are the "beaded color-coded necklaces of five principal deities—Eleguá, Obatalá, Changó, Oshún, and Yemayá . . . with these necklaces the initiate obtains the spiritual force of the orishas and their protection" (Fernández Olmos and Paravisini-Gebert 53). Sassafrass's desire to "keep company with priests and priestesses" reveals to us that she wants to consecrate her life, make it holy, and live for a much bigger purpose.[34] Shange implies that this possible purpose may be the healing of the community of those descended from Africans here in the New World. Referring to the music that accompanies the religious celebration for which Sassafrass is preparing, the author writes:

> Drums and chanting ran thru the lush backwoods of Louisiana. Sassafrass liked to think the slaves would have been singing like that, if the white folks hadn't stolen our gods. Made our gods foreign to us, so the folks in Baton Rouge never came near those "crazy fanatic niggahs" out there. (214)

In this passage, Shange directly addresses the suspicion and mistrust that often plagues practitioners of traditional African religions here in the Americas. Under the aegis of Christianity, those practices have been associated with devil worship, black magic, or at the very least, plain craziness. And yet here, she presents the celebration as an act of restoration, of honoring those who came before.

Shange identifies Sassafrass as being a child of Shango and Oshun. In addition to the qualities of which I have already made mention, both are entities that are associated with justice. Though Sassafrass desires to be a priestess of Oshun so that, in her words, she could "heal, bring love & beauty wherever she went" (215), the vision of Oshun we later see is one more characterized by wrath. Shange writes: "Sassafrass was in the throes of the wrath of Oshun. How dare you betray me? Her foot stomped. How dare you not recognize my beauty? Her hand brought forth the mirror wherein she admired herself. How dare you make no preparations for my child who is a gift of las potencias, the spirits?" (217). Here we see an entity who is very protective of her child, who demands, at minimum, respect for everything that she is, and, by extension, everything that her children are. She demands that preparations be made for Sassafrass, that there is recognition that this woman is a sacred being.[35] The questions asked are directed to Mitch, Sassafrass's lover, a jazz musician who has, in the words of Sassafrass's godmother "led [her] away from righteousness. [He is] a man unfit for the blessings of the spirits" (214). Oshun wants her child to find someone who is worthy of her, who can and will appreciate the beautiful creature that she is. This applies to the initiate who is consecrated to this specific *orisha*, and in fact to all human beings, for we are all children of God the Highest and His entities, the *orishas*. In this way, then, Shange urges healing on the level of both the individual, as in the case of Sassafrass, and also on the level of the community. We must all not only learn our own value but also exist within a community that respects said worth.

Shange's novel examines the lives of women of the African Diaspora. She establishes this focus with her first paragraph: "Where there is a woman there is magic. If there is a moon falling from her mouth, she is a woman who knows her magic, who can share or not share her powers. A woman with a moon falling from her mouth, roses between her legs and tiaras of Spanish moss, this woman is a consort of the spirits" (3). Shange clearly states that women are more intimate with the metaphysical, the magical. She also implies that each woman has a sense of her own agency: she can *choose* to "share or not share her powers" (3), provided that "there is a moon falling from her mouth" (3). The moon here signifies life, reproduction, as well as unspoken mystery. The moon also signifies wisdom; for Shange, then, a woman who knows herself, who has a deep understanding of her own mystery, who respects and acknowledges this as a source of life, this woman is magic.

It is in acknowledging the unknown and the unknowable that woman is able to consort with the spirits, for the African Diaspora is composed not only of those who live but also those souls whose lives were cut short, by enslavement, war, untenable working conditions, etc. She posits that women are the primary bearers of the spiritual in this group: they communicate better with the unknown, again, if they are fully themselves. The youngest daughter, Indigo, is the chief example of a female who understands herself, is true to herself at the risk of displeasing her mother. With her older sisters, we see a journey of reconciliation. Both Sassafrass and Cypress come to respect and acknowledge their own mysteries as women. While Cypress settles into a monogamous heterosexual relationship with Leroy, after dalliances with both men and women, the climax of Sassafrass's storyline is becoming a priestess in the Yoruba religion.

Audre Lorde, Sandra María Esteves, and Ntozake Shange, all call on the Yoruba religion and its New World variant of *Regla de Ocha* in order to underscore the role of the communal in the construction of their identities; both Lorde and Shange also appeal to entities of *Vodou* as well. All of these women propose identities that recall the expansiveness of the African Diaspora. In addition, Lorde, Esteves, and Shange each allow their interactions with the *orishas* to inform their sense of themselves as women in the Americas. They refute patriarchal definitions of womanhood in their writings, replacing flat representations of the Feminine with multifaceted characterizations of women that celebrate mind and body, secular and spiritual. In this way, then, both Lorde and Shange find in the New World Yoruba religion an effective strategy for personal and communal liberation.

In the next chapter, we will see a similar entreaty on the part of the protagonists of two novels written by U.S. Latinas. The study moves to two novels that feature multiple generations of the same family, all of whom are struggling to find their distinctive place in the world. While the older generations are portrayed to be discontented at the conclusion of the novels, wounded by their own mistakes and missed opportunities for healing, members of the youngest generation engage in this search within their families and to an extent in their surrounding communities. They who represent the protagonists of the novels find in their spirituality a sense of home.

TWO

The Search for Home

Cristina García and Loida Maritza Pérez

I enter a *botánica* on upper Park Avenue. I've passed the place before but I've never gone inside. Today, it seems, there's nowhere else for me to go.

—Pilar, in *Dreaming in Cuban*

Since being removed from her grandmother's care when she was two years old and leaving Cuba with her family in 1961, Pilar Puente has searched for home. Throughout her adolescence, she uses visual art as a means by which to express her feelings of uncertainty, anxiety, and uprootedness. While these feelings may be characteristic of adolescence for many, they are heightened for Pilar, who is a child of exile. Despite living in New York City since leaving Havana, she continues to feel as if she has no roots. At one point, she declares, "I'm not sure Cuba is [home], but I want to find out" (58). Until this moment in the narrative when she enters the *botánica*, Pilar has made no mention of an interest in the religion practiced by millions in her country of origin as well as in New York City.[1] Yet it is a spiritual system that is deeply identified with the Cuban nation. By entering this religious space, she moves one step closer to deepening her relationship with a community from which she has previously felt estranged.

In the epigraph of this chapter, Pilar makes a distinction between organized religion and rituals that are more natural, that have to do with the earth. For her, formal religion is theoretical and intangible; it does nothing to comfort her, to bring her peace, or to connect in any way with anything larger than herself. At this point in the narration, Pilar lives in Manhattan, a student at Barnard College; in the midst of the noise of the metropolis, she longs for something more organic. She stops to enter what presents itself as the only place she should be in that moment: a *botánica* is a store of religious goods that is closely associated with the *Lucumí* religion. There, one may find herbs, candles, rosaries, prayer books, and statues of Catholic saints, among other items used in the practice of the religion. Though not formally a building of worship, a *botánica* is not simply a place of commerce. Instead, it is a site of consultation, as the shop owner often offers advice to customers suffering from any number of ailments, whether they are mental, physical, or spiritual in nature. With this moment, García underscores the relationship between the *Lucumí* religion, also known as *Regla de Ocha,* and a sense of home. Engagement with the religion is a way of connecting with this feeling of belonging.

Cristina García and Loida Maritza Pérez are two of the authors that are part of the growing canon of U.S. Latino/a Literature. Whereas the 1960s and 1970s saw the emergence of new voices being published, thereby gaining access to greater modes of diffusion of their cultural production, the 1980s and 1990s saw a shift, as these gains won during the midst of the civil rights movement were threatened by the ensuing culture wars, in which conservative scholars and publishers denounced the value of works by U.S. ethnic writers. Instead, they championed the Western canon, to no avail, as multicultural U.S. literature continues to thrive in the present day. The 1990s saw an incipient boom in the publication of novels, short stories, and poems by writers of Latin American heritage; within the broad English-speaking market, new imprints were created, such as Rayo at HarperCollins, where smaller independent presses such as Arte Público continued to expand their offerings. The rapidly growing U.S. Latino/a population meant a growing market for consumer products, including literature. García and Pérez are representative of their respective immigrant groups: García arrived in the United States as a child in the aftermath of the Cuban Revolution, whereas Pérez arrived as a child shortly after the assassination of Rafael Trujillo, the dictator who governed the Dominican Republic for almost three decades. Both women grew up in New York City within the Cuban and

Dominican communities respectively; both of these populations put forth strong ethnic identities and yet maintain powerful ties to their islands of origin.

In their first novels, both Cristina García and Loida Maritza Pérez create young female protagonists who are part of the Caribbean Diasporas of New York City and who initially look to their families' islands of origin as their source of emotional, physical, and psychological well-being. Both novels, *Dreaming in Cuban* (1992) and *Geographies of Home* (1999) respectively, showcase these characters' relationships with syncretized religions of the New World. Both authors, writing at the end of the twentieth century, suggest that for younger generations, and specifically for women, of the Diasporic Caribbean[2] living in the urban United States, home is no longer explicitly identified with their Mother, either metaphorically (that is, the motherland) or literally (biological mothers). Instead, it is defined by one's cultivation of a holistic sense of self, a recuperation of that which was lost in the transit of exile. These characters develop a sense of home by engaging in spiritual systems that have survived for millennia. For these daughters, home is a process of healing broken psyches.

In their article "'The Bloodstream of Our Inheritance': Female Identity and the Caribbean Mothers'-Land," Ann R. Morris and Margaret M. Dunn find that for Caribbean women, notions of home, nation, and motherland are always tied to one's relationship to mothers. They write: "If a woman is able to claim a connection to both [land and one's mothers], she is well prepared for the journey toward self-identity and fulfillment. But if she has been denied a developmental bond with her own mother, then the 'mothers' land' itself may provide a surrogate" (218). Both Cristina García's *Dreaming in Cuban* (1992) and Loida Maritza Pérez's *Geographies of Home* (1999) suggest that the lands of origin for these women of the Diaspora do not adequately provide a surrogate for mothers. In both of these works, the authors link syncretic religious systems with a sense of homeland, of nation. Neither their mothers nor their countries of origin lend the young protagonists of these novels the sense of refuge one normally associates with home. Instead, it is the development of one's spirituality through interaction with entities of African diasporic religions that marks the protagonists' awareness of themselves as women. The authors employ the religion as a metaphor for liberation: they come to understand that they carry home within themselves.

Each novel present three generations of women in one family; for the mothers of both works, a sense of refuge and tranquility is elusive. Both Celia and Aurelia reveal an unwillingness to cultivate a spiritual practice that is rooted in recognizing the divine in nature and in positive portrayals of the female self. They reject these spiritual systems as a way of life, relying on them instead as a means of swift resolution to pressing troubles. In limiting their involvement with these religions, they implicitly limit themselves and their own ability to effect positive change in the lives of their families. They instead concede to social pressures that dictate they be less powerful beings. Both authors suggest that the older characters misunderstand these theologies, casting them as instant fixes and misusing them to their own detriment. Neither Aurelia nor Celia reaches a sense of peace; instead, they are lost and forlorn at the conclusions of the novels, alienated from daughters who choose not to compromise themselves but rather to honor their emotional and spiritual development.

A great deal of critical attention has been paid to Cristina García's first novel. A finalist for the National Book Award, it has been credited with igniting the attention of U.S. publishers of the strength of the U.S. Latino/a market.[3] The subject of more than fifty completed dissertations and numerous articles, it has brought new awareness to the representation of Cuban Americans in U.S. literature by women writers. *Dreaming in Cuban* is the story of three generations of the del Pino family. Celia and Jorge del Pino have three children, Lourdes, Felicia, and Javier. In the aftermath of the Revolution, Lourdes and her family (her husband Rufino and daughter Pilar) leave Cuba for the United States, later to be joined by her father; Celia and Felicia remain on the island, and Javier is sent to Czechoslovakia. While she focuses on Pilar and her search for an understanding of herself, García includes the histories of all of the women in the family: that of her grandmother and mother, her aunt, and her cousins who remain on the island. The novel, then, is a chorus of female voices.[4]

Critics have focused on the themes of memory, exile, and the effects of the Cuban Revolution on the family unit. Often, however, the religious subtext is ignored, misread, or mentioned in passing. Andrea O'Reilly Herrera mentions in the last paragraph of her article that García's use of the sea in the novel links Celia to the *orisha* Yemaya (90), but does not explore this connection further. She also views the inclusion of *Regla de Ocha* as indicative of García's "attempt to preserve a cultural and personal past which has been maintained, in part, through oral tradition" (79), but again, does not delve into this topic in any depth. Adriana Méndez-Rodenas's "Engendering the Nation: The Mother/Daughter Plot in Cuban-American Fiction" offers a psychoanalytic reading of the novel; following Marianne Hirsch's work on the mother-daughter plot, Méndez-Rodenas posits that García's representation of this relationship reveals an "'underside' of the Cuban nation" (48), one in which mothers and daughters have borne witness to historical events and who continue to be silent, unable to voice their perspective of those moments. She labels Felicia's fascination with coconuts a "fetish for maternal milk" (51), later claiming that her decision to undergo initiation in the *Lucumí* religion reflects a desire for the "pre-oedipal bliss" (52). By placing the representation of this African diasporic religious system under a Western critical gaze, Méndez-Rodenas makes a grievous error, in that she misses entirely the opportunity to explore the meaning behind the imagery that García presents.

Much less attention has been granted to Loida Maritza Pérez's first and only published novel. Like García's text, it tackles the enduring legacy of a dictator on the family unit, in this case that of Rafael Leónidas Trujillo Molina, who ruled the Dominican Republic from 1930 until his assassination in 1961. *Geographies of Home* concerns Iliana, youngest child of Papito and Aurelia, who leaves college at the end of her third semester to return home to her family in Brooklyn. She does so out of a sense of duty to her family, and yet Iliana struggles with the feeling that she has betrayed herself. The novel reveals how she attempts to balance her obligations to her family with her responsibilities to herself. It also details Aurelia's recovery of the spiritual legacy of her own mother, Bienvenida, as well as another daughter's episodes of madness, which culminate with a sexual attack on Iliana. Critics most often focus on the theme of violence in the work. Emblematic of the commentary is that of Lucía M. Suárez, who views the novel as a "critical site that reveals a number of sociocultural dynamics of violence against women" (154). For her, silence and secrecy are enduring legacies of the violence endured by Haitians and Dominicans; the novel is a testimony to the numerous cruelties that the women of Hispaniola suffer. Lyn Di Iorio

Sandín views the book as one that reveals the struggle of U.S. Latinas against their own patriarchal culture. She notes: "Ultimately, rebellion against the repressive rules of Latino patriarchy carries the unfortunate consequence of a *de facto* assimilation into a U.S. culture that requires women to take on individualist, and possibly, masculinist, qualities to be successful subjects" (63). While she takes note of the religious presence in the novel, for Di Iorio Sandín the religions in the book (Papito's Seventh Day Adventism and Aurelia's unnamed Afro-Caribbean beliefs) are representative of a larger struggle, one in which the matriarch and patriarch of the family turn away from their Dominican roots, thereby losing their origins. The novel, then, records how the youngest of Papito's and Aurelia's fourteen children, Iliana, comes to establish a sense of self without a firm grasp on the past, on her family's history.

While the focus of Bridget Kevane's study is the representation of religion in U.S. Latino/a novels, she is also distracted by the brutality present in Pérez's work. She writes: "So full of violence and abuse is Pérez's novel that on some level it reflects a microcosm of *trujillato* reign but within the spiritual practices of a contemporary Dominican family" (76). For Kevane, Pérez suggests Adventism itself as one source of this violence, which provides Papito the rules by which to survive. He converts to this system from Catholicism while living in a chaotic Dominican Republic. Pérez writes: "In a country where both [right and wrong] had shifted according to a tyrant's whims and little had offered relief or hope, religion had granted him salvation, unmediated access to the divine, and steadfast rules by which to live" (149). Out of the desire for order, then, emerges a cruel sensibility that negatively affects all of Papito's fourteen children, especially his daughters, who are terrorized by him. Iliana's sisters have little knowledge of their mother's religious beliefs and practices, and so are left vulnerable to Papito's domination.[5] Only Iliana, the youngest of her siblings (as Aurelia was the youngest in her family) inherits her mother's spiritual abilities. She intuitively knows that reality is nothing more than a question of perspective, a point of view that can be manipulated at will.

Arriving home from college, she questions all that surrounds her (the religious faith with which she grew up and the manner in which her family members live their lives, for example), eventually reaching the conclusion that she must depend on her own perceptions rather than on the opinions of others. Reliance on her own spirituality allows her to arrive at this deduction. Cynthia L. Palmer offers a reading about the representation of this unnamed spiritual system, writing: "La tradición espiritual feminocéntrica se representa en la obra como un discurso cultural contrahegemónico que sirve como base de la resistencia femenina a múltiples niveles de opresión de la mujer en una sociedad netamente patriarcal [The womancentric spiritual tradition is represented in the novel as a counterhegemonic discourse that serves as a foundation of female resistance to multiple levels of oppression of women in a purely patriarchal society]" (n.p.). Engagement in this spiritual tradition, then, allows for an appreciation of the whole self rather than an accommodation of the self to fit into patriarchal norms. In cultivating this sense of wholeness, both Aurelia and Iliana come to learn how they carry home within themselves: they begin to look within, to rely on their own instincts and presentiments as their guide for living.

In both of these novels, the authors link maternal figures with their lands of origin. Aurelia epitomizes confusion: she represents the Dominican Republic and its ambivalent attitude toward its African past most vibrantly symbolized by its African diasporic religious systems. These cosmologies go unnamed, a direct reflection of prevailing attitudes toward them. The novel's conclusion suggests that in order to regain one's sense of self, one must at the very least acknowledge the existence of this heritage. Celia represents Cuba, and the predominant tone of the representation of the religion in this novel is also one of uncertainty: when she finds herself in dire situations, she turns to the *Lucumí* religion; otherwise she mistrusts it. Both characters have daughters with differing reactions to these spiritual systems: Aurelia's oldest daughter, Rebecca, knows little about her spiritual heritage and so exhibits little awareness of it. Without knowledge of her birthright, she is rootless, adrift. She does not have this spiritual system at her disposal and so cannot protect herself from an abusive husband. Celia's oldest daughter, Lourdes, who moves to New York soon after the Revolution, embraces all that is of the United States, and rejects vestiges of her Cuban heritage. She does, however, embrace a spirituality that allows her to converse with the spirit of her dead father. In addition, García associates Lourdes with the *orisha* of sweet waters, Oshun. Celia's second daughter, Felicia, embraces the *Lucumí* tradition fully, becoming an initiate in the religion as a priestess of Obatalá, the *orisha* of wisdom. García's depiction of

Felicia is troubling, however: she is often associated with unusual behavior that betrays an underlying madness. It is left to the younger generation, to Pilar and Iliana, to recover, acknowledge, and celebrate these legacies. In doing so, we see a changing attitude, an acceptance, of these spiritualities. These religious systems therefore represent liberation on both a personal and a political level. Accepting them, or at the very least acknowledging the African heritage of both of these countries, suggests a more cohesive sense of nation.

Mothers

With the mothers of the two novels, García and Pérez provide portraits of women who feel ambivalence toward spiritual systems brought to the Americas by enslaved Africans. Though she often relies on the *Lucumí* religion in times of strife, Celia is never comfortable with the religion or its practitioners, at one point labeling them "witch doctors" (190). Aurelia rejects the spiritual system into which she was born, discarding her mother's legacy of communing with spirits for what she believes to be the relative safety of orthodox Christianity. Though both women feel peace when they are involved in the religions, they nevertheless are wary of these cosmologies, reducing them to social practices rather than principles that guide how one lives his/her life. Both women strive to find calm in their lives, only to discover that it remains illusory.

Celia

Throughout García's novel, Celia conveys insecurity and apprehension, not only toward the *Lucumí* religion but also in her life as a whole. Unlike her daughter Felicia and her granddaughter Pilar, Celia does not trust in this spiritual system completely. She depends on the support of priests during times of personal trouble, but only as a last resort, when there are no other options remaining. For Celia, the religion is magic rather than a system that guides the lives of millions. Home, then, remains elusive to Celia: though she, like all of the other characters, searches for this sense of peace, it remains out of reach.

Celia's quest for a sense of refuge stems in part from her estranged relationship with her own mother, who sends her to live in the capital with her great-aunt after she and Celia's father divorce when she is four years old (92). She forgets her mother on the journey to the capital: "On the long train ride from the countryside, Celia lost her mother's face, the lies that had complicated her mouth" (92). In characterizing this woman a liar, the narrator implies a strained relationship between the mother and daughter pair, suggesting a generational pattern that repeats itself until Pilar and Lourdes return to Cuba. Though she comes to adore her caregiver, Celia seeks a tranquility that eludes her until her death at the end of the novel, indicating that her ruptured relationship with her mother signifies instability. In spite of relationships with her husband, friends, children, and the Revolution itself, nothing brings Celia enduring peace. Her first interaction with the religion is after her Spanish lover abandons her, returning to Granada after their brief affair. After physicians concede that they cannot identify a reason for her illness, her aunt, a woman who derided faithful practitioners of the Catholic faith (93), calls in a *Lucumí* priestess who assures both women that Celia will survive. The narrator mentions in passing that the santera "draped Celia with beaded necklaces" (37): this implies that Celia receives *elekes*, beads of protection that represent several *orishas*. This is the first ceremony believers in this faith undergo on their way to priesthood; while there is no indication that she takes part in other rituals, nevertheless there is an awareness of the religion on the part of Celia.

Still, Celia remains suspicious of this spiritual system. The narrator notes: "Although Celia dabbles in *Santería*'s harmless superstitions, she cannot bring herself to trust the clandestine rites of the African magic" (90–91). Celia's unease with the *Lucumí* religion suggests Cuba's discomfort with its African roots. In Celia, García creates a character that is representative of many Cubans born at the beginning of the twentieth century. She was born in 1909, a historical moment in which Cuba was attempting to define itself as a modern nation after having won independence from Spain ten years earlier. The state suppressed the practice of Afro-Cuban religions, including the *Lucumí* religion, through the first two decades of the century, as practitioners were thought to be criminals who posed a threat to the infant Cuban nation. This spiritual system was disparagingly known in contemporary popular parlance as *brujería* (witchcraft), and there were numerous anti-*brujo* campaigns, all aimed at ending worship.[6] Christine Ayorinde notes that during all periods of Cuban history, "there has been an oscillation between the suppression and political functionalization of Afro-Cuban cultural and religious practices" (51). García's Celia is emblematic of this ambivalence.

Throughout the novel, Celia goes to priests and priestesses of this religious system to resolve her problems: when her lover Gustavo returns to Spain (36); when she languishes with a broken heart (37); and when Javier returns from Czechoslovakia and soothes himself with alcohol (159). Celia's skepticism culminates with her daughter Felicia's initiation into the religion. The first year of the priesthood in this spiritual system marks a rebirth of the initiate; Felicia instead falls seriously ill. Despite offerings made by fellow priests and priestesses, she dies in Celia's arms. Moments before her death, Celia storms the house and destroys Felicia's religious articles (190), a sacrilegious act for believers in the faith. The novel suggests that in taking this action, she ends the possibility of finding tranquility.

In spite of her rejection of the religion, García associates Celia with the *orisha* of salt waters and maternity, Yemanyá; this pairing is apt given her estranged relationship with her own mother. While she does not enjoy a close association with her biological parent, she does with the entity that guides her. The priestess who consoles Celia after Gustavo leaves her tells her that she has a "wet landscape in [her] palm" (7, 37). She lives near the ocean (7); at the opening of the novel she is guarding the coastline against invasion (3). When Pilar visits her, she envisions her grandmother underwater (220), and when she paints her, she does so using shades of blue (233). Pilar notes: "The aquamarines near the shoreline, the azures of deeper waters, the eggshell blues beneath my grandmother's eyes, the fragile indigos tracking her hands. There's a blue, too, in the curves of the palms, and the edges of the words we speak, a blue tinge to the sand and the seashells and the plump gulls on the beach. The mole by Abuela's mouth is also blue, a vanishing blue" (233). Blue, a color of the oceans and seas, is the primary color associated with Yemanyá.[7] The author suggests that active engagement with this religious system, a willing awareness and relationship with the faith, results in a harmonious life. Celia only finds rest at the end of the novel: after a life of unrest, she finally goes home when she walks into the ocean, joining the entity that has served as her spiritual guide.

In addition to her reliance on the *Lucumí* religion in times of trouble, Celia also makes use of telepathy to communicate with Pilar at key moments in her granddaughter's life. The narrator notes: "She closes her eyes and speaks to her granddaughter, imagines her words as slices of light piercing the murky night" (7). García here employs vaguely Biblical imagery, in that darkness cannot exist where light is, and that there is truth in light. Here, the night is not only literal (she is speaking to Pilar in the wee hours of the morning) but also a metaphor for the darkness that is the division in her family, the mistruths that her daughter Lourdes has told Pilar. Celia's talks are soothing to Pilar, who notes: "I might be afraid of [my mother] if it weren't for those talks I have with Abuela Celia late at night. She tells me that my mother is sad inside and that her anger is more frustration at what she can't change" (63). Telepathy, then, is a healing tool that Celia utilizes in order to calm her granddaughter's anxieties. It allows Pilar to forgive her mother, or at least sympathize with Lourdes; in allaying her granddaughter's fears, Celia reveals herself to be an agent of unification of her family.

Aurelia

Like García with Celia, in Aurelia Pérez creates a character who represents her homeland and whose failings stem from an unwillingness to engage in the spiritual system that surrounds her in her youth. Aurelia is born to a mother who earns a reputation as a spiritualist and a midwife. As a result of her younger brother's suicide, she spurns her spiritual heritage, casting it aside in favor of what she believes to be a more simple life, that of wife and mother to fourteen. The novel suggests that in abandoning her spiritual capacities, Aurelia betrays herself and her children, leaving them vulnerable to violence. When she revives her spiritual gifts, she mistakenly acts out of hubris, carrying out an act of brutality in the name of protecting her grandchildren. In focusing her attention on her daughter's husband, she leaves her youngest child Iliana defenseless to her sister Marina's aggression. Aurelia misuses her gift as a tool for vengeance; the novel implies that in doing so she invites violence into her life, upsetting the fragile home she has established with her husband. By the end of the novel, she is despondent, pleading for her daughter's forgiveness and yet aware of her own role in Iliana's attack. For Aurelia, the employment of her spiritual gift as a weapon heralds an opportunity for reflection on the true meaning of power. She comes to understand this concept not as domination but instead as the strength to honor one's own truth.

Though she rejects this lesson from her mother, she learns it from her youngest child. Resigned and fatigued, Aurelia comes to understand and accept both the responsibility and the beauty of her gift. Though not completely at peace, she recognizes her own agency, that is, her ability to change her own life; ultimately, engaging her spiritual gift brings about a painful, but necessary, lesson in self-accountability.

Like Celia, Aurelia is estranged from her own mother, Bienvenida.[8] Both Aurelia and her brother Virgilio inherit a spiritual gift from their mother: all three are able to communicate with spirits, to "perceive the invisible" (134).[9] Bienvenida is renowned in their village in the Dominican Republic as the local midwife who "was also the one who initiated rituals to appease the prematurely dead and give hope to their survivors" (132). She performs a sacred task, both initiating life and commemorating those who die. When her brother Virgilio commits suicide, Aurelia abandons the gift rather than succumb to what she sees as madness (134). In the wake of his death, she comes to believe that she cannot trust herself: "She wanted simply to live her life and, upon dying, to stand before God as one of the meek and not as one of the rebellious led astray by abilities she dared not trust" (134). This fateful decision leads her to marry Papito, a convert to Seventh Day Adventism, which is portrayed in the novel as hostile to women.[10] Fearing herself and her own abilities, then, leads her to abandon them. In the same moment, Aurelia rejects both her mother and the spiritual system with which she has always lived. She recognizes as much: "So many lessons she had refused to learn because they had been taught to her by her mother" (135). Because she disagrees with her teacher's way of life, Aurelia rejects the instruction. Though she creates a home with her husband and her children in New York, she comes to realize that in abandoning her spirituality, she has discarded a fundamental part of herself. The novel, then, is an account of her attempted recovery of those powers.

For Aurelia, recuperation of those abilities first begins by recognizing her loss. She notes: "It wasn't that she romanticized the past or believed that things had been better long ago. She had been poor even in the Dominican Republic, but something had flourished from within which had enabled her to greet each day rather than cringe from it in dread. With bare feet planted on familiar ground, she had *trusted her perceptions*" (23; my emphasis). Aurelia's spirituality is tied not to her current economic conditions or her geographic space, nor is it tied to a linear sense of time, whereby she glorifies her youth. It is instead linked to herself, to her ability to sense and therefore comprehend what is happening in the world. For her, this means understanding occurrences both seen and unseen. She admits: "For too long she had relied on God to grant her peace, reluctant to believe that He, in His infinite wisdom, had endowed the world and its creatures with the powers each needed to survive. It was these powers which she had spurned so many years before and which her soul had ached for with a constancy that prayers had not soothed" (135). Aurelia here implies that her rejection of her gift stemmed in part from a suspicion that these extrasensory abilities were not of God. Pérez once again tacitly acknowledges the stigma attached to having these abilities within the Dominican and Dominican American communities. Prayer to a distant deity was inadequate for someone with the ability and experience to commune with the spirit world. The practice of her gift soothes Aurelia: it is a return to her roots, to all that she left behind in the Dominican Republic as a young woman.

In the process of recovering her spiritual legacy, Aurelia learns the extent to which she has distanced herself from her family pedigree by conversing with her daughters. She is devastated to learn that her girl-children have thought her complicit in their father's domestic tyranny. In leaving her religious practices, she provides the opportunity for misogyny to flourish in what is to be their communal refuge, that is to say, their home. Papito focuses strictly on the preservation of the virginity of his daughters while they are teenagers, given that being decent young women is the highest form of praise, from his perspective. He notes: "Wary lest his daughters wind up whores and his sons in jail, he had wielded religion as sword and shield in their defense" (146). For Papito, a woman's sexuality is the most important aspect of her identity, to the exclusion of everything else. For Aurelia, however, there is the cultivation of one's personhood as a whole, including all of their abilities. Aurelia comes to acknowledge that in attempting to protect her children, she has erased a possible source of strength for them: "She also thought of the many more things she had never revealed to her children or her grandchildren. . . . The silence enveloping these legacies, the half-truths meant to gloss over and protect, the falsehoods uttered for fear of causing pain, and the inability or unwillingness to speak, now seemed to her to have inflicted greater harm" (298). In her analysis of this novel, Lucía M. Suárez identifies a history of silence and denial as characteristic of the nations of Hispaniola: both Haiti and the Dominican Republic have endured decades of brutality without confronting the repercussions of said violence, the trauma that it has caused.[11] Silence stymies action; in recovering her spiritual legacy, Aurelia reclaims not only her voice but also her willingness to act. Upon learning that her daughters perceive her to have been a passive witness to her husband's abuse, she resolves to take action.

She does so by killing her son-in-law in the name of preserving the integrity of her family, especially that of her grandchildren, Rebecca's children. Witnesses to their father's physical abuse of their mother, they adamantly oppose their mother when she attempts to return to her husband after seeking refuge with Aurelia and Papito. On Christmas Day, with her children and their spouses in the house, Aurelia envisions Pasión clearly; plucking the feathers of the chickens she had bought that morning, she revives the livestock with which Pasión surrounds himself in his house. With the power of her mind and her desire, she controls the birds so that they attack their caretaker: "They lashed out at Pasión, pecking at his face, his hands, his wrists, and any other bits of skin exposed as he crawled from the room to collapse on the third-floor landing" (256). The narrator describes Aurelia's action as an act of invocation: "Having conjured death, Aurelia stood respectfully in its presence" (256). Ever Bienvenida's daughter, she understands the gravity of her act; however, the author makes clear that Aurelia's feat is one that stems from hubris. She writes: "This feeling of invincibility permeated her entire being, lending her a self-assurance she had previously not possessed and persuading her that she could from then on avert misfortune and keep her children safe" (265). Aurelia justifies her actions in the name of safeguarding her family from all external threat; though the narrator describes this action as one that allows her to establish roots, more important is the characterization of Aurelia as "invincible." It provides her with a false sense of security. Employing her gift in this instance is an expression of power, of the same brute strength that her daughters commented that Papito had displayed throughout their adolescence. Though she removes the threat of violence in Rebecca's life, eliminating the external threat to her family, she fails to do away with the domestic threat that is

Marina, her daughter diagnosed as "bipolar manic-depressive who exhibits schizophrenic tendencies" (219).

Throughout the novel, this daughter shows unstable behavior, and for the family as a whole, she is a danger that is to be contained. When a doctor begins to recommend further assistance for Marina after her fourth suicide attempt, Aurelia rejects him out of hand, storming out of the office to see her daughter (140). Placing Marina in an institution offends her sensibilities as a mother, as she places premier importance on the ability to care for her family herself. Though she brings Marina back from a drug-induced haze merely with the sound of her voice, she cannot completely cure Marina. Her illness as a whole proves to be outside of Aurelia's purview of healing. In her arrogance, Aurelia uses her spirituality as a weapon against Pasión, who physically attacks Rebecca and their children. She fails to do the same with Marina, who sexually assaults Iliana. In neglecting to protect her youngest daughter, who inherits the spiritual legacy of the matrilineal line, Aurelia puts in danger the transmission of this tradition.

Aurelia is at a much lonelier place at the end of novel; though she is surrounded by her children, she knows that she has failed to protect her youngest. She lives with that guilt, as well as with the awareness that her daughters all castigate her for her husband's violence. The narrator notes: "[S]he balked at the thought that they had been terrified of their father and had not only doubted her ability to protect them from him but had also interpreted her silence as proof of her complicity" (267). She did nothing to protect them when they were children, and so resolves to do differently when they are adults. She absorbs this lesson: at the end of the novel, she interrupts Papito's attack on Iliana. The narrator reveals Aurelia's lesson: "[G]enuine power originated from a soul resilient enough to persevere against all odds" (300). After employing her spiritual gift as an implement of brute strength, she understands that it is to be used in support of the truth, as an instrument of love rather than murder. The novel begins and ends with a plea of forgiveness on the part of Aurelia. She comes to learn that she cannot control evil or madness. Instead, she can speak the truth—this is the lesson her mother had attempted to impart when she would say: "[T]he future can hurt you if you deny the past" (132). Ignoring Marina's strange behavior, both Aurelia and Papito are complicit in Marina's assault on Iliana, a violation not only of the female body but also of the home they have labored to construct.

For Aurelia, home looks like a very different place than it does for Iliana: for Aurelia, there is a tone of resignation, like an understanding and unwanted acceptance of her limitations at the end of the novel. She has yet to make peace with her own human frailty. She accepts it uncomfortably: "We tried our best" (315). She murmurs this while her youngest decides to leave the house. Home is not a comfortable space, then, not even metaphorically, for Aurelia. It is not uplifting or empowering; instead, it is a place of fatigued acquiescence, of learning to accept one's limitations. Pérez writes: "Only now did she understand that her soul had yearned not for a geographical site but for a frame of mind able to accommodate any place as home" (137). She realizes that her spirituality is her home—it is a state of mind, a consciousness that is not dependent upon material conditions that surround her but instead on her relationship with herself.

First Generation of Daughters

Lourdes and Felicia of *Dreaming in Cuban* and Rebecca of *Geographies of Home* are the intermediary generation in these novels: they are neither the mothers with whom the young protagonists feel an affinity nor are they those protagonists themselves. Like Celia and Aurelia, Lourdes, Felicia, and Rebecca are both mothers and daughters at the same time. This analysis focuses on their relationship with different spiritual systems of the Spanish Caribbean. All three of them live in the Caribbean until adulthood. Lourdes and Rebecca immigrate to the United States as young adults, leaving behind the chaotic political situations of their home countries, while Felicia remains in Revolutionary Cuba. Each character has a complex relationship with her mother; engagement with spiritual systems provides an opportunity for the healing of that relationship.

Lourdes

Celia's oldest child has been estranged from her mother since her birth: having left his young wife with his own mother and sister, Jorge returns to discover that they have terrorized her, leading to Celia's breakdown. "In the final dialogue with her husband, before he took her to the asylum, Celia talked about how the baby had no shadow, how the earth in its hunger had consumed it. She held their child by one leg, handed her to Jorge and said, 'I will not remember her name'" (43). Lourdes grows up with the impression that her mother rejected her, and so remains distant from her. In spite of her strained relationship with her mother, Lourdes has a very close relationship with her father, one that continues after his death. Throughout the novel, Lourdes is associated with the river,[12] which itself carries the essence of Oshun according to the *Lucumí* system of belief. While García does not explicitly develop this connection, she offers a representation of Spiritism, where a living human being communicates with spirit guides who may or may not be his/her ancestors. Lourdes hears her father forty days after he has been buried; he not only offers her advice (136), he checks on her well-being (170), and tells her stories about her mother to which she had no previous knowledge (195–96). In conversation with Lourdes after his death, Jorge reveals to her his mistreatment of Celia: "I tried to kill her, Lourdes. I wanted to kill her. . . . I wanted to break her, may God forgive me. When I returned, it was done" (195). A traveling salesman, Jorge leaves his young wife with his mother and sister, in full knowledge that they would be abusive to her. He does so out of jealousy: he marries Celia after she has been abandoned by her Spanish lover. In spite of this desertion, Celia maintains her love for this man, Gustavo, writing the epistles that interrupt the narrative. Jorge continues: "I took you from her while you were still a part of her. I wanted to own you for myself. And you've always been mine, *hija*" (196). In confessing his complicity in causing the estrangement between mother and daughter, Jorge, as a spirit, brings about an opportunity for healing. In the afterlife, he presents an opportunity for reconciliation that he did not facilitate while he was alive, in all of his human frailty. With this characterization, García underscores the role of spirits in the lives of their charges: to assist them so that they live in balance with their surroundings, whole and self-realized.

After admitting his role in separating Lourdes from Celia, Jorge goes on to mention Lourdes's violation at the hands of Revolutionary soldiers on her husband's land some thirty years prior to the conversation. At the time pregnant with her second child, she confronts the two soldiers who have come to claim the land for the government. One soldier scars her, carving his initials on her flesh with his knife. She tells no one of this incident, leaving Cuba with her husband and daughter soon after. Having recounted it to no one, it comes as a surprise when her father says that he knows of the rape. In the spirit world, there is an access to omniscience, to knowledge beyond human comprehension. In revealing his knowledge of this life-altering incident, her darkest secret and another moment that has come to define her life,[13] Jorge assures his daughter of his love for her. He then reveals to Lourdes that her mother had loved her (196), a disclosure that goes against everything Lourdes has thought about Celia. Her feelings of abandonment by her mother had to this point dominated Lourdes's conception of herself; with her father's admission and his encouragement, she returns soon after to Cuba to visit her mother for the first time since she left the island. García underscores how healing for this daughter does not come in reconciliation either with her mother or with the mother country; on the contrary, it comes about at the intervention of a spirit, a father whose love continues into the afterlife. Home, then, is not found either in a geographical place or in one person but instead within oneself and the guides with which one walks.

Felicia

Unlike her sister Lourdes, Celia's other daughter, Felicia, finds tranquility and comfort in the *Lucumí* religion. García primarily characterizes this figure by her unorthodox behavior, obscuring the roots of this comportment. Celia's second daughter has the misfortune of being named for a victim of homicide: while in the asylum, Celia befriends a woman who killed her husband. Soon after, she dies of incineration (51). The novel suggests that in naming her child after her murdered friend, Celia bestows upon Felicia a life of tribulation. On the day of her wedding to her first husband, she makes a sexual advance, only to be choked to near-unconsciousness (81). She is seven months pregnant with twins at the time. A merchant marine, Hugo is frequently away at sea: upon his return, he brings her several infections, including syphilis (82). The narrator mentions this diagnosis in passing in the course of the novel (47, 82, 90), focusing instead on Felicia's delusions, her eccentric behavior, and her suicide attempts. Pregnant with her third child, she tries to kill her first husband by burning him with a greased rag (82). Within four days of meeting and marrying her second husband, he dies in a fire (149). She has no memory of meeting, let alone marrying her third husband, who the narrator implies dies after falling from a roller-coaster car that he is sharing with his wife (155). There is no mention of treatment for the syphilis, leading the reader to conclude that Felicia's increasingly erratic actions are the result of the advancement of the illness.

Her interaction with the *Lucumí* religion begins when she is a girl: in her first meeting with Herminia at six years of age, she asks this daughter of a *babalawo*[14] to save her (183). Throughout the years, she depends upon her friend for her assistance. In her eponymous chapter, which she narrates, Herminia highlights her appearance: "The other children shunned me and called me *bruja*. They made fun of my hair, oiled and plaited in neat rows, and of my skin, black as my father's" (184). Herminia, then, represents the Afro-Cuban element of the Cuban nation, that which has been uneasily accommodated in the national historical discourse in the twentieth century.[15] Through her friendship with Herminia, the novel implies that Felicia learns to combat the implied tragic legacy of her namesake. Her engagement with this religious system has curative effects, as Herminia notes: "Our rituals healed her, made her believe again. My father used to say that there are forces in the universe that can transform our lives if only we'd surrender ourselves. Felicia surrendered, and found her fulfillment" (186). The culmination of her concession to these protective forces is her initiation in the religion.

García's portrait of Felicia's ceremony and ensuing year of initiation is problematic in that it implies that the religion is to blame for Felicia's subsequent demise. Soon after she undergoes the formal procedure to be a priestess of Obatalá, she begins to weaken physically, a process that Herminia observes is not standard: "When you make a saint, the saint takes good care of you. But Felicia showed none of these blessings" (189). Rather than appear vibrant, she withers away, losing weight as well as her eyesight. This illness recalls Celia's heartbreak after her married lover abandons her, in which she is characterized by her list-lessness and her will to die. Whereas Celia is resolute on dying, having lost her will to live, Felicia is determined to be a commendable priestess: "She wanted to prove to the *orishas* that she was a true believer, serious and worthy of serving them, so she continued her rituals" (188). In her commitment to these entities, then, Felicia has found a reason to continue living; she finds her peace in serving her guiding spiritual entities. She dies serenely, in her mother's arms (190). The religion, then, brings a peaceful conclusion to what had been a tortured life; passing away while being cradled by her mother, she finds her refuge.

Rebecca

With her portrait of Rebecca, Pérez highlights the plight of the female immigrant who lives without a sense of spirituality. That she is female is significant: in *Geographies of Home*, spirituality passes from mother to daughter, from Bienvenida to Aurelia, from Aurelia to her girls. Without this sensibility, Rebecca is without roots and therefore without peace. Bienvenida raises Rebecca, Aurelia's firstborn daughter, until she is eight years old, and from her grandmother she learns to appreciate the miraculous in both the natural and human realms (56). The narrator observes: "She had been raised on miracles, taught from early childhood to believe. In the Dominican Republic she had walked hand in hand with her maternal grandmother who had pointed out trees that appeared to have rotted from the inside out but had nonetheless branched out to bloom with leaves" (56). Bienvenida introduces her grandchild to the marvels of nature, to the wonders that the environment presents to her, underscoring that human beings are but one part of life on this planet.[16] As an adolescent, she would escape the family's house and retreat to nature: "She had flung these [clothes] off to sprawl naked on the earth cooled by midday rains" (205). There, away from everyone, Rebecca would masturbate, retreating from the demands of her parents or her younger siblings, for whom she has to care. With this description of a young girl's burgeoning sexuality, Pérez underscores the importance of sensuality in the development of one's identity. Within her home, any expression of sensuality is strictly forbidden, as Papito is determined that his daughters will not be "whores" (146). With this, Pérez implies that their house in the Dominican Republic is just as confining as the one they share in the United States. Being outside, under the "low-hanging leaves of papaya trees" (205), Rebecca can explore these urges. When she pleasures herself, she has the opportunity to think only of herself and her aspirations, rather than the demands of her family. With Rebecca, the novel suggests that a strictly orthodox Christian upbringing negatively affects women, who are limited to the role of mother and wife.

In the present-day narration, Rebecca is forty years old; a virgin until she is thirty, she is in a relationship with one man, Samuel, for two years, then marries her husband, Pasión, with whom she has three children. The novel implies that Rebecca does not have an identity until she marries; this, in spite the fact that she is the first in the family to move to the United States, working in order to secure entrance visas for the admission of her parents and siblings into the country (62). Like Iliana, Rebecca also feels the obligation of family; her efforts go unacknowledged, as Papito resumes his place as the head of the family once he arrives from the island. Though she is the oldest girl-child, she is not the first to marry, watching two younger sisters achieve that goal (203), and so she escapes by living with a violent man who needs to establish residency. Pérez implies that the loss of a firm relationship with the matriarchal heritage of spirituality results in Rebecca's loss of herself: at the outset of the novel, she is in an abusive relationship that she chooses not to leave. In the face of violence to her personhood and those of her children, she remains in her marriage, in part because she depends on her husband for an acceptable identity: she is someone's wife. Without access to the spirituality of her matrilineal line, Rebecca struggles to find a way of being in the world.

(Grand) Daughters

With Pilar and Iliana, García and Pérez provide portraits of independent young women who discover for themselves new modes of womanhood by interacting with African diasporic spiritual systems. Neither is satisfied with the examples of living that their mothers (and in Pilar's case, grandmother) reveal to them. Instead, they find refuge in religious systems that offer broader definitions of womanhood. Both characters come to embrace those beliefs; in doing so, they learn to accept themselves, finding within themselves the peace and tranquility they had previously identified with their families and their countries of origin. Home for both of these women lies within.

Pilar

Throughout this novel, the protagonist expresses a desire to return to the island where she spent her first two years, and to her grandmother: for Pilar, both Cuba and Celia mean home, that is, they both convey feelings of safety and refuge. Her parents leave the island after the

Revolution; during the course of the narrative, she longs for Celia, with whom she has a special relationship. They communicate telepathically in the dark of night: "She closes her eyes and speaks to her granddaughter, imagines her words as slices of light piercing the murky night" (7). Later, Pilar notes that Celia shares the story of her own life with her granddaughter (28–29), and she encourages her to live her dream of being an artist (29). From her earliest memories, then, Celia gives Pilar permission to be herself; she demonstrates to her young granddaughter unconditional love, accepting her for herself. Celia's spiritual abilities, therefore, are the vehicle through which she can attempt to heal her dispersed family. Following Celia's example, Pilar learns to accept her own spiritual abilities once they begin to reveal themselves.

During her visit to the *botánica* with which this chapter opens, Pilar selects a red and white beaded necklace, and lifts a cane designed with a woman balancing a double-headed ax (200). Both the double-headed ax and the combination of red and white are associated with Changó, the *orisha* of thunder. In doing so, she reveals an affinity for this entity, and indeed, in conversation with the owner of the store, he confirms for her that she is a daughter of Changó. Telling Pilar that she "must finish what [she] began" (200), the storeowner prescribes nine days of spiritual baths, assuring her that clarity will come afterward. On the ninth day, she calls Lourdes with the news that they must return to Cuba. With the inclusion of this moment in the narrative, García underscores that this religious system brings clarity to those who have faith in its precepts. Pilar intuitively feels comfortable speaking with the owner of the store: "I rub the beads in my left hand and feel a warm current drifting up my arm, across my shoulders, down between my breasts" (200). With this description we see the unifying of Pilar's mental intuition and her embodied knowledge: it is her body, her physical reaction to the words of the store owner, that relays to her the assurance that she should follow his advice.

In addition to the clarity that comes after she finishes her baths, she also experiences heightened awareness of her surroundings. Pilar notes: "I can hear fragments of people's thoughts, glimpse scraps of the future. It's nothing I can control. The perceptions come without warning or explanations, erratic as lightning" (216). At no point does she fear this ability; on the contrary, Pilar acknowledges it and welcomes it. With this sentence, she presages the further development of her spirituality in

Cuba. Once there, she reunites with her grandmother and learns more about her family. Her return to the island allows her to understand herself not solely as her mother's daughter but within a larger context of family.

Soon after arriving on the island, Pilar insists on meeting Herminia, Felicia's best friend. Ivanito recounts their encounter: "We [Pilar and Ivanito] listen to stories about my mother [Felicia] as a child, about her marriages to my father and to other men, about the secret ceremonies of her religion and, because Pilar insists on every detail, about my mother's final rite, and her last months on Palmas Street" (231). In asking questions about her aunt and the initiation ceremony Felicia undergoes, the narrator indicates the depth of interest Pilar has about the religion. Herminia then welcomes Pilar into a back room, recognizing her as a daughter of Changó.[17] She begins to question the Revolution in a way that she had not done while she was in New York. An avid supporter of Fidel Castro as a teenager in the United States, on the island she sees the effects of the Revolution. She notes: "I have to admit it's much tougher here than I expected, but at least everyone seems to have the bare necessities" (235). In conversation with her grandmother, Pilar raises the issue of the role of art: she learns that the only acceptable art is that which does not attack the state (235), an unacceptable compromise for a daughter of the United States. In returning to the island, Pilar returns to the place that she has to some extent identified as home. While she is there, she comes to the realization that she can no longer categorize it as such: "But sooner or later I'd have to return to New York. I know now it's where I belong—not *instead* of here, but *more* than here" (236; italics in the original). No longer does Pilar romanticize Cuba; instead, she concedes the political realities of the island, as well as the hardships suffered by its inhabitants. The *Lucumí* religion has facilitated her return to the island: by engaging this spiritual system, she begins to understand her fierce independence and herself. With this, she recognizes that home is not a geographical location or idealized vision; instead, it is that which she carries within herself.

Iliana

At the onset of *Geographies of Home* (1999), we meet Iliana, the protagonist of the novel, who returns to her family home in Brooklyn after

eighteen months at a university in upstate New York. The daughter of
Dominican immigrants, she is the first female in her family to attend
college as well as the first female to leave home unmarried. She encounters numerous acts of racism on her campus, where she is one of only
a few black women. She decides to return home after being summoned
by a "disembodied voice" (2) that would bring her the latest news of
her family. She comes to identify this voice as belonging to her mother,
who communicates with her telepathically. The voice imparts her life
story, tells her from where she comes. Pérez writes: "On nights when
the radiator in her room gave off little warmth, the voice transported
her to a Dominican Republic where summer days were eternal, clouds
evaporated in the scorching heat, and palm trees arched along beaches
of fiery sand. It spoke of her birth immediately following her grandmother's death. . . . the voice reassured Iliana of her own existence and
kept her rooted" (4). Aurelia soothes her youngest child by recalling
earlier times, rendering nostalgia an effective tool for dispelling her
daughter's fears and anxieties. The Dominican Republic she evokes
is one that is seemingly unpopulated: there is no mention of social,
political, or economic realities. Instead, Aurelia appeals to the beauty of
the country's natural landscape, of the heat, the beaches, and the palm
trees, all of which are a striking contrast to the cold in which Iliana lives
in the winter of upstate New York. As she calls for her youngest child to
return home, Aurelia implicitly conveys the message that Iliana would
be closer to that idyllic space if she were to move back to Brooklyn. She
soon learns otherwise.

In identifying the voice as belonging to her mother, Iliana goes
against her own upbringing. The narrator notes: "Everything Iliana had
been brought up to believe denounced the voice as evil. Yet her instincts
persuaded her it wasn't so" (4). This moment establishes the tension
in the novel: Iliana must decide between behaving according to the
dictates of her family or learning to trust herself and her perceptions.
In communicating with her youngest, Aurelia is asking Iliana to discard
all that she has learned from her family and follow her instincts instead.
Aurelia does not tell either her husband or her own children about her
brother or indeed about her own capabilities, which is why she confuses
Iliana, who also inherits the gift. Iliana has to choose between relying
on herself, on her own instincts, as she had done as a child before being
socialized to abandon those abilities, or continue to rely on her family,
which is defined by her father, who absolutely does not believe in such

things. In the end, she realizes that she must choose herself and her abilities, that both of her parents are fallible, indeed that her father fears his surroundings much more than she ever has. She realizes this after she suffers two sexual assaults by her sister, a diagnosed "bipolar manic-depressive [who] exhibited symptoms of schizophrenia" (219). Iliana disassociates from her body after the first attack, attempting to rationalize what has happened. She reasons that the moment of the attack is only a moment of her existence, and while she makes an effort to remain aware solely of her thoughts, her body calls for her focus. She observes: "She was far more than the sum of her spilled blood and her flesh that had been pierced. She was the breaths seeping from her lips, the heart resounding in her chest, the anima enabling her to perceive" (287). Iliana makes an interesting distinction between her material self, her flesh and blood, to a more abstract identity. She concentrates on her respiration, which signifies life itself, as well as on the muscle that pumps blood throughout her system. Finally, she concentrates on her soul, which allows her to sense and understand that which is occurring. In the novel, Iliana struggles to make peace with her intuition: in this moment, she comes to accept its soundness, its authentic role in her life and in her conception of herself. Iliana recognizes that her intuition is a valid source of knowledge for her.

This understanding is reaffirmed after Marina attacks her again. In spite of her best attempts, once again it is Iliana's body that reacts physically to her sister's invasion. Marina's assault is insidious; the narrator notes that "Iliana concentrated on holding herself erect, concentrated too on keeping her limbs from severing and her head from rolling off" (290). She does all she can to maintain her body's integrity, giving attention to her limbs, her extremities. Assured that the attack has rendered her invisible, she moves to clothe her exposed self; at the sound of her sister's voice affirming that she is fine, Iliana's body reacts. The tone of this voice conveys not only Marina's hatred for Iliana but also her conviction that she understands the extent of her violation. The narrator notes: "Her body shuddered, jerked forward, shook spasmodically and did not still" (290). Iliana feels the extent of her sister's hostility toward her, not only because of the attacks themselves but also because of the reaction of her body.

Ironically, it is the attack on her physical self that brings about Iliana's healing in that it confirms for Iliana that she possesses spiritual gifts that others do not. It confirms for her the premonition she had prior to leaving her college campus (11). It also serves to unite her intuition with her embodied knowledge. While she has struggled with her perceptions in the novel, she has also been distant from her body. Though other characters describe her as physically beautiful,[18] Iliana perceives herself as awkward and uncoordinated, ugly (43). Shy, she commands attention with her physique. She has a confident stride: "[H]er hips thrust forward and swayed as if unhinged. Her friend Ed had described the stride as regal, her sisters as whorish" (5). Though she is not aware of her beauty, Iliana's physical presence conveys confidence and self-assurance. She is a walking contradiction, then, fragmented in that her conception of herself does not match what she unknowingly conveys. After the two assaults by Marina, she suffers another attack at the hands of her father, who beats her after she arrives late the Sunday night of the confrontation with her sister. In the moment that she feels the blows, the narrator notes: "Her soul reclaimed every inch of her body as her thoughts coalesced into a scream of silent vows. *"NoNo. I will not fall or flinch. I will not let you or anyone else ever knock me down again. I may have been molded from your flesh but this body is mine and mine alone. You will not make me ashamed of it as my sister did"* (313; italics in the original). With this third assault, then, Iliana releases the bonds of guilt and obligation that dictated her return to the family. She claims ownership of her body, her thoughts, and her soul. She understands that she cannot depend on her family for protection or love. Instead, she takes full responsibility for her own life, with the recognition that she has all of the tools necessary to live a full and vibrant existence.

Conclusion

She would leave no memories behind. All of them were her self. All of them were home.

—Iliana, in *Geographies of Home*

In both of these novels, the protagonists confront the instability of "home," which is identified as a specific geographical space (for García, it is Cuba, and for Pérez, most immediately it is a house in Brooklyn and then more remotely, the Dominican Republic). At the conclusion of the novels, both come to understand that this place does not exist outside of themselves, but rather, within each young woman. Both young women had previously identified maternal figures with home (Pilar with her grandmother Celia, Iliana with her mother Aurelia); by the end of each work, they realize that this association no longer functions for them. Instead, they come to rely on themselves, on their own intuition. Both Cristina García and Loida Maritza Pérez associate this instinct with an unnamed religious presence. These religions facilitate the maturation of both Iliana and Pilar in that they come to realize that they can depend on themselves. In Pilar's case, after suffering two violations by her sister, it is clear that she has no other choice. The romanticized versions of home fade, and they realize that they carry home within themselves.

In the next chapter, we will see a phenomenon similar to that which we have seen so far: a poetic voice invoking these spiritual entities and a female protagonist who is led on a journey of self-discovery by these same beings. The depiction of these spiritual systems differs greatly in the representative Latin American novels presented in this study: U.S. authors continue to refer to these religions as if in code, that is, elusively. These works show a cosmology that is to be discovered, unearthed, and recovered. In both Cuba and Brazil, however, the characters of the novels written by white women of those societies interact directly with the *orisha*s, who are characters themselves integral to the plots of these works. The women writers of African descent in both countries, however, refer more obliquely to these entities, suggesting a radically different relationship not only with the religious traditions themselves but also with the inclusion of these religions in their literary works.

⇃ THREE ↿

Love, Revolution, Survival

Nancy Morejón and Daína Chaviano

quién soy / que voy de nuevo entre las calles, entre orichas, /
entre el calor oscuro y corpulento
— Nancy Morejón, "Amor, ciudad atribuida"

who am I / that I go again through the streets, among orichas, /
through the dark and corpulent heat
—"Love, Attributed City"

A los tiranos les encanta controlar hasta los orgasmos de sus
súbditos; pero no por puritanismo, sino porque no soportan que
nada escape a su control. Por eso la cama es el único sitio donde
los preceptos de las dictaduras son burlados a ultranza.
—Eri, in *Casa de juegos*

Tyrants love controlling even the orgasms of their subjects; not
because of puritanism but because they cannot bear that anything
escapes their control. For this reason the bed is the only place
where the rules of dictatorships are fought tooth and nail.

Nancy Morejón may be the most famous poet to emerge from Revolutionary Cuba; winner of the Premio Nacional de Literatura in 2001, she is lauded not only for her virtuosity as a poet, that is, for her lyricism and her imagery, but also for writing the black woman into the Cuban national imaginary, primarily with her widely anthologized poem "Mujer negra" (1975). She has published several poetry collections, including *Mutismos* (1962); *Amor, ciudad atribuída* (1964); *Richard trajo su flauta y otros argumentos* (1967); *Parajes de una época* (1979); *Octubre imprescindible* (1983); *Cuaderno de Granada* (1984); *Piedra pulida* (1986); and *Paisaje célebre* (1993). In addition to her poetry, she is a well-respected literary critic in her own right, as well as a translator. As one of the most visible Cuban artists recognized outside of the country, Morejón is also widely criticized, principally by literary critics based in the United States, for continuing to support the Cuban Revolution, as she makes clear in writings and interviews, as well as in her decision to continue living in Cuba. In poems such as "Un patio de La Habana," "Los ojos de Eleggua," and "Amo a mi amo," and in this brief fragment from her love poem to her beloved city of Havana, Morejón highlights the omnipresence of the ancestors and the *orishas* in her homeland, reminding her audience of a legacy of insurrection and revolt that predates 1959. For her, Cuban men and women of African descent, the descendants of the enslaved Africans who transported their religion during the Middle Passage, they are the true rebels of the country; they serve as the conscience of the Revolutionary project.

For Daína Chaviano, the Revolution is now at its nadir; she clearly establishes the three related themes of *Casa de juegos*, published the same year that Cuba was celebrating the fortieth anniversary of the Revolution, sex, power, and freedom. In juxtaposing the three, she provides a formula by which power may be undermined in order to reach some semblance of freedom. She proposes that the only true liberation practice for those living under dictatorship is sex. In a country where the populace is wholly dependent on the government to provide for every aspect of one's life (food, shelter, education, employment), where nothing escapes the notice of the neighborhood guard, only the most basic of human functions evade the regime's reach. In this conversation, the protagonist of the novel, Gaia, a university student, learns that her sexual partner, Eri, has saved her from expulsion from school without her knowledge. Throughout the novel, he repeatedly says that he wants to heal her: after the death of a previous lover, she experiences a marked lack of sexual drive for several years. In the course of that time, she becomes troublesome as she insists on questioning the absurdity of the system in which they live. In one instance, she refuses to sign a petition circulating in the university denouncing anyone or anything that proves to be inconsistent with Marxism-Leninism (110). Only upon serious persuasion on the part of her classmates, who insist that their signatures mean nothing, does she join in their pledge of fidelity to the regime. So long as Gaia, the protagonist, remains sexually inactive and toes the party line, she is the perfect Cuban citizen: contained, voiceless, and controlled. Her lover aims to heal her by revealing that the best form of rebellion is through sex: only in this way does one gain a voice. It is the sexual act culminating in orgasm that eludes the government's grasp. The most revolutionary act against the now-battered Revolutionary regime in Cuba is not armed revolution, such as that which brought the regime into power in the first place, but the physical and spiritual union of two beings. In doing so, the participants of this union are unleashing the power of the erotic, that which Audre Lorde identifies as the "assertion of the lifeforce of women; of that creative energy empowered, the knowledge and the use of which we are now reclaiming in our language, our history, our dancing, our loving, our work, our lives" (55).[1] She goes on to state: "The erotic is the nurturer or nursemaid of all our deepest knowledge" (56). Throughout her oeuvre, Daína Chaviano utilizes the image of the sexual act as the sites of multiple discourses: here, it is most accessible means to a sense of freedom.

The Cuban Revolution of 1959 is one of the defining events of the twentieth century, not only for Cuba itself but for the Americas as a whole. Early reforms included the reduction of rents and utilities, the construction of low-priced public housing, the raising of wages, and land redistribution. Legal discrimination was outlawed within the first three months of 1959; as historian Louis A. Pérez Jr. observes, "The reform measures were dramatic and historic, and all provided immediate relief to those sectors of Cuban society that demanded relief immediately" (321). He goes on to state that a disproportionate segment of those without employment were men and women of African descent, and so they were among the primary beneficiaries (321). Sweeping changes in the areas of health, education, and nutrition resulted in a better educated, more healthy population, one that could contribute and participate in the Revolution. In 1958, only 25 percent of the Cuban population as a whole had attended school, with the remaining 75 percent having never completed primary school. Four years later, as a result of widespread literary campaigns, the adult literacy rate in the country had risen to 96 percent.[2] Offerings on the secondary and university level were expanded, so that hundreds of thousands more students were attending school. Levels of poverty dropped dramatically, as mandatory and free health care resulted in an increase in life span; food rationing meant that everyone in the country had access to food. These reforms resulted in the flight of tens of thousands of members of the middle class and the elite: by 1962, almost two hundred thousand Cubans had left the country, with a great number being professionals, skilled workers, landowners (Pérez 335). Those who left had been deprived by the sweeping changes made by the government, especially in terms of the widespread seizure of land; a great number of those who remained in that first decade of the Revolution benefited materially, having made gains in education, employment, health care, and housing. They became primary stakeholders in the success of the Revolution.

Nancy Morejón

Born in Havana to politically active parents (her father was a member of the Communist Party in the 1930s), Nancy Morejón grew up in the capital city surrounded by extended family. As the daughter of communists, she was raised a secularist, and yet she was fascinated by the vibrant Afro-Cuban culture that enveloped her.[3] Indeed, Morejón grew up in the 1940s, when African culture and the contributions made by Africans to the country were being celebrated in the realms of literature, music, and the visual arts. Beginning in the 1920s, there was a concerted effort on the part of the scholars, writers, and artists to discover the "authentic" in their country; Fernando Ortiz, Lydia Cabrera, Alejo Carpentier, Nicolás Guillén, and Wilfredo Lam all participated in efforts to celebrate the Cuban of African descent, and they did so by studying and promoting information on Afro-Cuban religions such as *Regla de Ocha, Palo Mayombe,* and *Abakuá* (in the case of Ortiz and Cabrera), and by incorporating entities of these religions in their work (in the case of Carpentier, Guillén, and Lam). Though these religions were officially outlawed until the 1980s, there was a celebration of these religious

practices, at least in the realm of culture.[4] In a 1994 interview with Ruth
Behar and Lucía Suárez, Morejón comments:

> Yet religion in Cuba, in its popular sense, is fundamental—Santería,
> Spiritism, the religious beliefs which are now called magico-religious
> systems. These practices were so commonplace that they existed in
> and around the world within which we moved. Not exactly in our
> house, but where I lived and went to school. *I have always said that
> these religions constituted a focus of cultural resistance for the slaves.*
> That shaped me. It was a world I could enter and exit, in which I
> could feel a song, listen to a chorus of slaves, listen to a *guaguancó*,
> a *rumba*, a *guaracha*, or a *toque de santos*. This is the world that, many
> years later, I realized I had not learned about from anthropological
> sources, or in lectures by Fernando Ortiz. This was a reality that
> belonged to my uncles, my distant uncles. *It was seen as a religion,
> but at the same time it was a form of cultural expression.* (626–27; my
> emphasis)

For Morejón, then, the influence of the *Regla de Ocha* extends beyond
just the religious sphere to life itself. This is a spiritual system that
undergirds the Afro-Cuban community, for much of whom it is not
just a set of practices that are to be observed once a week but instead
is an ongoing conversation with ancestors and *orichas*. This continuous
dialogue with the entities that serve as spiritual guides to humanity is
present in several of her poems.

Morejón underscores the commonality of this interaction with the
spiritual realm in "Un patio de La Habana." In this poem, Morejón
juxtaposes material luxury with spiritual wealth; in the first stanza,
Morejón establishes the plainness of the space she describes. It is not
grand in any obvious way: there are no high walls or decorations with
flowers that recall the majesty or romanticized vision of southern Spain
as offered by poets such as Antonio Machado.[5] Instead, the value of the
space lies in that it is a resting place for the relatives who have died
("conserva los huesos de los muertos"). Whether understood as the
literal burial site for the ancestors or as a space through which older
generations of men and women in the family have passed, the patio
moves from simply an architectural extension of the house to a sacred
space. The poetic voice identifies these beings as the source of wealth

for the surviving members of the family, who in their recognition of those who have died honor their memory. Morejon's use of the word *labrador* indicates that this is not a wealthy family but instead one whose members have worked the land; in a Cuban context, this more often than not alludes to an African heritage. This continuing ancestral presence guides and protects the present generation; they have ascended to the next level of existence, whereby they can continue to watch over their family members.

Morejón's inclusion of sacred entities includes allusions not only to the ancestors but also to the *orichas* themselves. In most of her poetry, she only suggests the presence of these entities through references to nature; one of the few in which she plainly includes an *oricha* is "Los ojos de Eleggua." Leslie Feracho reads the poem as a redefinition of the Cuban homespace with the acknowledgment of the Afro-Cuban heritage, as symbolized by the entity associated with the crossroads; Alan West sees the poem as an example of Morejón's insistence on Cuban transculturation: "A Yoruba orisha, symbol of destiny, chance, and justice, merges with the power of faith and miracles (St. Anthony), racial harmony and social justice (St. Martin de Porres), and the total nourishment of El Niño de Atocha" (18).[6] With this poem, Morejón offers a warning to the Cuban populace about the future of the country: Elegguá, the entity associated with destiny, is unhappy and uncertain about the direction he is going in the poem. Cuba is the source of the *Regla de Ocha* in the Americas; the disappointment of that entity with which one both begins and ends all religious ceremonies within this spiritual tradition augurs a somber future for the island.

The poem begins *in medias res*. The first stanza suggests that the poetic voice is taking part in a ritual celebration of the *orichas*, a *toque* or drumming, whereby the faithful (which includes both those who have been ordained formally as well as those who keep the traditions without ceremonial consecration) have gathered. Because the practice of Afro-Cuban religions was officially declared illegal for most of Cuban history, these kinds of festivities would often occur in personal dwellings;[7] here we see that the poetic voice returns to the house in order to see Elegguá in person, an indication that the entity has mounted one of his priests and is indeed present. All who are in attendance at the gathering can therefore speak with this entity personally.

LOS OJOS DE ELEGGUA[8]

esta noche
junto a las puertas del caserón rojizo
he vuelto a ver los ojos del guerrero
eleggua
la lengua
roja de sangre como el corazón de los hierros
los pies dorados desiguales
la tez de fuego el pecho encabritado y sonriente

acaba de estallar en gritos
eleggua salta
imagina los cantos
roza el espacio con un puñal de cobre
quién le consentirá
si no es la piedra
o el coco blanco
quién recogerá los caracoles de sus ojos

ELEGGUA'S EYES

tonight
before the doors of the big red house
I've seen the eyes of the warrior again
eleggua
tongue
red with blood like the heart of irons
gold feet one larger
the fiery roof the rearing beaming chest

bursting out in shrieks
eleggua leaps
imagines song
grazes space with a copper dagger
who will consent to him
if not the stone
if not the white coconut tree
who will gather the shells of his eyes

Elegguá is a warrior: as one of the first *orichas* that practitioners receive in ceremony, he is the entity that guides humanity. One appeals to him to assist in the clearing of obstacles of one's roads in life; he will fight on behalf of those who honor him and recognize him as playing an instrumental role in their lives, hence his position as guard near the door in the homes of practitioners. Morejón presents Elegguá here as an ominous presence: screaming, jumping, moving through the space as if to prove that it belongs to him and no one else. He has come to earth unhappy, then, feeling the need to remind those in attendance of his nature as a warrior. Elegguá is also mischievous, hence his reputation as a "trickster"; it is this characteristic that most often appears in literary representations of this figure, as well as in religious ceremony. That Morejón presents him here strictly as intimidating is also indicative of his unhappiness. With the verses "quién le consentirá / si no es la piedra / o el coco blanco / quién recogerá los caracoles de sus ojos," Morejón references the implements used in religious ceremony to divine the future. There are a number of ways to communicate with the *orishas* outside of drummings, one being the use of the coconut, another being through the use of Elegguá's shells. Here, then, the *oricha* is reminding his audience of who he is: the master of the crossroads, he to whom one speaks when wanting to know about the future. It appears those in attendance may have forgotten.

Morejón continues this portrait marked by disappointment and outrage in the final stanzas:

> ya no sabrá de Olofi si ha perdido el camino
> ya no sabrá de los rituales
> ni de los animales en su honor
> ni de la lanza mágica
> ni de los silbidos en la noche
>
> si los ojos de eleggua regresaran
> volverían a atravesar el río pujante
> donde los dioses se alejaban donde existían los peces
> quién sabrá entonces del cantar de los pájaros
> el gran eleggua ata mis manos
> y las abre y ya huye

y bajo la yagruma está el secreto
las cabezas el sol y lo que silba
      como único poder del oscuro camino (66)

soon he won't know if Olofi has lost his way
      and nothing of the rites
nor of the animals that honor him
      nor of the magic sword
nor of the whistlings of the night

if eleggua's eyes look back
they will look back across the stinking river
where the gods drew off into the distance
where fish swam
      who then will know the birdsongs
the great eleggua ties my hands
unties them now runs away
and under the yagruma tree
the secret lies
heads the sun and something whistling
      the sole power of the dark road.

Olofi is the manifestation of the Supreme Being Himself; this third stanza puts forth the possibility of Eleggúa no longer performing his responsibilities. What if he no longer can communicate with God clearly? What if rituals are lost? (Again, in appealing to him at the beginning and end of every ceremony, practitioners are asking for his assistance, thereby hoping to avoid possible obstructions.) What if humanity loses contact with him, never to hear the sound of his whistle again?

Weaver's translation fails in the final stanza in that she translates "pujante" to mean "stinking"; it does not, it means "powerful," "thriving." This failure is important because it changes the meaning of the final stanza; if one interprets her translation, one would be led to believe that the entity associated with the river, Oshún, is also upset with the population that has allowed her waters to become contaminated and therefore smell badly. Instead, the word means "powerful," indicating that this population will perhaps need to appeal to Oshún in order to draw these entities near to them again. Indeed, "alejaban" indicates that they have retreated from humanity, to a divine clearing where they no longer have anything to do with human beings. The poem concludes in ambivalence, with Eleggúa revealing to the poetic voice how easy it is to both complicate her life as well as assist in living with ease ("el gran eleggua ata mis manos / y las abre"). He then flees, hiding under a sacred tree that signifies a number of other *orichas* and that signals to the reader both that they are all unhappy as well as that the resolution is to return to him. The final image of the dark road ("oscuro camino") underscores the uncertainty of the future.

Morejón published "Los ojos de Eleggua" in her 1967 collection *Richard trajo su flauta y otros argumentos*. The optimism with which a great deal of the Cuban populace greeted the Revolution had subsided, as it became clear that Fidel Castro was a dictator who led autocratically. In the years after the failed invasion at the Bay of Pigs in 1961 and the aversion of nuclear war in 1962, he consolidated his power with the financial backing of the Soviet Union. 1967 marked the death of Che Guevara in the jungles of Bolivia, which strengthened Castro's hold on power. A year later, Heberto Padilla, a prominent poet, dared to be critical of the Revolution in print and was subsequently arrested and made to denounce his poetry. For much of the 1970s, Morejón's poetry was not published and there is a twelve-year gap between the publication of *Richard* and her next collection, *Parajes de una época* in 1979; this pause has led critics to speculate that her involvement with issues of race led to an unofficial ban on her work.[9] Nevertheless, 1975 saw the publication of her most famous poem, "Mujer negra," which has garnered the greatest amount of critical attention regarding her work; it is a retelling of Cuban history from the perspective of an enslaved African woman. Morejón challenges the master discourse in which the African presence is ignored or elevated solely on the level of culture to remind her audience that black women have also contributed to the nation, that in fact, it was the black woman that gave birth to the Cuban nation.

Another poem in which Morejón rescues the figure of the black woman from obscurity is "Amo a mi amo." Like "Mujer negra," "Amo a mi amo" has received positive critical attention; for Marciela A. Gutierrez, "the poem reveals how, in spite of her physical chains as a slave and as a woman, the female narrator is spiritually free" (213). In an essay about Morejón's womanism, Linda S. Howe asserts that the protagonist's rebellion happens in a dream (165). For Lorna V. Williams, "Amo a mi amo" is an example of Morejón's writing against a *negrista* portrait of black woman as a highly sexualized object: "Instead, in her work, terms of sexual difference often become signifiers of oppression" (135). Critics have overlooked the obvious allusions to the *oricha* Oshún in this poem; indeed, Morejón includes "miel," "girasoles," and "campanas," all three signifiers of Oshún in a Cuban context. The irony that Alan West notes increases exponentially when one considers that the "love" that the poetic voice expresses is insincere: this is not romantic love. Oshún prepares her sacrifice, one that will avenge the cruelty and torture inflicted on the hearts, bodies, and souls of the enslaved.

AMO A MI AMO

Amo a mi amo,
recojo leño para encender su fuego cotidiano.
Amo sus ojos claros.
Mansa cual un cordero
esparzo gotas de miel por sus orejas.
Amo sus manos
que me depositaron sobre un lecho de hierbas:
Mi amo muerde y subyuga.
Me cuenta historias sigilosas mientras
abanico todo su cuerpo cundido de llagas y balazos
de días de sol y guerra de rapiña.
Amo sus pies que piratearon y rodaron
por tierras ajenas.
Los froto con los polvos más finos
que encontré, una mañana,
saliendo de la vega.
Tañó la vihuela y de su garganta salían
coplas sonoras, como nacidas de la garganta de Manrique.
Yo quería haber oído una marímbula sonar.
Amo su boca roja, fina,
desde donde van saliendo palabras que no alcanzo a descifrar
todavía. Mi lengua para él ya no es la suya.

I LOVE MY MASTER

I love my master.
I gather brushwood to start his daily fire.
I love his blue eyes.
Gentle as a lamb,
I pour drops of honey for his ears.
I love his hands
That threw me down on a bed of grasses.
My master bites and subjugates.
He tells me secret tales while
I fan all his body,
running with wounds and bullet-pierced
from long days in the sun and plundering wars,
I love his roving pirates' feet
that have pillaged foreign lands.
I rub them with the softest powders
I could find, one more,
coming from the tobacco fields.
He strummed his ornate guitar and
melodious couplets soared,
as though from Manrique's throat.
I longed to hear a marimbula sound.
I love his fine red mouth
that speaks I can't understand
for the language I speak to him
still isn't his own.

In the opening lines of the poem, the poetic voice declares her admiration for her master's eyes; she also presents herself as unthreatening, "gentle as a lamb" (4). While the lamb does signify docility, the animal is also one that is often used in religious ceremonies across religious traditions, not only within African diasporic ones but also within Islam and Judaism. The practitioner of these religious traditions uses the lamb as an offering to God, as an acknowledgment of His role in his/her life. The poetic voice here prepares the sacrifice: "esparzo gotas de miel por sus orejas" (5). The poetic voice goes on to describe their lovemaking; here, Morejón makes vivid the oft-used metaphor of the female body as representative of land. In the same way that he subjugates her, he conquers territories ("Me cuenta historias sigilosas mientras / abanico todo su cuerpo cundido de llagas y balazos / de días de sol y guerra de rapiña"). Though he has suffered physical pain (his body carrying the wounds of war), nevertheless he continues in his pursuit of more land, more wealth: the musical instrument he mentions is indicative of his wealth, as is the fact that he owns the tobacco fields ("vega") in which they have sexual relations; the poetic voice also mentions "cañaveral" at the conclusion of the poem, indicative that he owns both tobacco and sugar fields.[10] His avarice is simply one reason for which he is sacrificed at the conclusion of the poem.

Another is his treatment of the enslaved on his property: though he himself has suffered bullets, he continues to torture the workers. She learns of his maltreatment by overhearing the older men on the property:

> Y la seda del tiempo hecha trizas.
> Oyendo hablar a los viejos guardieros, supe
> que mi amor
> da latigazos en las calderas del ingenio,
> como si fueran un infierno, el de aquel Señor Dios
> de quien me hablaba sin cesar.

> And the silk of time is in shreds.
> Overhearing the old black overseers
> I learned how my lover
> doled out whip-blows
> in the vatroom of the sugar-mill,
> as if it were a hell, that of the Lord God
> they harped upon so much.

Within the myriad cultures of the African Diaspora, older men and women are considered sacred, because they have attained the wisdom of life. Though living, they are also considered ancestral presences, and so are honored by younger generations. The master's violations are multiple, then; men and women young and energetic enough to work with the cauldrons are being whipped there, at the site of unbearable heat.[11] In addition, the older generation sees this mistreatment and can do nothing to protect the young, robbing them of their agency. Finally, there are multiple attempts to convert her, but what she witnesses is the mistreatment of her compatriots in a manner that creates a hellish existence on earth.

In response to these abuses, she curses not only the master himself but also everything that connotes slavery, the clothes he makes her wear; the tasks that take her away from the sunflowers; the language he has imposed that does not fit in her mouth, the breasts that no longer give milk; the womb slashed by the whip; and her own heart.

> Maldigo
> . . . .
> Amo a mi amo, pero todas las noches,
> cuando atravieso la vereda florida hacia el cañaveral
>   donde a hurtadillas hemos hecho el amor,
> me veo cuchillo en mano, desollándolo como a una res
>   sin culpa.
>
> Ensordecedores toques de tambor ya no me dejan
> oir ni sus quebrantos, ni sus quejas.
> Las campanas me llaman . . . (74,76)
>
> I curse
> . . . .
> I love my master but every night
> When I cross the blossoming path to the canefield,
> the secret place of our acts of love,
> I see myself knife in hand,
> flaying him like an innocent animal.
>
> Bewitching drumbeats
> now drown his cries, his sufferings.
> The bells of the sugar-mill call . . . (75,77)

Comparing the use of the verb to Caliban's lament that with Prospero's language, he learned to curse, Marilyn Grace Miller notes: "'Maldigo' is the contradiction, both in tone, and meaning, of the declaration of love at the poem's outset; it is the invocation of a new litany of rebellion" (9). In one fell swoop, the poetic voice, Oshún herself, curses all that has allowed this system to flourish. In the penultimate stanza, she envisions herself knife in hand, ready to dissect him; initially, she seems to qualify this statement by saying that this is a recurrent vision, one that she has nightly. Yet the last stanza intimates that this killing takes place, with no remorse. Morejón leaves us with images of the drums and the bells; while Kathleen Weaver's translation adds that the bells originate from the sugar-mills, Morejón last line only mentions the bells without stating a source.

In a 2000 interview with María Dolores Alcantud Ramón, Morejón reveals that she considers the poems "Mujer negra" and "Amo a mi amo" to be prayers. When asked if the poems are the evils of history, Morejón responds: "No, son rezos. Aunque metafóricamente sí son verdugos, dirigidos a los que fueron los verdugos, pero son poemas liberadores [No, they are prayers. Although metaphorically yes, they are tyrants, they are directed at those who were tyrants, but they are poems of liberation]." With these poems, Morejón demonstrates her love for her country; she does not separate her identity as a woman of African descent from her nationality as a Cuban, any more than she could isolate her gender from her race from her class from her nationality. Whereas she communicates her reservations about the Revolution (though never in an obvious manner), she conveys without hesitation her love for the *mestizaje* that created modern Cuba. Her work honors her ancestors, those men and women of African descent forgotten and therefore silenced by history; it is a testimony to her belief in the Cuban nation, more so than in the Revolution.

Daína Chaviano

Born in Havana, Cuba, Chaviano established a name for herself on the island as a science fiction writer. She was awarded the David Prize for Science Fiction for her first publication, a short story collection *Los mundos que amo* (1979). She published several works in that genre before moving to Miami in 1991. *Casa de juegos* (1999) is the second novel in Chaviano's *La Habana oculta* series. While the first work of the series, *El hombre, la hembra y el hambre* (1998) has received the lion's share of critical attention, the remaining three have garnered almost none. Writing about the first novel, Michi Strausfield declares: "[E]s una novela construida con dosis de sexo, oposición política, ganas de exilio, prostitución y hambre, en proporción idónea como para gustar a lectores poco exigentes. Yo diría que es una obra fabricada, dominada por el oportunismo de su autora y destinada al consumo superficial [(It) is a novel composed of a dose of sex, political opposition, a desire for exile, prostitution, and hunger, in direct proportion to the likings of readers who do not demand much. I would say that it is a fabricated work, dominated by the opportunism of its author and destined for superficial consumption]" (19). Readers find many of the same characteristics that Strausfield lists in *Casa de juegos* as well. Though the explicit sex scenes may be jarring, the reader soon recognizes that in composing those episodes, Chaviano challenges him/her, questioning his/her sense of decorum. This same challenge is faced by the novel's protagonist, Gaia, who through the course of the novel comes to reassess her relationship with her own ideals and desires, and the city in which she lives. The novel engages its reader on two levels, then: at the same moment that the story recounts Gaia's adventures of healing, it openly toys with the reader as well, forcing the reader to reconsider larger definitions of the sacred and its role in one's everyday existence.[12]

As the novel opens, we find her still mourning the death of her only lover three years after his death. Though she masturbates to his memory, she notes that "los meses comenzaron a transcurrir sin que su libido diera señales de vida [months passed without her libido showing any signs of life" (31). A friend soon takes her for a spiritual reading with a *Lucumí* priestess, where she learns of the offerings necessary to relieve her of languor. There, she also discovers that she will receive the assistance of Inle, a husband of Oshún's. Through the course of the novel, a beautiful woman leads Gaia to a mysterious house where she meets another guide, Eri, and experiences rituals that assist in reviving her latent sexuality. The reader comes to learn that they are incarnations of two *orishas*, Oshún and Erinle. Though the novel is sexually explicit, it is more than simply a text of provocation. On the contrary, with her work Chaviano emphasizes the much-needed re-union of mind, body, and spirit. Her text is a call to reexamine the metaphysical power of sexual intercourse. Chaviano reveals the spiritual potential of female sexuality, as well as the relationship between the two in female subjectivity formation. In naming her protagonist after the Greek entity that represents the Earth, Chaviano puts forth that a healthy and vibrant sexuality, one that acknowledges the spiritual component, is necessary for the survival of the human species. She does so by incorporating Afro-Cuban traditions in the text: the representation of these spiritual entities (who, notably, do not appear by their syncretic names of the Virgen de la Caridad de Cobre or San Rafael) signifies an interruption of traditional narrative discourse. By including them in her novel, she uses them not as metaphors but instead is deliberately calling on these entities as a means to instruct her reading audience.

In addition to an allegorical rendering of the call to heal the planet, the novel also questions the reader's notion of liberty and privacy. As Michel Foucault highlights in the first volume of *The History of Sexuality* (1978), the shame of sex, not only of the act itself but also of one's sexuality, is a product of an official discourse of control. We see from this work the tendency to flee personal responsibility, as the protagonist attributes her participation in sexual activities often to witchcraft and forced intoxication. This pattern breaks only when she becomes accountable to herself for her desires. In doing so, she becomes truly free, able to survive amid the social and political reality of a Cuba that censures her.

The Ambience of Cuba

Though the author does not incorporate specific historical dates into the narrative, the reader gets a general sense that we are in the Special Period of the early 1990s, when, following the collapse of its Soviet patron, Cuba suffered severe shortages in food, medicine, and energy. As a means to combat the economic downturn, the government turned to tourism as a revenue source, barring citizens from five-star hotels that were built to attract a mostly European audience. At the conclusion of her reading with Lisa's godmother, Gaia learns that she is to look for a savior, someone to end her unintentional celibacy, in the Vedado section of Havana (41). Vedado is the center of commercial life in the city, as well as of university life, as it is the site of the University of Havana, and of tourism, as many hotels are located there. When she gains entrance to one of the hotels without harassment, Gaia views it as miraculous; she had prepared to be refused admission given that the hotel is explicitly for tourists and diplomats. She notes: "Encargó un Mojito, aún sin creer lo que estaba viviendo; pero hizo un esfuerzo por comportarse a la altura de las circunstancias, es decir, como si no sucediera nada fuera de lo común [She ordered a Mojito, still stunned at what she was experiencing; but she made the effort to acclimate herself to her surroundings, that is, as if nothing out of the ordinary was happening] " (42). Throughout the novel, entrance into a prohibited space creates a dreamlike daze for Gaia; Chaviano highlights this state with images of shadows and indistinct figures. The reader is therefore never sure as to whether the course of events the protagonist recounts are "real" or an extension of Gaia's imagination.

This underscores the atmosphere in which the Cuban citizenry live: the novel suggests them incapable of discerning reality because of the circumstances in which they exist. That is, their reality is one that falls outside of norms of verisimilitude. During the course of the novel, the island is characterized as "surrealist" (47); as "onírica y engañosa, seductora y fraudulenta, embustera y libertina [dreamlike and deceptive, seductive and fraudulent, liar and libertine]" (113); one that wears a "perennial mask" (177); where one must lie because there is no other choice (192). The narrator observes: "[Cuba es] una sociedad capaz de engañar al resto del mundo, pues incluso a sus propios ciudadanos le resultaba difícil descifrar los atroces mecanismos de su funcionamiento [(Cuba is) a society able to trick the rest of the world, but even to its own citizens it was proving difficult hiding the vicious mechanisms of its workings] (113)." Chaviano levels her criticism therefore not only at the Cuban government but also at the rest of the international community for accepting a mythology that has destroyed the physical, emotional, psychological, and spiritual well-being of the populace. The novel offers an image of a country that remains outside of time and reason for its inhabitants, who try to accommodate the lunacy that invades their lives at any given moment.

While she is a native of the city, Gaia's immediate surrounding is the university. About the school she notes: "La universidad no era aquel parnaso descrito en los libros [The university was not that Parnassus described in books]" (17). With an allusion to Mount Parnassus, ancient home of the Muses, she implicitly makes the argument that a university should ideally be a place of the arts, literature, poetry, and free thought.[13] Instead, "Gaia jamás se habría quejado ante Lisa de la aridez de sus asignaturas, y Lisa no se hubiera lamentado de cuán pocos temas podía debatir con alguna libertad [Gaia would never complain about the dryness of the assignments in front of Lisa, and Lisa would never bemoan the few topics that one could debate with some freedom]" (17).

The failing regime has corrupted the principles of this once-safe space for intellectuals, instead churning out graduates who pledge loyalty to Marxist-Leninist doctrine in order to survive the system. Though they have been friends since early childhood, they remain circumspect about what they share even with each other, as paranoia and suspicion guide their lives. They are representative of a population that has learned to veil their thoughts and emotions; instead, they must proclaim allegiance to the whims of the failed revolutionary regime. To do otherwise would mean to call undue attention to oneself and risk imprisonment.[14]

Emblematic of the country is Gaia's lover, El Pintor, who preys on her desire for intellectual stimulation: "De ahí que pudiera entender perfectamente la pasión de Gaia por mamar de fuentes iconoclastas, y por eso no escatimó esfuerzos en proporcionar a la joven todo tipo de estímulos a su fantasia [From there he could understand perfectly Gaia's passion for drinking from sources of iconoclasts, and for that reason he spared no expense in encouraging her fantasy]" (19). He seduces her by appealing to her desire to learn something more, something greater than the party line. The narrator notes that he also enjoys seducing adolescents and Gaia possessed the necessary prerequisites: "diecinueve años y una actitud de perpetuo desamparo [nineteen years old and an attitude of perpetual helplessness]" (29). He takes advantage, therefore, of the power differential between them: an older man, he takes pleasure in molding young girls. During their first sexual encounter, he asks her to pledge obedience to him, which she does (25). In the course of their relationship, he recounts his affairs with other women, passing them off as his whims as an artist; the narrator notes that in doing so, he creates a conditioned response in her, so that she becomes excited only upon hearing these stories (30). She therefore becomes wholly dependent upon him and his adventures for mental and physical stimulation. The narrator observes that Gaia becomes amoral, or rather, he affects her sense of morality to the extent that she no longer cares about moral behaviors or judgments. Chaviano's portrait of El Pintor evokes comparisons with Fidel Castro: an older figure that exploits the yearnings of a more vulnerable being that makes clear his/her desire to learn, grow, and evolve. As the Revolution has continued, the populace has learned adaptive behaviors so as to better submit to the whims of El Líder. This has resulted in the already commented upon deception of the population, who must lie and pretend in their public lives in order to survive. In destroying Gaia morally and taking advantage of her physically, El Pintor leaves her spiritually and physically bereft: "Ese angustioso torbellino de ideas no fue nada comparado con la oscuridad que la invadió después, como si su espíritu se hubiera transformado en una sustancia volátil y devastada [That anguished turmoil of ideas was nothing compared to the darkness that invaded her afterward, as if her spirit had transformed into a volatile and devastating substance]" (31). She is a hollowed shell after his death, her body a vessel that has been deprived of its life force. The text suggests an intervention is necessary in order for the Cuban nation to withstand the fifty-year-old assault on her spirit: short of an overhaul of the political system, Chaviano calls on the spiritual systems that have prospered in Cuba in spite of political persecution since the arrival of enslaved beings from Africa shores.[15]

Intervention of Spiritual Systems

Chaviano's novel reveals the struggle to maintain a sense of personal freedom within a repressive environment that insists on the existence of solely official truth. She uses myths of both Greek and West African origin; while she more fully incorporates the latter by including two *orishas* as characters of her story, there are numerous allusions to the first, beginning with her protagonist, who shares a name with the Universal Mother of Greek myth.[16] In his study on this figure, Mark Munn writes: "Because she is omnipresent to all living things, and because all depend on her, Gaea is often named first of all deities as witness and as enforcer of oaths. She is rarely depicted as an active personality among divinities. . . . [She is also] the original source of prophecy" (33). Gaia, or Earth, is simply life: she is the force that emerges from Chaos. She is the primordial energy that brings forth all of existence. Jean-Pierre Vernant notes: "La Tierra ya no es ese espacio vacío, esa especie de caída oscura, ilimitada e indefinida. A la confusión, a la tenebrosa indiferenciación del caos, se enfrenta la claridad, la firmeza, la estabilidad de Gea. Sobre la Tierra todo aparece dibujado, visible, sólido [Earth is no longer empty space, that kind of dark, limitless, undefined drop. In the face of confusion, of the dark indifference of chaos, one is confronted with the clarity, the strength, the stability of Gea (sic). On Earth everything appears drawn-out, visible, solid]" (15). Reading the character through this filter, we come to understand the extent to which Gaia is out of balance at the opening of the novel.

She describes her efforts to revive her flagging libido in the following terms: "Abandonó todo esfuerzo cuando se convenció de que explorar aquel vacío era como intentar revivir un cadáver [She abandoned all efforts when she convinced herself that exploring that emptiness was the same as trying to revive a cadaver]" (31). In the aftermath of her lover's death, the protagonist has become the antithesis of her name. In using the term *vacío*, Chaviano refers to Gaia's existential emptiness, which recalls chaos, that out of which the universe consisted prior to the appearance of the Universal Mother.

In Greek myth, Eros emerges after the creation of the Earth. Vernant notes: "El primer Eros es una manifestación de la energía cósmica. De la misma manera que la Tierra ha surgido del Caos, brotará de ello lo que contiene en sus profundidades. . . . Lo que la Tierra entrega y manifiesta es lo mismo que permanecerá, envuelto en el misterio, en su seno [The first Eros is a manifestation of cosmic energy. In the same way that Earth has emerged from Chaos, Eros arises from that which Earth contains in its depths. What Earth gives and manifests is that which will remain, wrapped in the mystery, in her bosom]" (17). Eros is not at first romantic love, that which is often represented in modern times as heterosexual coupling; it is instead a life force that materializes from the Earth, a product of Earth's energy.[17] Chaviano's story of the revival of the earth is therefore in some ways a rewriting of Greek myth.[18] Erinle identifies Eros as the unnamed spirit that steers Cuba (170). Gaia being representative of the planet, the healing that comes about through sexual activity was inevitable, for according to myth, eros is but a natural energy source of the earth. Chaviano's contribution to the discussion is the role that she assigns the *orishas* in her narrative.

Chaviano's inclusion of the spiritual entities of *Regla de Ocha/ Lucumí/Santería* follows a Cuban literary tradition that has been greatly overlooked within criticism.[19] She joins novelists such as José Lezama Lima and Severo Sarduy, among others, in doing so.[20] She features several of the main *orishas* of this religious system as characters in the novel, including Obba, Oyá, and Shangó, with references to Elegguá as the guardian of the crossroads. The most important are Oshún and Erinle, for they guide Gaia in her healing so that she may live fully on the island. The presence of entities that are associated with feminine and masculine elements indicate an aim of balance and wholeness. The portrait of Oshún in the novel accords with her presentation in religious legends (*patakís*) particular to the Caribbean, which speak to the region's cultural syncretism. She is a *mulata,* of mixed African and European heritage, whose beauty mesmerizes all who see her: "[L]a figura de esa mujer violaba todas las normas clásicas . . . las miradas respondían con fervor religioso. Era imposible ignorarla [(T)he figure of that woman violated all classical norms . . . the looks responded with religious fervor. It was impossible to ignore her]" (83). Within Cuban literature, the *mulata* exemplifies beauty, supposedly incorporating the best of her inheritance in terms of skin tone and physiognomy.[21] The author emphasizes this aspect in her characterization of the *orisha* as well;[22] she does so in order to provide for the protagonist a complete portrait of femininity. Her beauty does not solely depend on her physical attractiveness but also on her guiding principle:

> —¿Nunca has querido conocerte?
> —Sé bien quién soy.
> —Pero no quién puedes llegar a ser. . . . —No deberías
>   renunciar al placer de ser tú misma. (14)
> —Have you never wanted to get to know yourself?
> —I know well who I am.
> —But not who you could be. . . . You should never
>   abandon the pleasure of being yourself.

This exchange reveals an interest in constant evolution and consistent growth on the part of the character personifying the *orisha.* In allowing El Pintor to appropriate control of her life, she surrenders all to him: his death brings about a metaphysical demise that paralyzes her. Oshún's statement acts as a clarion call, both for the protagonist as well as for the reader: the novel, then, becomes an account of Gaia's restoration, as she learns to take pleasure in herself. With Oshún, Gaia interacts with a woman older than herself, one who demonstrates for her a womanhood marked by confidence, not helplessness. She serves to usher her young charge into a more mature phase of her development.

While Gaia's relationship with Oshún is formative, the novels focuses greatly on her interaction with Erinle.[23] The author offers that he is: "medico y pescador [doctor and fisherman]" (39). He "protegía de todas las aflicciones y padecimientos [protected against sorrows and sufferings]" (187). Like Oshún, the narrator characterizes him chiefly by his beauty: "Era hermoso, mucho más hermoso de lo que intuyera en la penumbra; de una piel acanelada y tersa. . . . Tenía los ojos de un verde leonado [He was beautiful, so much more beautiful than she sensed in the shadows. . . . He had smooth cinnamon-colored skin . . . and hazel eyes" (50). Though he and Oshún share physical attractiveness (to the extent that they resemble each other), Erinle's good looks threaten Gaia: Oshún warns her that anyone who looks at the *orisha* directly may lose control of their will (79). Erinle, then, is another male figure, like El Pintor and Fidel Castro before him, to whom Gaia submits her will: Chaviano distinguishes him from the other two in that the *orisha* speaks to her about trust, about needing to believe in him (57, 131). Her sanction comes not from coercion but from her own free will: the relationship only advances when Gaia assents to his propositions, when she seeks him out after a three-month absence. Each assertion of consent, the author would have us believe, is an effective exercise of personal autonomy.

In her meetings with Erinle, he insists on solely wanting to heal her. While the stated malady is her frigidity (this is the ailment that spurs her childhood friend Lisa to take her to the *Lucumí* priestess for a divination session), another condition that affects her is that of shame. In the aftermath of a sexual encounter, she feels alternately rage, fear, embarrassment, as her body responds to physical pleasure while her rationale tells her to deny it (23, 77, 99, 142, 167). She notes: "No era una experiencia agradable. Semejaba la cercanía del vacío: daría un paso y se hundiría en una brecha que la llevaría al infierno [It wasn't a pleasant experience. It resembled the imminence of chaos: she would take a step and sink into a hole that would lead her to hell]" (99). Expressions of her sexuality are illicit, even to herself. She feels she has taken leave of her senses, functioning outside of her own sense of reason; this despite her enjoyment during these episodes. Her noted conflict between the pleasures of the body and the pleasures of the mind reflects a general sense of fragmentation that is characteristic of a Western culture that predominantly casts these parts of a self in opposition. She reveals a distrust of sexuality, triggering the need to guard against the dangers it presents, as well as a suspicion of her body in general.[24] Erinle's grand lesson is to teach her to accept her pleasure, revel in the enjoyment of her body.

He does so in a methodical way, in that he appeals directly to her senses—the visual, the auditory, the tactile, the olfactory, and the gustatory. During their first meeting, she enjoys several courses of seafood dishes; they are in a prohibited space (a restaurant in a hotel where only tourists and diplomats are legally allowed to stay), and she eats food that is unavailable to her.[25] For the protagonist, the mere act of ingesting these foods, which she describes in great detail because they are both beautiful in presentation as well as in scent and taste, causes pleasure: "Eran procesos que despertaban en ella un ansia remota e indescifrable como el anticipo de un orgasmo [They were processes that awakened in her a remote and unfathomable yearning resembling the anticipation of an orgasm]" (47). He therefore almost immediately begins to cure the malady that is her frigidity, beginning with her gustation.[26] Their first meal together is an act of transgression, then: though she is aware of the dangers present, she finds pleasure not only in the food itself but also in the illicitness of the gathering. Following the meal, he massages her, thereby appealing to her sense of touch. She does not speak, instead allowing herself to feel once again the hands of someone else on her skin: "¿Cuánto tiempo hacía que nadie le tocaba? Se abandonó a una dulce soñolencia [How long had it been since someone had touched her? She let herself drop into a sweet drowsiness]" (54). In allowing herself to receive the pressure from Erinle's hands, she surrenders to a world of sensation, where she does not examine, analyze, or interrogate her response to him.

During her nap, he ties her hands and feet: as the memory of her former lover arises in the midst of her massage, Erinle counteracts this by using vibrators for both vaginal and anal penetration. He therefore isolates her pleasure, so that her orgasm is a purely physical response rather than one that he brings about through direct contact.[27] In bringing her to orgasm, Erinle exorcises the memory of El Pintor: Gaia no longer associates pleasure with her former lover, nor does she relate it to his touch. Here, technology stimulates the protagonist; while it is impersonal, it facilitates her ability to take pleasure in herself.

As he appeals to her senses, he attempts to limit her ability to rationalize the situations in which she finds herself by asking that she not ask him questions, to which she assents. Though frustrated by his unwillingness to satisfy her inquiries, she continues to spend time with him. While upon first glance, this would appear to mean that Chaviano subscribes to the silencing of the female, the text itself suggests an alternate reading. In her previous relationship, Gaia's lover appealed solely to her intellect, easily manipulating her to bend to his will. With Erinle, she must trust him completely, literally without question, instead relying on her body to communicate her comfort level with him, her confidence in him, as well as her discomfort in any given situation. She comes to lean not only on her physical sensations but also on her intuition in order to guide her (187).

Shame disappears from Gaia's sexual experience; whereas it dominates the descriptions of earlier scenes, by the conclusion she admits that it passes rather quickly (167). Chaviano therefore uses it as a barometer of her healing. The protagonist comments:

> El sexo era un recurso poderoso: al contener tabúes milenarios, resultaba también liberador; y en una prisión social podía adquirir trascendencia catártica. No importaba cuán monstruosa fuese la represión: para alguien sin posibilidades de sublevarse, forzar los límites de su erotismo se convertía en un mecanismo de cordura porque se estaba rebelando contra algo que sí podía vencer.

> [Sex was a powerful resource: though it holds millennia-old taboos, it was also liberating; and within a social prison it could acquire cathartic transcendence. It didn't matter how monstrous the repression: for someone without the possibility of rebelling, pushing the limits of his/her eroticism became a method of common sense because s/he was rebelling against something that they could in fact defeat.] (167)

Chaviano posits here that repressed sexuality reflects the political situation surrounding someone who lives under tyranny, as it is but another aspect of life that the government regulates. Broadening one's sexual preferences and practices is necessary, therefore, to combat the overarching reach of dictatorship, if only to serve as a reminder to that person that s/he remains a free being.

Chaviano's formula for the maintenance of a sense of freedom under oppressive rule is reminiscent of Audre Lorde's construction of the erotic as a source of knowledge. For Lorde, rationality has been overemphasized as the sole measure of intelligence, which has limited how one processes the world. Humans in modern Western culture, which was born in the age of the Enlightenment, have been indoctrinated to believe that thinking is separate from feeling.[28] For her, these are not separate modes of experience, but rather distinct approaches to be used in combination. For Lorde, it is not a question of thinking versus feeling but rather identifying the impetus from which one lives. In her essay, "Uses of the Erotic," she writes:

> When we live outside ourselves, and by that I mean on external directives only rather than from our internal knowledge and needs, when we live away from those erotic guides from within ourselves, then our lives are limited by external and alien forms, and we conform to the needs of a structure that is not based on human need, let alone an individual's. But when we begin to live from within outward, in touch with the power of the erotic within ourselves, and allowing that power to inform and illuminate our actions upon the world around us, then we begin to be responsible to ourselves in the deepest sense. (58)

Lorde's formulation of life presumes the existence of an eternal truth that is accessible to each person. One reaches this truth by continually honoring its prompts, following its directives. In doing so, one arrives at a new level not only of self-knowledge but also of an awareness of the world surrounding them. One begins to understand the role the supra-structure, all that surrounds you, plays in your life. For those living under conditions that limit free movement and possibility, they are able to more easily identify those external impulses that have nothing to do with each person's needs and desires, which Lorde also presumes to be universal. In her estimation, then, one awakens to the possibilities of life as one becomes emboldened by his/her own truth.

Prior to her interaction with the *orishas*, the text suggests that Gaia was living according to the precepts of a script: university student that rebels against a system that limits the knowledge available to her; female who is initiated sexually when she is young and who is manipulated by older men. Ostensibly, Gaia has no power in either scenario: as both a student within the university and as a young woman, she cannot change either her position within the established structure. Both situations place her in a vulnerable position, one that she attempts to alter using rationality, only to fail at any lasting change. Instead, Erinle teaches her to take cues from the entirety of her being, trusting herself and her needs, rather than simply reacting to external stimuli. The novel suggests that this reliance on essential truth, which is accessible through the erotic, is critical to empowerment and freedom.

Problematic Racial Imagery

Chaviano's inclusion of *orishas* as the messengers in her narrative highlights a lived reality. While the most widely acknowledged religion remains Catholicism on the island, the practice of Afro-Cuban religions such as the *Regla de Ocha*, *Palo Mayombe*, and *Abakuá* is notable. With the addition of spiritual entities from the *Regla de Ocha* system, Chaviano underscores the different kind of reality that exists in her native land. What for others may be "magical realism"—that is, the introduction of fantastical elements into a reality that more or less resembles verisimilitude—is simply lived reality on the island. It is not a separate category of existence whereby magic intrudes upon a quotidian existence; rather, it *is* the quotidian. The interaction with these spiritual elements in the novel allows Cubans, practitioners and nonpractitioners alike, to experience a different kind of reality: "Y es que el poder de los orishas era una realidad de la cual no escapaban católicos ni ateos [And it is that the power of the *orishas* was a reality that neither Catholics nor atheists could escape]" (85). Chaviano's novel serves as a call for greater recognition of that which is autochthonous to the nation;[29] these beliefs provide an alternative perspective on life, one that provides a functional formulation of freedom.

In her study *Voices out of Africa in Twentieth-Century Spanish Caribbean Literature* (2009), Julia Cuervo Hewitt argues that Spanish Caribbean writers often include references to African-derived beliefs, figures, and language among other cultural codes, so as to acknowledge Africa as an integral component of their Caribbean culture. They nevertheless undercut this by also negating a direct African heritage. The Spanish Caribbean therefore displays a distinct African-ness that is simultaneously not African any more but rather Caribbean. Caribbean identity is therefore layered and multiple (18). Chaviano reveals a similar tendency in her own writing: while her inclusion of these figures serves as recognition of Africa as a primary contributor to Cuban culture, Chaviano's language at times reveals a problematic portrayal of African-ness. When referring to African diasporic aspects of her native land, she resorts to imagery of primitivism. Upon the protagonist's return to the *Lucumí* priestess for a second divination session, she comments on the language with which the *santera* prays. She does not name the language as *Lucumí*, she simply refers to it as unintelligible (153). Observing that *Lucumí* is the second most commonly used language in Cuba, she notes: "[E]ra un dialecto apegado a la naturaleza. . . . Las palabras se retorcían como serpientes, saltaban entre los labios o se quebraban en fragmentos con un crujido de ramas rotas [(I)t was a dialect that adhered to nature. . . . The words twisted like serpents, jumping between lips or snapping in fragments with the cracking of broken branches]" (153). Aside from the curious metaphor claiming that the language sounds like nature, Chaviano's allusion to serpents is awkward, given that the immediate historical referent for the serpent within religious literature in a Judeo-Christian tradition is the devil. Also, she emphasizes destruction and fragmentation, again when she is speaking about a language that derives from West Africa.

Another challenging moment is in her reference to the presence of the *orishas* on the island: "Y para desmentir su presunta sencillez estaba la magia de los angeles/orishas . . . porque no dudaba de que tales criaturas hubieran invadido su isla [And in order to refute her presumed simplicity was the magic of the angels/*orishas* . . . because she did not doubt that such creatures had invaded her island]" (188). Using "invasion" to describe the presence of religious beliefs carried to the territory by enslaved humans who had no choice in their migration is a poor choice of words at best. Some of these men and women were victims of invasions carried out on the African continent by marauders who then sold them: Chaviano's language in this instance is striking because it speaks to an apparently suppressed thought that Africans had somehow conquered Cuba historically. "Invasion" implies violence and the theft of something to which you have no right; it is curious, then, that this author, who infuses her narrative not only with representations of the spiritual entities of an African diasporic belief system but also with the legends from this cosmology, that she implicitly accuses those that carried this religious system with them as having assaulted the island. This is the same author who ascribes to the *Lucumí* priestess with whom her protagonist interacts a Galician heritage (35, 155): the primary "human" characters (Gaia, Lisa, and Rita, the priestess) are

white women of European heritage.[30] The primary *orishas* who guide
Gaia are described as *mulatos* who are cinnamon-colored (59). The
only figures that she describes as dark-skinned in the entirety of the
novel are Shangó and Oyá. Chaviano names neither character, but her
descriptions are in keeping with *patakís*. She writes:

> En dos ocasiones su mirada tropezó con la de un gigante negro
> que parecía seguirlas, arrastrando consigo a una joven mestiza
> totalmente ebria y a otra mujer tan negra como él. Iba descalzo y
> vestía unos pantalones rojos que encendían más el brillo de su torso.
> La mestiza era muy hermosa, pero el pañuelo ensangrentado con
> que se cubría la cabeza le daba un aire deslucido y triste. La otra
> mujer, en cambio, se desplazaba con toda la majestad del mundo
> sobre sus hombros y una expresión gélida en las pupilas.
>
> [On two occasions her glance came across that of a giant black
> man who looked as if he were following them, dragging with him
> a young mestiza who was completely drunk and another woman
> as black as he was. He went barefoot and wore a pair of red pants
> that reflected the sheen of his torso. The mestiza was very beautiful,
> but the bloody headscarf with which she covered her head gave her
> an air of filth and sadness. Conversely, the other woman carried
> the majesty of the world on her shoulders and moved with an icy
> expression in her eye.] (70–71)

Oshún identifies the man as her husband; by deduction, the reader
is able to identify the remaining two women as Obba and Oyá. The
description refers to a well-known legend in which Obba, eager to
please her new consort Shangó and jealous of her sister Oshún's cooking
prowess, asks Oshún advice about his favorite dish; the latter recom-
mends a soup of ears. Obba cuts off her own ear and feeds it to him in a
soup; Shangó is horrified when he makes the discovery, allowing Oshún
the opportunity to seduce him (Vadillo 59). Here, Obba is the *mestiza*
(woman of European and indigenous heritage), a tragic character who
evokes the sympathy if not the pity of the reader. Shangó appears as
a silent brute who drags a woman as they walk on the grounds of the
casino. This recalls a stereotype of the black man as a *mandingo*, the
well-endowed man of African heritage who is characterized by his
physicality. That Oyá, another wife who fights alongside him at war,

is described in terms of her majesty does not redeem the description: in all, these three figures, each representative of different phenotypes not otherwise included in the novel, are all silenced, marginal in a text ostensibly about freedom in the face of oppression.

Finally, the tone with which she sometimes refers to the *orishas* as part of a religious system is at time scornful. In the same moment that she speaks of the power of the *orishas*, she refers to witchcraft (85). In fact, her mentions of witchcraft punctuate the text: each time she goes to the casino, either with Oshún or Erinle, she believes that she is under a drunken spell (16, 121, 135). She posits that Havana itself is bewitched,[31] subject to vampires,[32] and compares it Dante's rendering of hell.[33] At one point, she claims that the city is both demonic and tempting[34] ("demoníaco y tentador" [86]), primarily due to the annual celebration of the founding of the capital city. The festivities take the form of honoring the ceiba, a sacred tree to practitioners of the *Lucumí* religion because they recognize it as Iroko, the birthplace of the *orishas*. Gaia comments: "La ceiba era Iroko, la mansión de los orishas; y celebrar el nacimiento de La Habana reverenciando a ése árbol, no hacía más que perpetuar su potencia [The ceiba was Iroko, home of the orishas; and celebrating the birth of Havana worshipping that tree did nothing more than perpetuate its power]" (86). The irreverence that Chaviano employs to write about this religious system serves to disturb the dependence on any religion as a source of salvation; that she includes characters that she presents as *orishas* incarnate is almost irrelevant. The author uses this same technique when writing her sex scenes.

Chaviano's Sexual Discourse

In the first volume of *The History of Sexuality*, Foucault writes: "If sex is repressed, that is, condemned to prohibition, nonexistence, and silence, then the mere fact that one is talking about it has the appearance of a deliberate transgression. A person who holds forth in such language places himself to a certain extent outside the reach of power; he upsets established law; he somehow anticipates the coming freedom" (6). As a Latin American woman in general and a Cuban woman specifically, Chaviano writes against social norms that dictate that it is indecorous for a woman to write of such things. Beginning in the 1970s, however, these customs began to change as a result of the women's movements in different societies.[35] Daína Chaviano has written erotically in the majority of her publications. Commenting on a collection of poetry published a decade prior to the appearance of this novel, one critic finds that Chaviano's eroticism is a natural consequence of a Revolutionary emphasis on gender equality. For Margarite Fernández Olmos, Chaviano utilizes blunt language in order to reveal a female sexuality that revels in its own pleasure; it does not exist as subordinate to male desire (146–47).[36] Explicit sex scenes are found throughout this novel, as Chaviano details Gaia's encounters first with a ballet dancer as a young schoolgirl, with El Pintor, and with several *orishas*, including Erinle, Oshún, and Shangó. In all of the scenes, Chaviano focuses solely on Gaia's reactions and responses to her lovers' touch. Her sustained emphasis on her protagonist's gratification indicates a valorization of the female experience. It also represents a challenge to the reader who may still be unaccustomed to frank depictions of female sexuality.

Chaviano's sexual scenes confront the reader's comfort level not only because of the directness of her language but also because she often includes a number of taboos, such as double penetration, sadomasochistic imagery, as well as sacred images in sexual settings, almost daring the reader's definition of profanity.

> Sintió, muy a pesar, que gozaba hasta el paroxismo con aquella doble acometida que la mantenía clavada en su sitio, como una santa crucificada o una emperatriz que se ofreciera a sus esclavos para que éstos la disfrutaran más por ese acto de profanación que por el placer que su cuerpo les brindaba. Así soportó ella la embestida de los miembros hasta que de ambos brotó el maná, espeso y bullidor como la lava: riachuelos que la glorificaron bautismalmente.
>
> [She felt, lamentably, that she enjoyed even the convulsions from the double attack that kept her nailed in her place, as if she were a crucified saint or an empress that offered herself to her slaves so that they could enjoy her, more for this profane act than for the pleasure that her body could bring them. In that way she bore the onslaught of those members until they both gushed their manna, thick and bubbling like lava: streams that glorified her as if in a baptism.] (75–76)

Here she compares crucifixion, the common method used to kill thieves in the ancient Roman Empire and the way in which Christian faithful believe Jesus Christ to have died, to Gaia's inability to move because two men are penetrating her simultaneously.[37] Her series of contrasts uncovers a continual shifting in the dynamic of power: a crucified saint is a martyr, a person believed to be at fault in his/her time but whose virtue is later rewarded with sainthood; an empress who bears her body not to a consort or lover but to those humans who must obey her, satisfying her every whim. In presenting this series of comparisons in quick succession, she reveals a bold humor, as she delights in mocking her audience's beliefs in the sacred.

Chaviano also satirizes possession, a key feature of *Lucumí* religious celebrations: in some instances, Gaia uses equestrian imagery to describe herself in moments of passion. Alternately her lover reins her in (25) or she is ridden bareback (176).[38] Within *Regla de Ocha*, the *orisha* mounts the person during possession; that person is then known as the horse of the *orisha*. Again, Chaviano takes what is known to be sacred language for a wide swath of the Cuban population and contorts it, almost daring her audience to take offense. In juxtaposing the religious with the sacred, she underscores the false division that separates the two. She also serves the same purpose for the reader as Erinle does for Gaia in that she asks her audience to confront their own self-imposed limits. Her candid language does not function as mere titillation, entertaining as it is; rather, she goads the reader to confront his/her personal limitations. By continual questioning and resetting of these boundaries, Chaviano suggests, one is able to access a personal source of freedom.

Conclusion

A comparison of the poems by Afro-Cuban writer Nancy Morejón and white Cuban Daína Chaviano reveals disparate approaches to the inclusion of these entities in these literary works. Morejón speaks directly about the ancestors, whose enduring presence reassures the Cuban population. Her poems about the *orishas* are more disconcerting, primarily because of the subtlety of her discourse. Morejón is reassuring her reading public that there is justice for those who have suffered wrongs. In both poems, the *orishas* are present to avenge abuses, warning that there are consequences for ignoring their admonitions. "Amo a mi amo," in particular, suggests that the governing class, those that have benefited from the land and who have tortured men and women who have worked it will be brought to judgment accordingly.

Morejón's vision, therefore, is on the Cuban nation as a whole. *Casa de juegos*, in contrast, offers a story where spiritual entities assume human form in order to save a single individual. Through a series of ceremonies, these incarnated beings succeed in healing the protagonist by leading her to recognize all aspects of herself. This self-awareness brings about a sense of personal liberation, one that allows her to disregard the political crisis in which she lives. In the face of such all-encompassing tyranny, she must adopt an attitude of indifference in order to flourish on a personal level. Only when she understands herself as a whole, rather than as distinct parts that continually conflict with each other, is she free. In the next chapter, we see a similar phenomenon in works by three Brazilian women, one of European heritage, the other two of African descent. Whereas the European author highlights individual salvation, the two of African descent evoke the larger Afro-Brazilian population.

⋝ FOUR ⋜

Sacrifice and Salvation

Helena Parente Cunha, Sônia Fátima da Conceição, and Conceição Evaristo

Aos poucos, vou desatando um nó, desamarrando um laço, depois as malhas da rede, por fim me livro de todas as correntes. O meu corpo ilimitado e demovido desemboca em rios imprevistos, transpõe barreiras insuspeitadas.

—Eu

Little by little, I am undoing a knot, casting off a chain, then the mesh of the net, finally I free myself of all restraints. My limitless and liberated body flows into unforeseen rivers, crossing unsuspected barriers.

—I

A menina nunca tinha sido dela. Voltava para o rio, para as águas-mãe.

—Maria Vicêncio

The girl was never hers. She was returning to the river, to the Mother-Waters.

—Maria Vicêncio

In her introduction to the 1994 edition of Ruth Landes's seminal text *The City of Women* (1947), Sally Cole offers the following observation about the relationship between women and *Candomblé*: "Candomblé makes visible women's experience, and offers women well-defined roles, personal access to a multiplicity of spirits who speak to women's needs, and access to extended personal networks and material resources" (xiii). The river inspires liberation; for both the protagonist of Helena Parente Cunha's first novel *Mulher no Espelho* (1983) and the mother of the protagonist of Conceição Evaristo's first novel *Ponciá Vicêncio* (2003), the cool river waters signify personal freedom and more importantly, autonomy. In the course of the novels, both protagonists discover and assert the right to be fundamentally who they are, sloughing off restrictive definitions of Brazilian womanhood confined by societal definitions of race, class, and gender. Instead, they take their cues from the entity identified with the river in *Candomblé Nagô*, Oxum, and *Candomblé Angola*, Ndanda Lunda.

The 1960s and 1970s marked a pivotal moment in the history of women's literary production in Brazil; though the country had seen the rare publication of writings by women since its existence as a colony of Portugal, only in the twentieth century were women recognized by their male counterparts as legitimate contributors to cultural production. Writers such as Rachel de Queiroz in the 1930s, and Clarice Lispector and Lydia Fagundes Telles in the 1940s published short stories and novels that are seen as a counternarrative to the dominant discourse written by their male counterparts, one in which women (irrespective of race and class) were seen as marginal. The military dictatorship plunged the country into political chaos beginning with the coup d'état of 1964 and ending twenty-one years later in 1985; in that span, tens of thousands were detained by the government. Many, including the sitting president, Dilma Rousseff, were tortured by military police, with thousands forced into exile.[1] Activists on the political Left, though victims of increased censorship (especially after the passage of the Institutional Act Number 5, which allowed for the suppression of political rights of individuals and groups deemed as threats to national security), fought for the reestablishment of their civil liberties. The formation of the dictatorship also coincided with the global women's movement, as nations across the world, including Brazil, saw the political activism of women as they demanded full equality in the face of the law. The United

Nations declared 1975 to be International Women's Year, inaugurating the Decade of the Woman; women's groups such as the Movimento Feminino pela Anistia (the Women's Movement for Amnesty) and Nós Mulheres (We Women) gained greater prominence. Women across racial and class lines made these demands, confronting a culture in Brazil in which women were (and are) explicitly eroticized and conceived of as little more than sexual playthings. Those in support of the equality of men and women in the eyes of the law saw the women's movement as part of the greater human rights movements. The publication of literature was therefore a critical mechanism through which political alliances were fortified, as more women across racial and class lines offered differing perspectives on life in the supposed racial democracy.

Literature is most explicitly political in the hands of the women who take part in writing groups that grew out of the local black nationalist movement of the 1970s, the most famous one being Quilombhoje. Emanuelle Oliveira examines the relationship between the political events of late-twentieth-century Brazil and the flourishing of Afro-Brazilian literature in her study *Writing Identity: The Politics of Contemporary Afro-Brazilian Literature* (2008). For her, there are three critical events over the last four decades that have contributed greatly to the development and dissemination of this body of knowledge. They are: the founding of *Cadernos Negros* (*Black Notebooks*), a journal in which Afro-Brazilian writers self-published their poems and short stories; the creation of Quilombhoje, the São Paulo–based writing group from which many writers published in *Cadernos Negros* emerged; and later, beginning in the mid-1990s, the professionalization of the group. For her, both the group and the journal emerged from a specific political moment in which marginalized groups within Brazil strengthened, clamoring for democracy in light of a weakened military dictatorship in place since 1964.

Within this context in which more women authors were giving voice to their own visions of life in their poems, novels, and short stories, Helena Parente Cunha won the 1982 Prêmio Cruz e Sousa, for her first novel *Mulher no Espelho* (1983). This work offers the world of *Candomblé* as a means by which to combat patriarchal definitions of womanhood. In the novel, this religious system serves as an instrument that actively encourages the development of female agency, irrespective of ethnic background. The protagonist, a white woman who belongs to the upper middle class of Bahian society, moves from a sense of psychic fragmentation to a reconciliation of all aspects of her personality.[2] She does so after she goes into a trance at a *Candomblé* ceremony and learns the identity of her guiding *orixá*, Oxum, a defining moment in her life that inspires her to reclaim an African heritage her family had denied for generations. *Candomblé* therefore serves as an alternate system of knowledge for the protagonist, a mirror that provides a different set of images and prototypes of womanhood.

More than a decade after the publication of Parente Cunha's novel, *Enfim . . . Nós: Escritoras Negras Brasileiras Contemporâneas / Finally . . . Us: Contemporary Black Brazilian Women Writers* was published in 1995. This marks the first collection of poetry written by Afro-Brazilian women writers; edited by Miriam Alves and Carolyn Richardson Durham, the bilingual volume features the work of sixteen poets. Alves is one of the most prominent members of Quilombhoje; in her opening remarks to the collection, she writes: "A nossa escrita existe: no afã da contestação da situação histórica da população escrava, na indignação e na denúncia de nossa marginalização e extermínio mais ou menos oficial nestes séculos; numa luta constante de afirmação do ser humano nas suas infinitas formas [Our writing exists: in efforts of rebellion in the historical situation of the slave population, in the indignation and in the denunciation of our marginalization and more or less official extermination in these centuries; in the constant struggle to affirm the human being in all of his/her infinite forms]" (6). For Alves, then, and indeed for all of the writers in this collection, their efforts are deliberately political: they are combating the reality of marginalization, giving voice to millions who exist on the periphery of Brazilian society.

Founded in 1980 in São Paulo, Quilombhoje continues to write and publish with the goal of revising the image of the Afro-Brazilian man and woman in Brazilian literature by adding multifaceted portraits to the collective imaginary. Theirs is a concerted effort to reveal the complexities of Afro-Brazilian life, recover lost histories, lost stories, and change perceptions of this community. The name of the group is a combination of two words: *quilombo*, the space created by Africans escaping enslavement, and *hoje*, today. By invoking this heritage, these writers not only communicate the sentiment that their community remains enslaved by endemic racism, sexism, and resulting discrimination, they also impart that they create as self-determining beings, agents of their own future. Indeed, in the face of a literary establishment that overlooks them, in effect silencing these artists, they decided to create their own opportunities, giving voice to themselves and their own stories.[3]

Pertinent to this particular study is the poets' treatment of a religious system traditionally practiced by many Afro-Brazilians, *Candomblé*. The sole poet to plainly invoke this system within the collection is Sônia Fátima da Conceição, who, in three of her poems references the worship of the *orixás*; there we see a relationship characterized by longing and limitation. Conceição highlights a critical distinction between the use of *Candomblé* as a motif of difference in literature, which characterizes Parente Cunha's usage, and as a feature of a culture that continues to be marginalized. For the poetic voice of these poems, *Candomblé* is not an alternate system of thought but a system that undergirds life for tens of millions of practitioners of African descent in Brazil. This population has suffered continued harassment, prosecution, and persecution for these religious beliefs. For them, *Candomblé* is not a sign of rebellion against a patriarchal hegemony but a way of life.

Almost a decade after the publication of several of her poems in *Enfim . . . Nós*, Conceição Evaristo published her first novel, *Ponciá Vicêncio* (2003). In this work, Evaristo offers the story of a young Afro-Brazilian woman who leaves her family in the country so as to make a life for herself and her family in the city. In uprooting herself, she abandons all that sustains her: not only her nuclear family (which consists of her mother and her brother) but also her spirituality, her engagement both with the *nkisis*, primarily Ndanda Lunda, and with her ancestors. While the desire for economic security compels the migration of both the eponymous protagonist and her brother, it also occasions a disruption of the sustenance of a vibrant spirituality that is characteristic of her community. Only when the family reunites is the spiritual system that guides each member recognized and celebrated. With the inclusion of *Candomblé* and the honoring of ancestors, Evaristo communicates both continuity and change; though material conditions of life may or may not evolve, the belief systems held by this family continue to serve as a support, even when ignored by the individuals themselves.

These three authors provide both very different portraits of *Candomblé*: for Parente Cunha's protagonist, the religion is a means by which she can reclaim previously rejected parts of her heritage and her womanhood. She understands herself in a new way, reveling in her sensuality and forgiving herself for her past mistakes. For Conceição, the religion represents a possible and yet unattainable respite from the quotidian conditions in which many Afro-Brazilians live; the poetic voice in her works aspires to a freedom that would allow this population to worship these entities openly and to live in comfort, that is, without concerns that stem from racism and endemic poverty. In addition, Conceição recognizes the mystery that continues to surround the religion in Brazil, and so, much like Sandra Maria Esteves in her early poetry, she alludes to misunderstood religious practices within this tradition so as to suggest the power of a dismissed and marginalized population. Finally, Evaristo recognizes the enduring spiritual nourishment of these religious traditions for the Afro-Brazilian community; her novel suggests that the abandonment of these practices, especially in pursuit of personal advancement, leads to certain tragedy.

The Fragmentation of Patriarchy

Desde já, se estabeleça a separação. Ela
é ela. Eu sou eu.

—Eu

The separation was established long ago.
She is she. I am I.

—I

Mulher no Espelho is a dialogue between the protagonist, "eu" (I) and her reflection in her mirror, *"a mulher que me escreve"* (the woman who writes me).[4] The representation of these two voices underscores the protagonist's crisis of identity: *"a mulher"* rejects all that the woman's first person voice ("eu") has become, an upper-middle-class white housewife whose life is dedicated to her husband and sons. From the perspective of *"a mulher,"* "eu" is a cliché, one that embodies the ideals of her class. Instead, *"a mulher"* repeatedly urges "eu" to become more interested in herself and her own thoughts, emotions, and desires. She slowly does so by reclaiming the African diasporic religion of *Candomblé*. These African elements of Brazilian culture that she was urged to leave behind in her childhood take the split protagonist on a journey from fragmentation to a greater sense of integration. Thereafter, she recovers aspects of her identity that she had previously learned were unseemly, such as the enjoyment she receives from sexual pleasure. Throughout the text, the protagonist interacts with the *orixás* Iemanjá, Xangô, Iansã, and Oxum; this study focuses primarily on her association with the latter.[5] Because of this relationship, she comes to speak in a single, rather than a multiple, voice, with the ability to proclaim at the conclusion of the novel, *"sou eu"* (175). In choosing to reclaim an African-based consciousness, she effectively navigates herself out of the series of male-dominated relationships to which she had been previously accustomed. She learns that she has an opportunity to live her life anew, as a woman not divided by loyalties to her father or her husband or her sons, but indeed, one who is true to herself, to her own needs and desires.

Similar to the protagonist of *Mulher no Espelho,* Helena Parente Cunha was raised in Salvador in what she calls a "very strong structure within the traditional pattern for Bahia" (Szoka 47).[6] She began publishing in the late 1970s, after the collapse of the military dictatorship in Brazil, and after making her life in the academy as a professor of literary theory at the Universidade Federal do Rio de Janeiro. Though she has written, and garnered praise for, her poetry and short stories, *Mulher no Espelho* is Parente Cunha's first novel, and the only one in which she utilizes Afro-Brazilian motifs. While this text has garnered significant critical attention (which I discuss below), critics often overlook the African elements of the novel. Only Cristina Sáenz de Tejada has examined them in considerable depth, in both an article (1997) and in her book-length study (1998). However, she fails to investigate the representation of Oxum in the novel, which is the focus of this study.

One of Oxum's most important implements is the mirror; while critics have failed to recognize this relationship, many have analyzed the novel utilizing Jacques Lacan's mirror-stage of psychological development to reveal how Parente Cunha engages with literary theory. For Carmen Chaves Tesser, the novel is a direct response to poststructuralist theory: she proposes that the narrator is the personification of language itself as it attempts to define who it is and how it functions (595). She writes: "As a post-structuralist, [Lacan] saw the decentering of thought as natural in his famous 'mirror stage'—the point at which the child realizes that his arms, legs, are part of a whole, a separate being from his mother. The mirror stage is also the point at which language begins to fill voids" (595). In comparison, for Khadija Safi-Eddine, the reflection in the mirror, "*a mulher*," is the protagonist's conscience, which allows her to gain a greater understanding of herself (48). Naomi Lindstrom considers the way in which Parente Cunha blends these theoretical considerations with the "presentation of personal and social concerns" about womanhood (141),[7] and for Laura J. Beard, the novel represents the self all the while underscoring the futility of the exercise (103). I agree with the critics who read the novel as one that fully develops the Lacan's mirror stage of individual development, thereby seeing "*a mulher*" as something that aids the protagonist to reconcile disparate parts of herself. However, I do so with one critical distinction: I posit that "*a mulher*," the personage in the mirror, is actually the *orixá* Oxum, in which case the novel is one that traces the gradual recognition by the protagonist that this entity guides her life.

Obedience and Self-Sacrifice

At the opening of the story, the protagonist finds herself at an impasse. During the course of her marriage, she has attempted to follow what she perceives to be the dictates of her society regarding the roles of daughter, wife, and mother. In the process, she has restrained her own thoughts and feelings. Despite her best efforts, however, she loses her family. We learn at the outset that her husband is a known philanderer, and her three adult sons alternately ridicule and ignore her. The men in her life have all left the house in which they once lived as a family, leaving her alone and at a loss as to how to comport herself.[8]

For the protagonist, a chief characteristic of womanhood is acquiescence: indeed, she learns to assent to the whims of those surrounding her. Early in the novel, we learn that the protagonist's father was the central figure in her younger life. She describes her relationship to him as follows: "Insignificantes éramos todos nós, em volta dele, todo-poderoso, mandando e antimandando, e nós, aos seus pés, submissos, submetidos, subjugados, submergidos, subtraídos [We were all insignificant around him, all-powerful, ordering and demanding, and us, at his feet, submissive, subdued, subjugated, submerged, subtracted]" (33). The protagonist makes clear that her father was like a god to her. The image she conveys is similar to that of the deity of the Old Testament, in that he is someone who remains distant from those who surround him and who demands that everyone succumbs to his will. She discloses that her father was "um homem do interior, filho de coronel, dono de terras, acostumbrado a mandar, chicote na mão, esporas nos pés, ele também por criação e temperamento sabia fazer-se obedecer [a man from the interior, son of a colonel, landowner, used to ordering, whip in hand, spurs on his feet, by upbringing and temperament he knew how to make himself be obeyed]" (59–60).[9] As the child, and more importantly, as the daughter, of this man, she is expected to obey without question until she marries a man of the same class who will then replace her father in her life.

In marrying her husband, the protagonist does in fact find a man who is very similar to her father. She acknowledges this (66), and reveals the similarity in her behavior toward both men: "Aceitei meu pai com a boca em linha reta. Com a boca esvaziada de porquês, aceito meu marido e meus filhos. Aprendi a agir como ajo com minha mãe. Minha mãe viúva, que eu amo e admiro. A sua voz pouca e leve. O seu silêncio denso. O altíssimo silêncio seu [I accepted my father with his mouth in a straight line. With a mouth emptied of 'why's?' I accept my husband and my sons. I learned to behave as I do with my mother. My widowed mother, who I love and admire. Her voice low and slight. Her dense silence. Her greatest silence]" (34). Notably, her mother is a woman that the protagonist chiefly characterizes by her silence, to which she assigns depth and height. It is from her mother that "eu" learns to simply accept all that the men in her life do, without the benefit of asking why. Her primary model of femininity lived her own life in this way, and so, without question, the protagonist follows the unspoken rules. In the face of all authority, she accepts.

There are moments in the narrative in which the protagonist conflates her husband and her father. She understands herself to be a woman upon whom these men depend, to the extent that she takes pride in being relied upon. This compliancy is the chief characteristic of her identity: her sense of self is determined by her ability to be reliable for these men who seemingly are able to take care of themselves. Yet in the last line of the passage, she communicates a quiet discontent with her position, an acute awareness perhaps that she deserved better treatment, both from her father and her husband.

Among the repeated themes in this novel are those of obedience, submission, and sacrifice. *"A mulher"* reveals that the protagonist was unwanted, or rather, that her father's preference for a son led to the protagonist's submissive behavior: "Esta foi a sua primeira sensação de culpa. Por causa desta decepção primordial que você deu a seu pai, você procurou sempre, inútil tentativa, compensá-lo pela perda. A partir daí, você começou a traçar o seu caminho de obediência e submissão [This was your first sense of guilt. Because of this primordial deception that you gave to your father, you tried always, useless attempts, to compensate him for his loss. From that point on, you began to mark your journey of obedience and submission]" (67). Her commitment to quiet surrender, therefore, is rooted in her inability to repent for the seemingly unpardonable sin of being born a girl. From childhood, then, she assumes the blame for something that she could not change, her sex. Almost from the beginning of her life, therefore, she learns to bow to the wishes and desires of everyone surrounding her, rather than to her own will. "Eu" writes: "Aceitei que meu pai gostasse mais de meu irmão. Aceitei que meu marido não permitisse que eu saísse sozinha. Aceitei viver disponível para meus três filhos. Aceitei, aceitei, risco e perda, solitário ganho [I accepted that my father liked my brother more. I accepted that my husband didn't allow me to go out by myself. I accepted living always available for my three sons. I accepted, I accepted, the risk and the loss, I win the game]" (24). Once again, we hear the insistent repetition of her acceptance, almost like a steady drumbeat. The passage recalls the moment in the Catholic mass when, during the presentation of the Eucharist, the congregation repeats three times it is its fault that Christ was crucified. In accepting the blame for that act, there is a presumed recognition that redemption and transcendence is achieved through suffering.

Gender and the Catholic Church in Latin America

Throughout the text, in fact, Parente Cunha offers a sustained attack on the ideological influence of the Catholic Church. In an article about this novel, she writes: "Quando se pensa na identidade da mulher brasileira captada através da narrativa femenina contemporânea, faz-se indispensável incluir um traço comum a muitas escritoras—a culpa— sem dúvida, parte do legado deixado pela ideologia da Igreja Católica

[When one thinks of the identity of the Brazilian woman as seen through contemporary female narrative, it becomes essential to include a common feature—guilt—without a doubt, part of the legacy left by the ideology of the Catholic Church]" (119). The Church, she suggests, informs all aspects of daily life in Brazil, even though one may not be an active participant in the rites of the institution. The protagonist's willingness to place the needs of the men in her life before her own recalls the concept of *marianismo*, as introduced by Evelyn P. Stevens in her 1973 essay entitled "*Marianismo*: The Other Face of *Machismo* in Latin America." There she writes that in their aspiration to be like the Virgin Mary, Latin American women gain a great amount of spiritual strength that leads to a kind of superiority over men. This allows for "an infinite capacity for humility and sacrifice. No self-denial is too great for Latin American woman, no limit can be divined to her vast store of patience with the men of her world" (94–95). In fact, according to this line of thought, men must be humored, because "everyone knows that they are *como niños* (like little boys) whose intemperance, foolishness and obstinacy must be forgiven because 'they can't help the way they are'" (95).

Stevens states that Latin American women have power in their relationships with men, and although those men might act disrespectfully, their wives and mothers understand that they do not have the spiritual fortitude to act correctly. Nowhere in her study, however, is there any mention of happiness, fulfillment, or contentedness felt by the women she examines. There is no hint at the reality of their emotional lives. In contrast, the protagonist of this novel provides an intimate portrait of the fictionalized reality of one Latin American, specifically Brazilian, woman. In describing her family, she says, "Meu marido acha que devo viver exclusivamente, totalmente, exhaustivamente para ele. Isso me faz muito feliz. Na opinião de meus filhos, toda mãe tem obrigação de se dedicar de modo absoluto a quem pôs no mundo. Esta é a razão da minha vida [My husband thinks that I should live exclusively, totally, exhaustively for him. This makes me very happy. In the opinion of my sons, every mother has the obligation to dedicate herself in an absolute way to the people she brings into the world. This is the reasoning of my life]" (26). At this point in the text, she does not question whether her husband or her sons have the right to demand that she live for them. She reveals that she is accustomed to a lifetime of service to her father:

"Renunciei a tudo por amor a meu pai [I renounced everything for my father's love]" (61). Upon marriage, the protagonist transfers that attention and devotion to her husband.

Though she hints that unrelenting devotion might have caused her pain and fatigue, "eu" insists that she welcomes pain into her life: "[E]ntreguei mãos e pés aos laços e aos nós que me amarram. Entre os laços e os nós, meu limite de liberdade. Minha escolha, minha liberdade [(I) gave my hands and feet to the ties and to those that would bind me. Between the ties and the knots, my boundary of freedom. My choice, my freedom]" (26). Though she uses images of restraint to reference freedom, "eu" does not recognize the implicit contradiction. Instead, the reference to being bound recalls the suffering of Christ, to the extent that His followers are supposed to take up His cross. Again, the text presents the notion that there is redemption after suffering. In the same way that God so loved the world that He sacrificed His only Son, the protagonist does the same for her family. She says, "Há momentos em que eu tenho a impressão de que eles estão sugando o meu próprio sangue [There are moments when I have the impression that they are sucking my very blood]" (35). Similar to the figure of Christ, the protagonist sacrifices herself for the presumed good of everyone else. She expounds upon her idea of love when she says, "Só quem vive profundamente o amor, pode entender as ilimitadas compensações do sacrífício, a alegria de doer de tanto amor. É por muito amar que eu me divido entre meu marido e meus três filhos. Cada qual me disputando um do outro. Amar é também fazer doer e sangrar [Only s/he who lives love profoundly can understand the limitless compensations that come from sacrifice, the happiness of suffering such love. It is through much loving that I divide myself between my husband and my three sons. Each one fighting the other for me. Loving is also suffering and bleeding]" (35). The protagonist evokes a form of Catholicism that believes in the spiritual value of physical pain. It is the principle that in suffering like Christ, we will join Him in heaven. Again, she ignores the apparent contradiction between love and pain, insisting instead that at times, those terms mean the same thing.

With her critique on the supposed spiritual value of pain for women, Parente Cunha calls attention to the fact that Brazilian culture, influenced by the Church, does not make similar demands of its men. On the contrary, such behavior could be deemed "unnatural," even "unmanly."

In her 1989 study, Brazilian theologian Ivone Gebara comments on the continued power of patriarchal thought in Latin American Christianity (22). This, in spite of the development of liberation theology in the 1960s which puts at its center the emancipation of all regardless of gender, race, or class. In a study published three years earlier, however, she calls attention to the *terreiro* of *Candomblé* where women are not submissive but rather are in positions of power:

> No que tange a esta experiência religiosa primordial, seria de grande importância refletirnos sobre a função da mulher no Candomblé, particularmente no Nordeste brasileiro. Lembro apenas esta realidade para color e relevo o fato de que mesmo em culturas machistas como a nossa, no Candomblé, a mulher tem um lugar especial no exercício oficial de tarefas religiosas. A "mãe-de-santo" é "rainha" em seu terreiro. Recebe o desejo do santo o da santa, transmite-os, preside e coordena cerimônias religiosas.

> [With regard to this fundamental religious experience, it would be of great importance for us to reflect upon the role of the woman in Candomblé, particularly in the Brazilian Northeast. I remember only this reality to highlight and emphasize the fact that in the same machista cultures such as ours, in Candomblé, woman has a special place in the official exercise of religious tasks. The 'mãe de santo' [godmother] is a queen in her *terreiro* [religious compound]. She receives the wishes of her saint, she transmits these wishes, she presides and coordinates religious ceremonies.] (13)

Here she reminds her audience of the possibilities of liberation that *Candomblé* presents to its female practitioners. Parente Cunha's inclusion of this religious system in her novel suggests that she also recognizes the emancipating possibilities *Candomblé* presents for women and, in fact, proposes it as a means by which to combat patriarchal thought.

Birth of a New Self: Daughter of Oxum

The most noteworthy aspect of this novel is the idea that the recognition of an African heritage allows the white protagonist to reintegrate her fragmented self, so that by the end of the work there is no longer a distinction between the various voices but rather one unified voice.

Parente Cunha suggests that the European values of patriarchy are destructive to women, who should instead look to the world of *Candomblé*. There, one can find women not only as female energies who are worshipped, such as Iemanjá, Oxum, and Iansã, but also women as priestesses who do not remain quiet and subservient to their male counterparts. As critic Cristina Sáenz de Tejada points out: "Es significativo señalar el papel primordial que ocupa la mujer en estas ceremonias a través de la figura de la 'mãe-de-santo' que controla y regula el ritual religioso. Asimismo actúa como la transmisora de las tradiciones de su cultura [It is critical to point out the prime role that woman takes on in these ceremonies through the figure of the 'mãe-de-santo' who controls and regulates the religious ritual. In this way she acts as the transmitter of the traditions of her culture]" (47). In simply participating in the rituals of this religion, then, the protagonist of the novel finds a system of thought that places women in the forefront, in a position of power rather than one of submission.

According to the *Enciclopédia brasileira da diáspora africana*, Oxum is the

orixá iorubano das águas doces, da riqueza, da beleza e do amor. Segundo alguns relatos tradicionais, é divindade superior, tendo participado da Criação como provedora das fontes das águas doces. É o nume tutelar do rio Óshun, que nace em Ekití, no Leste da Nigeria. . . . É a Venus dos iorubás, famosa por sua beleza e por seu grande cuidado con a aparência . . . [ela] é descrita como divindade que *gosta muito de se banhar, que está sempre se mirando num espelho*.

[Yoruba orixa of sweet waters, of wealth, of beauty and of love. According to some traditional stories, she is the oldest divinity, having participated in Creation as the provider of the fonts of sweet water. It is the name of the Oshun River, that begins in Ekiti, in eastern Nigeria. . . . She is the Venus of the Yorubas, famous for her beauty and for her great care with her appearance . . . she is described as the divinity that *likes bathing herself, that is always looking at herself in the mirror*. (505; my emphasis)

Oxum is the sole *orixá* in the pantheon of entities within this religion that carries the mirror, which she uses to appreciate her own beauty and sensuality. She is the quintessence of femininity. In examining Yoruban oral literature, Diedre Badejo finds that she is the entity that governs fertility, that which allows for the continuation of the human race. She writes: "As a female deity, she possesses the power to withhold the life-force which activates humanity through the male principle. That singular power emphasizes that without the female principle, the male principle is rendered impotent" (74).[10] Oxum, then, is an entity that represents and embodies all aspects of womanhood. She defends the power that all women inherently possess. In including this specific deity in the novel, Parente Cunha is proposing an alternate version of womanhood, one that should stand alongside the Virgin Mary in popular representations of the feminine. After the men in her life leave, the protagonist learns the identity of the *orixás* who guide her.

Throughout the novel, "eu" refers to Oxum, Xangô, and Iemanjá; in memories of her childhood, she recalls asking her nanny about these and other *orixás* (43, 68–69), only to have her attention be drawn somewhere else. Though we learn early in the novel that we are in the city Salvador da Bahia (8, 26), there is little doubt that the protagonist and her family belong to the white landowning upper class. She is well aware of social stratification and one's proper place in the hierarchy. She notes: "Naquele tempo, na casa de meu pai, era feio se falar, era feio se pensar em candomblé, coisa em que branco não se mete [In those days, in my father's house, it was ugly to talk about, ugly to think about *Candomblé,* something in which a white person didn't involve himself]" (150). According to the rules of behavior established by her father, not only was it unbecoming to speak of the religious system identified with the Afro-Brazilian population, it was considered "ugly." Her father emphasizes beauty in his dealings both with the protagonist and with her mother; engaging in *Candomblé* at any level would therefore be a serious transgression, in that she would be moving beyond her assigned place.

Nevertheless, as the novel progresses, the references to her nanny and Afro-Brazilian culture increase, as she recovers more of her childhood memories. The protagonist declares at one point: "Mas painho, eu não sou branca, eu sou morena [But Daddy, I'm not all that white, I'm brown]" (150). This assertion of what could later develop into racial pride goes unnoticed by the majority of the critics of this work, many of whom focus on psychoanalytic readings of a presumed white female protagonist. Cristina Sáenz de Tejada writes that the novel "analiza la problemática de una mujer mulata de clase media-alta que, una vez separada de su marido y de la ideología branqueante que éste defiende, inicia un regreso cultural a sus orígenes africanos [analyzes the problems of a *mulata* of the upper middle class who, once separated from her husband and the ideology of whiteness that he defends, begins a cultural return to her African origins]" (46). Sáenz de Tejada brings light to another possible motivation for the protagonist's submission to her husband: in order to allay anxiety about her heritage, she would obey both him and her male children, thereby ensuring that her presence does not upset the established social order.

"Eu" goes on to question her ancestry: "E os avós dos meus avós? De onde vem a minha pele morena? Da atenuação dos tons da Nigéria? Do soprar dos ventos quentes da Guiné? Ao som de quais tambores começou a correr o meu sangue? [And the grandparents of my grandparents? Where does my dark skin come from? From the weakening of skin tones from Nigeria? From the blowing of hot winds from Guinea? The sound of which drums made my blood run?]" (150). Referencing the history of *branqueamento* in Brazil, "eu" questions the source of the family's financial prosperity.[11] The protagonist's turn to *Candomblé,* then, is not merely the assumption of a spiritual system that is one of the most prominent signifiers of African heritage in Brazil, it is also an act of retrieval as she regains a lost heritage within her family.

While in trance at a *terreiro*, she discovers she is the daughter of Oxum:

Ela pertence a Oxum. Iansã é dona dela. Ela tem de fazer a cabeça. Ela vai morrer, se não quiser ser cavalo de Oxum. Se não quiser ser cavalo de Iansã. A força das aguas. O poder dos ventos e das tempestades. Oxum. Iansã. A graça do passo. O grito do guerra. Oxum. Iansã. Ela sabe a mansidão. Ela espalha os temporais. Os amarelos de ouro. Os vermelhos de sangue. Oxum. Iansã. Ela pertence a Oxum. Iansã é dona dela. Ela vai morrer, se não fizer a cabeça.

[She belongs to Oxum. Iansã is her mistress. She has to crown. She will die if she does not want to be Oxum's horse. If she does not want to be Iansã's horse. The strength of the waters. The power of the winds and the storms. Oxum. Iansã. The grace of her step. The shout of war. Oxum. Iansã. She knows gentleness. She scatters the storms. The yellows of gold. The reds of blood. Oxum. Iansã. She belongs to Oxum. Iansã is her mistress. She is going to die if she doesn't crown.] (164)

Here the protagonist learns that she must initiate into this religion ("tem de fazer a cabeça") as a means by which to avoid facing death. To this point, she has sacrificed herself without any thought as to the harm she has caused herself; living in an environment that actively encourages women to surrender their will for the good of the men in their lives, she has previously given little thought to the metaphors of blood and suffering that she uses to describe love. She understands love to mean something that brings about her own suffering, but for the sake of a greater good, namely that of her family. For "eu," renunciation of her self (her thoughts, dreams, emotions, will, etc.) would bring joy to the lives of everyone around her. Throughout the novel, though, *"a mulher,"* who, I would emphasize, is the reflection of "eu" that appears in her mirror, encourages "eu" to think of herself first, to place herself at the forefront of her own life. Suddenly, in trance, the protagonist learns the identities of deities that will persuade her to do the same.

While the protagonist reveals that she is a daughter of Oxum late in the narration, there is strong evidence that Oxum has always been present in her life. A critical part in the protagonist's journey to integration is the recognition of her sexuality and the role that her body has played in her life. As a child, she did not know the meaning of virginity: "Pensava que ser virgem era ser boa como a Virgem Maria. Na minha cabeça, virgindade representava bondade, humildade, delicadeza, altruísmo. Eu me considerava distante desses sentimentos, incompetente para a virtude [I thought that being a virgin meant being good like the Virgin Mary. In my head, virginity represented goodness, humility, kindness, altruism. I considered myself detached from those sentiments, incompetent for virtue]" (81). Again, we see the grasp of the Catholic Church, as its only model for womanhood is a mother who reproduced without having sex. *"A mulher"* takes pains to point out how "eu's" ignorance of the sexual act continued until she was seventeen years old (81), and while she experienced stirrings of her desire, she had no acceptable outlet because she was not married. Later the protagonist continues: "Eu era uma menina ingênua e sozinha, sem ninguém que me ajudasse a ter coragem de romper o cerco das proibições de meu pai, sem ninguém que me explicasse o que significavam palavras como virgindade, que nem de longe eu suspeitava o que fosse [I was a naive lonely girl, without anyone to help me have the courage to break the barriers of my father's prohibitions, without anyone explaining to me the meaning of words such as virginity, which I couldn't begin to suspect]" (82). Her genuine lack of knowledge regarding her own sexuality underscores the situation in which many young girls find themselves: without encouragement to explore their own bodies, they remain unaware of what brings them pleasure or discomfort until they are with their sexual partners.

Reclaiming the Body

In her influential essay "The Laugh of the Medusa," Hélène Cixous highlights the relationship between the power of writing for women and its effect on women's sexuality: "To write. An act which will not only 'realize' the decensored relation of woman to her sexuality, to her womanly being, giving her access to her native strength; it will give her back her goods, her pleasures, her organs, her immense bodily territories which have been kept under seal" (351). Throughout her novel, Parente Cunha includes explicit descriptions of the protagonist's relationship with her body, both during her marriage, when she believes it to be something of which she should be ashamed, as well as after all of the men in her life leave her. The manner in which she treats her body reveals her location on her spiritual journey from psychic fragmentation to a reconciliation of all aspects of her personality.

As a wife and mother, "eu" denies the existence of her own sexual pleasure in favor of her husband's: "Eu simplesmente me assisto, sem espelhos, neutra e vaga, cada vez mais consentida [I simply attend to myself, without mirrors, neutral and vague, each time more agreeable]" (48). According to Evelyn P. Stevens, "the ideal [of *marianismo*] dictates not only premarital chastity for all women, but also postnuptial frigidity. 'Good' women do not enjoy coitus; they endure it when the duties of matrimony require it" (96). The protagonist articulates her unhappiness when she says: "Meus seios solitários, minhas nádegas vazias de carí-cias, meu sexo ermo. Em chamas [My solitary breasts, my buttocks free of caresses, my lonely sex. On fire]" (48). Rather than accept that she, the "eu" voice, has admitted to something less than happiness, she quickly blames *a mulher que me escreve,* thereby denying responsibility for her own feelings. She continues to do so until the conclusion of the novel, when the two voices become one.

While the protagonist's sense of self is not defined by her body, her spiritual integration is furthered once she has an active relationship with her body, that is, once she no longer denies herself pleasure or feels embarrassment when she enjoys herself. Her involvement with *Candomblé*, a religion that eschews the mind/body problem of Catholicism and much of Western thought, promotes this process. Early in the text, the protagonist hints at the passionate woman that lies within the woman who tires from attempting to please all of the men in her life. She says that when she dances alone, she can enjoy herself: "No pulso do ritmo, deduzo a minha quota de liberdade, desfruto de uma sensualidade que desconheço, gozo de uma beleza física que me restaura [In the pulse of the rhythm, I take my share of freedom, I enjoy a sensuality that I don't know, I enjoy a physical beauty that restores me]" (47). This recalls several of the defining characteristics of Oxum, she who loves to dance ("a graça do passo"), who in the movement of her body personifies sensuality and beauty. Alone, the protagonist allows herself to experience pleasure, and achieves sexual release without depending on her husband: "entro no chuveiro e deixo a água correr pelo meu corpo satisfeito, após o orgasmo que me concedi [I enter the shower and let the wáter run along my satisfied body, after the orgasm that I reached]" (47).[12] In the water, this daughter of Oxum feels free enough to let go and release. Later, she says, "Muitas vezes gosto de me ver nua, sozinha no quarto, nos mistérios do meu corpo que o infinito dos espelhos cruzados me estendem, me prometem, me acenam. Espreito pelas frestas do que me foi negado. Do que me neguei. A minha nudez me atrai, me excita, me assusta [I often like seeing myself nude, alone in my room, in the mysteries of my body that the infinity of the folded mirrors extend to me, promise me, offer me. I peek through the cracks to see what was denied me. What I denied myself. My nudity attracts me, excites me, scares me]" (47). At the same time, then, that she fascinates herself, she also scares herself, most probably because she has not yet integrated her sexual self with her conception of wife and mother. And yet, she uses the mirror, one of Oxum's chief implements, to study herself, to learn about the mysteries of her own body, to develop a greater sense of her own sensuality. In this way, she recalls Oxum herself, who revels in her own reflection in the mirror.

Certainly, the protagonist's relationship with her own body is symbolic of her relationship with Oxum. She has ignored it, repressing her most basic desires in order to satisfy someone else. And yet, the deity who governs beauty and love, who encourages the sensuality of women, is always present, lying dormant, awaiting recognition. Significantly, "eu" describes being away from mirrors when having perfunctory sex with her husband (48). After the men in her life leave, "eu" takes a moment to look at herself in those mirrors. Initially she only sees "uma imagem deprimida, o rosto contraído, os ombros encurvados, as mãos caídas, as pernas entreabertas, em busca de mais chão [a depressed image, a shy face, curved shoulders, fallen hands, legs apart, looking for more ground]" (113). Once she ascertains that her body is all there, that there is nothing physically missing, she begins to laugh.[13] Standing naked in front of her countless mirrors, she says, "Uma sensação boa de liberdade percorre as minhas imagens. Apalpo os meus seios, apalpo o meu sexo. Vivos. Ansiosos. Um sorriso lúbrico surpreende o meu rosto no espelho. Olho fixamente. Sorrio mais no meu sorriso lúbrico e me reconheço [A sensation of freedom runs through my images. I touch my breasts, touch my sex. Alive. Anxious. A sensual smile surprises my face in the mirror. I stare. I smile more at my sensual smile and I recognize myself]" (114). She revels in her own beauty, enjoying her own sensuality. She recognizes the reflection in the mirror as herself. From this point, the voice of "eu" dominates the narration: no longer does the voice of "a mulher," again, originally identified as the reflection in the mirror, appear as often. This implies that "eu" no longer looks outward for guidance regarding her behavior as she had previously done with her father, husband, and sons; instead, she draws on herself as the source of her identity.

The protagonist thereafter begins to enjoy her body, recognizing that she is, in fact, desirable. This is contrary to what her husband has told her during the course of their marriage. Alone, she appreciates that she has "um belo corpo não jovem, à espera do prazer a que tem direito [a beautiful body, not young, waiting for the pleasure to which I have a right]" (115). In the face of a Western culture that insists on beauty being synonymous with youth, this mother of three young adult men recognizes her own desire to experience pleasure. She details each caress; in touching all the parts of her body previously only touched by her husband, the protagonist reclaims herself. She demonstrates that she is presently concerned primarily with her own pleasure rather than that of someone else. She can now affirm her self, her being: "Sim, eu sou eu [Yes, I am me]" (115).

The Companion of Oxum

In addition to allusions to the *orixás* themselves, Parente Cunha refers to the protagonist's neighbor, "o menino preto filho da cozinheira [the little black boy, son of the cook]" (43). Throughout the novel, he becomes synonymous with the *orixá* Xangô: "O menino preto filho da cozinheira da casa do lado ia para o quintal e gritava e erguia os braços e dizia que era o rei dos trovões [The black little boy, son of the cook next door, used to go out to the yard and yell and raise his arms and say that he was the king of thunder]" (23). Storms characterized by lightening and thunder are symbols of Xangô, who uses them as weapons. In *Flash of the Spirit,* Robert Farris Thompson writes about the Yoruba entity, Shàngó: "He became an eternal moral presence, rumbling in the clouds, outraged by impure human acts, targeting the homes of adulterers, liars, and thieves for destruction" (85). In Brazil, this entity maintains this reputation as the arbiter of justice: "Xangô é pesado, íntegro, indivisível, irremovível. . . . Seu raio e eventual castigo é o resultado de um quase processo judicial, onde todos os prós e os contras foram pensados e pesados exaustivamente—a famosa balança de Justiça [Xangô is substantial, whole, indivisible, unmovable. . . . His lightning and eventual punishment is a result of a quasi-judicial process, where all of the pros and cons are thought of and considered exhaustively—the famous balance of Justice]" (*Os Orixás* 7, 9).

The little boy next door is a constant presence in the novel, one to which the protagonist returns in her recovery of Afro-Brazilian culture (40, 43, 50, 58, 68, 103–104, 111). Her frequent allusions to him remind the reader that Xangô is a husband of Oxum's; this suggests that throughout her childhood and into adulthood, the protagonist was under the protection of this *orixá* as well as her own. In spite of the dominant authoritarianism of first her father and then her husband, there remains a reassuring male spiritual presence surrounding her. As she enters new relationships after the dissolution of her marriage, she encounters a man she identifies as her neighbor, now an adult (150–51). While the other sexual encounters are short-lived, she presents the one she has with the son of Xangô as inevitable: "Meu destino, minha escolha. O preto bonito, filho de Xangô. Minha escolha. Meu destino. Meu destino de pertencer ao destino dele [My destiny, my choice. The pretty black man, son of Xangô. My choice. My destiny. My destiny to belong to his destiny]" (170). Calling him "bonito" reminds the reader of her father's designation of everything associated with *Candomblé* as ugly; as an adult woman, she rejects the limitations of her past imposed by her upbringing, seeing instead the beauty of this man and his religious beliefs. With this union, Parente Cunha suggests a replacement of worldviews: whereas the protagonist had previously lived according to the hierarchical stratification of race, class, and gender, in this relationship she breaches those restrictions, permitting herself instead to live according to her own sensibilities.

Reemergence in the World

While the protagonist is engaged on her quest for fulfillment, her children, who are accustomed to her attention, languish. Her oldest son enters a rehabilitation clinic, her middle child is arrested for attempted murder, and her youngest spends his days drunk (109). While she asks herself if she is to blame for their actions, she accepts that there is very little she could have done to prevent them: "fiz o que pude. Sacrifiquei a minha vida e a minha morte [I did what I could. I sacrificed my life and my death]" (109). After years in which she has tried to make the lives of her husband and children easier, she adopts a tone of regret. However, she does not blame herself for their misfortunes. On the contrary, she recognizes that she has done all that she could for her family. Significantly, she points to both a life and a death, an indication that the wife and mother that she was no longer exists: she has, instead, borne an entirely new version of herself.

She next mentions her children when her youngest son interrupts a meeting she has with a lover, forcing himself into the house, drunk, and demanding to know the identity of the man she is entertaining. Resembling a jealous lover himself, he puts his hands on his mother and calls her a whore. She asserts herself when she screams, "Sinto-me com toda a autoridade, ouviu bem? Sinto-me com toda a autoridade para lhe dizer a verdade. Para lhe dizer que você é um perdido. Cansei de lutar por você. Por você e seus irmãos. Me sacrifiquei. Me imolei. Virei cinza.

Agora basta [I have the authority, did you hear me? I have the authority to tell you the truth. To tell you that you are lost. I tired of fighting for you. For you and your brothers. I sacrificed myself. I harmed myself. I turned into ashes. Now it's enough]" (142). This may be the first instance in his life in which the protagonist has not cowed to her husband or to a child, and so he ignores her. In admitting her fatigue and her pain, she finally gives voice to all that she had suppressed previously. She now recognizes the damage she did to herself in the course of her marriage, and so refuses to resume that behavior for the sake of placating her son. She continues: "Eu, sua mãe, faço o que quero e não admito que filho meu venha me dizer o que é certo, o que é errado [I, your mother, do what I want and I do not admit that my son can come and tell me what is true, what is mistaken]" (142). From her words, we learn that her son believes that he has the authority to correct his mother's behavior, much in the same way as her father or her husband would. She maintains, "E se estou andando com muitos homens, é problema só meu. Você não tem nada a ver com este caso [And if I am going out with many men, it is only my problem. You have nothing to do with this]" (142). With this declaration, she challenges everything she has taught her son to believe about the role of men and women in his society. Like her mother before her, she previously lived in silence, attempting to satisfy the desires of her husband and children in order to keep the peace. Here, this daughter of Oxum claims a right to her own sexuality, recognizing that she is sole owner of her body: she refuses anyone else's claim to it.

The response of her son to his mother's newfound confidence is to show her a gun that he has been carrying. The manner in which she deals with him changes completely; her tone moves from one of defiance to one of soothing: "Não faça bobagem, meu filho. Não. Me dê essa arma. Filhinho, a mamãe está pedindo. Venha cá, meu benzinho [Don't be silly, son. No. Give me the gun. My little boy, your mommy is asking. Come here, my baby]" (142). In order to remove the weapon, she finds it necessary to placate him by assuming a voice to which he is more accustomed. She humors him, saying that she will introduce him to her guest, thereby effectively removing the possibility that he is in fact her lover. By taking up a reassuring presence, the protagonist temporarily mollifies her son. With this scene, Parente Cunha reveals yet another aspect of Oxum. Recognizing the threat that her son poses, the protagonist resorts to flattery in order to calm him, effectively ending the danger. Badejo writes: "Women's power is unequivocal because, like the womb itself, women are a mysterious matrix of internal synergism where spirit and body first meet. To defeat women is to defeat the awesome power of life itself" (85). While her son lives by the societal definition of manhood that dictates he utilize brute strength in order to destroy what he deems to be his (namely, his mother), the protagonist already lives according to the religious system of *Candomblé,* whereby women are empowered beings. Able to draw on her own inherent might, she reveals the possibilities open to women if they were to live by this system of thought.

The Face of Justice

In the aftermath of her confrontation with her son, there is another disagreement, one which results in his death, after he returns to the house to force another altercation. The protagonist says: "Por que meu filho veio bater à minha porta, tão tarde da noite? . . . Continuo imóvel sobre o sofá. O mesmo cansaço. O tédio absoluto. . . . Dois homens falando, gritando, brigando. Conheço estas voces? Vozes cravadas na noite suspense. Tiros riscando a noite. Muitas vozes no silêncio escorregadio. Movimento na rua madrugante. Não me mexo [Why did my son come knocking on my door, so late at night? . . . I stay on the sofa, not moving. The same fatigue. The absolute weariness. . . . Two men talking, yelling, fighting. Do I know these voices? Voices piercing the suspenseful night. Shots slicing the night. Many voices in the slippery silence. Movement on the dawning street. I don't move]" (173). Having already reclaimed formerly discarded parts of her identity and personality by this point in the narrative, "eu" here associates fatigue and immobility with her husband, her children, everything that accompanied how she used to live. Though she hears commotion at her door, she does not welcome it by allowing the disturbance to enter the space she has created separate from the family that has abandoned her. Her apartment now serves as an area of her protection and well-being; granting her son entrance would mean disruption and a demand for her to return to the submissive mother that he knows. For critics who address this scene, there is consensus that this death is a consequence of the protagonist's self-realization.[14] Joanne Gass contextualizes his murder as an attempt on the part of the state to regulate his mother's behavior: "The price of trying to forge an identity outside of ideology is very high; one might think too high" (73). An examination of the scene itself reveals that punishment is not directed at the protagonist but instead directly at her son.

She continues: "Ligo o rádio. Não escuto o que escuto. Morte na madrugada. Jovem tresloucado. Reputação da mãe. Atirou. Fugiu. Encontrado o corpo [I turn on the radio. I do not hear what I am hearing. Death at dawn. Deranged young man. Mother's reputation. They shot. They fled. Body found]" (173). The announcement leaves ambiguous the identity of the shooter, though it suggests that there was some justification, as the young man came to personify madness, a threat that is not tolerated within general society.[15] Earlier in the novel, "eu" establishes that her sons are demonstrating "deviant" behavior, involved with drugs, alcohol, violence, and homosexuality (36–37, 95–96). The classification of deviancy is a reflection of a given society's mores;[16] whereas the defense of a mother's reputation could be considered a noble pursuit, here, it is portrayed as a signifier of mental imbalance. With his death, such danger is put to an end.

Reconciliation of the Selves

After her son's death, the protagonist expresses resignation (174), and yet in the last paragraph of the novel, the mirror of the title breaks, and with it, the voice of *"a mulher."* No longer do we have the division between the two voices that have offered conflicting narratives. Instead the protagonist says, "Olho um rosto inteiro num pedaço de espelho. Um rosto só. . . . Meu rosto. Inteiro. Sou EU [I see a whole face in a piece of the mirror. Only one face . . . my face. Whole. I am ME]" (175). The protagonist is no longer fragmented; instead, she speaks in a singular voice. She has now subsumed the identity of *"a mulher,"* she who consistently encouraged her to live as a self-realized woman, one not divided by loyalties to her father or her husband or her sons, but indeed, one who is true to herself, to her own needs and desires. And because of this, we are left to ponder the true identity of *"a mulher que me escreve"*: is she, as Naomi Lindstrom claims, a feminist novelist? Or could she possibly have been the voice of Oxum all along? Though the mirror is destroyed, the task is complete: no longer sacrificing herself for the benefit of others, the protagonist can easily claim: "Sou eu."

In this novel, we find the journey of a woman who begins by defining herself in terms established by her father, her husband, and her sons. After these men leave her, she finds herself in a position where she comprehends that she has the capacity to construct her identity for herself. From the beginning of the novel, she acknowledges that no one knows her true self, that, in fact, it is an impossibility for anyone to truly know anyone: "Por acaso, alguém sabe alguém, carne e grito sob a capa do rosto, ordenado e composto em carapaça? [By chance, does anyone know anyone, flesh and cries under the cover of their face, an ordered and composed shell?]" (17). And while she asserts that she exists only in her own imagination (18), she does not know herself at the beginning of the text. In fact, this feeling of unease prompts the writing of her life story. In doing so, the protagonist slowly comes to the realization that she is more than just someone who can be identified by the roles she plays in the lives of the men surrounding her: more than just "daughter of," "wife of," "mother of." The protagonist has to confront not only the memory of her own biological father, but also the patriarchal society in which she lives. She does so by engaging in the religious rituals of *Candomblé,* through which she learns that she is the daughter of Oxum. This entity leads her to begin integrating her disparate selves, those elements of herself that she believes to be objectionable, namely, her own wants and desires. In heeding the voice of Oxum, the protagonist succeeds at speaking in a singular voice, one that integrates her multiple identities.

Yearning for Peace

Esboço um sorriso / trajo a alvura / dos dentes. Na espreita / aguardo / ternuras / afagos . . .

—"Esperança"

I put on a smile / I wear whiteness / of teeth. / On the lookout, / I wait for / tenderness / caresses . . .

—"Hope"

Born in Araraquara, São Paulo, Sônia Fátima da Conceição is one of the prominent writers of the Afro-Brazilian writing collective Quilombhoje. A sociologist by training, she has published poems and short stories in numerous editions of *Cadernos Negros;* her work has also appeared in *Enfim . . . Nós* and *Mulheres Escrevendo: Uma Antologia Bilingüe de Escritoras Afro-Brasileiras Contemporâneas / Women Righting: Afro-Brazilian Women's Short Fiction.* She has also published a novel, *Marcas, sonhos e raízes (Marks, Dreams and Roots)* (1991).[17]

For the poetic voice in the poem that serves as an epigraph of this section, there is effort in the seemingly simple act of smiling, an action that communicates optimism that there may come softness. Nevertheless, there is guardedness as well—she exerts energy, watching for a gesture that conveys kindness and gentleness. She also suggests a subversive sense of humor, revealing that the only whiteness present is that which she puts on her teeth; this is a verse that recalls an imaginary of stereotypical representations of men and women of African descent, figures of dark skin, full nose, and white teeth. Hope does not mean aspiring to material wealth but instead to a basic recognition of humanity from those who look past hers. In the three poems that follow, Conceição reveals a tone of melancholy in her portrayal of *Candomblé;* while for Parente Cunha, the inclusion of this spiritual system signified difference and liberation for her upper-middle-class white protagonist, Conceição cannot reach the freedom implicit in the system, due to societal limitations placed on her due to race, sex, and widespread poverty. For the poetic voice in her poems, there exists a yearning for basic human rights. In "Quem dera" / "If Only I Could," she writes:

Ver o mundo com meus olhos	To see the world with my eyes
quem dera	If only I could recognize again
reconhecer de novo	
ervas, sentimentos,	herbs, feelings,
desvendar	to unmask
o que tráz o curso	what the course of the winds
dos ventos	brings
reverência eguns na noite	to venerate the spirits in the night
saber da ávore	to know the tree to the root.
a raiz.	
tocar a terra feira à	to touch the earth made to
minha medida	my measure
dançar sem receio aos Orixás	to dance without apprehension for

	the Orixás
curar lumbrigueiro	to cure tape worm
dizer aquela reza forte	to say that strong prayer
e curar, curar	and to cure, to cure
mazelas, sequelas	ailments, consequences,
invejas, mau-olhado	
	old age, the evil eye
ignorâncias	ignorance
curar . . .	to cure . . .
que dera. (214)	if only I could. (215)

"Quem dera" is a poem of the subjunctive mood, of this mode that expresses that which could possibly happen in some undetermined time and space. She presents a series of actions that she would perform if she were able: recover lost knowledge and feelings ("reconhecer de novo / ervas, sentimentos"); regain the ability to know the future ("desvendar / o que tráz o curso / dos ventos"); interact with the ancestral presence ("reverência eguns na noite"); commune with nature ("saber da ávore / a raiz."); fully praise the *orixás* ("dançar sem receio aos Orixás"); and be a source of healing ("curar, curar"). She identifies illnesses that are physical ("lumbrigueiro," "mazelas," "invejas") as well as spiritual ("sequelas," "invejas," "mau-olhado," "ignorâncias"). Listing this succession of efforts that she would accomplish given the opportunity begs the question, Why is she not able to do these things? What forces are impeding these actions? The poetic voice implicitly indicts Brazilian society: she cannot worship as fully as she would like due to discrimination against those who practice *Candomblé*. While *Macumba* and *Umbanda* are religious practices that have as a foundation the *orixás*, these African diasporic religions also combine Kardecian spiritism; they are therefore considered less purely African in practice, and are more popular with a greater majority of the Brazilian population.[18] Were she able, she would be in balance with all that surrounds her: recognizing that a human being is only being a part of nature rather than an owner of it, she would have at her disposal the knowledge that nature provides. This is a more holistic approach to life, one that criticizes the Enlightenment discourses that define knowledge as the province of the logical, rational mind and that discard other kinds of intelligence. Tapeworm is an ailment suffered by impoverished peoples of Brazil, and a significant portion of the Afro-Brazilian population continues to live in extreme poverty. If she were able then, Conceição would heal those sicknesses that ail her community, freeing them to live in health of mind, body, and spirit.

She continues this train of thought with another of her poems, "Desejo" / "I Want":

DESEJO

> deslizar em águas de rio
> abraçar sombras de cachoeiras
> saudar orixás nas florestas
> me enfeitar de estrelas
> cintilar na noite
> sorrir   (218)

I WANT

> to slide into the river waters
> to embrace the shadows of waterfalls
> to greet the orishas in the forests
> to adorn myself with stars
> to sparkle in the night
> to smile   (219)

Again, the poetic voice expresses a desire to be in communion with nature; we see the *orixás* residing in the forest, signifying that they reside away from the urban centers that populate her country but instead in their elements. The rejection of the urban in preference for the rural hearkens back to the sacred space established by those who escaped slavery, the *quilombo*, which exist just outside of the margins of the cities.[19] References to the rivers and waterfalls serve as entreaties to Oxum, who represents both of these bodies of water. To be surrounded by beauty, to live in it and draw life from it, would bring her joy. We are left to wonder why she would prefer this mode of escape from the daily realities of life: while the poem is rather innocuous, read together with "Quem dera" and "Invasão," we see once more a yearning for something which eludes her, and from which she cannot flee.

INVASÃO		INVASION	
Energizemos as cidades		Let's energize the cities	
(é o momento)		(it's the moment)	
ressoem os atabaques		let's beat the drums	
santo sacrifício		holy sacrifice	
sacrifique		sacrifice [20]	
(um bode)		(a goat)	
na Santa Eucaristia		in the Holy Eucharist	
santo sangue		holy	
nos cobra		blood	
a todos		covers us all	
AXÉ	(228)	AXÉ	(229)

In this poem, which serves as a call to action, Conceição takes advantage of the fears and stereotypes about African religions by invoking those prejudices and threatening an attack. These are historic fears that go back to colonial times, when, in the aftermath of the Haitian Revolution of 1791–1804, drums were outlawed in societies throughout the Americas. There was recognition that Africans used drums to communicate with each other and with their spiritual entities; the fear was that the call for insurrection could be announced through this medium, hence these instruments were declared illegal. The comparison of the "Santa Eucaristia" (7) with the sacrifice of the goat (5–6) reminds the audience that Jesus Christ, He who is the Holy Eucharist, was himself a sacrifice, the Lamb of God. With these verses, Conceição manages to put *Candomblé* on equal footing with Christianity. The image she calls upon, though, that of inhabitants of the cities covered in the blood of the sacrifice (8–10), challenges those who would accuse this religious system of primitivism. She dares the reader to be afraid of the act meant as an offering to the *orixás*, an action that is meant to awaken them and give them life ("Energizemos as cidades"). The final word of the poem acts as "Amen" does at the end of prayer of the Christian tradition; not only does it close the prayer, there is the unspoken message of "May it be so."

Comparing Parente Cunha's novel with the poems of Sônia Fátima da Conceição, we note the stark difference in the employment of *Candomblé* in their art. Although *Mulher no Espelho* (1983) features this system of belief prominently, it does so as a signifier of difference: this religious system allows "eu" and *"a mulher que me escreve"* to escape the restrictions placed upon women of upper-middle-class Bahian society. Parente Cunha utilizes *Candomblé* as a means by which to challenge the predominance of patriarchal thought in early 1980s Brazil, when the military dictatorship that had ruled the country since 1964 was weakening, only coming to an end in 1985. Conceição's inclusion of this system of belief underscores all that is not available to Afro-Brazilian communities around the nation: the ability to worship fully and freely, without harassment and persecution; to have access to clean water and soil (tapeworm infections occur when water or soil is contaminated with human feces); to have their beliefs acknowledged as legitimate systems of knowledge rather than as outdated superstitions. The longing for integration that marks Parente Cunha's text remains for the poetic voice in the art of Conceição. For her, there is little salvation available; despite the presence of the *orixás*, there remains an inability to access them and practice as fully as she would like. The sacrifice, then, is remaining in a country that cannibalizes the contributions made by enslaved Africans and their descendants in the realm of culture (*samba, capoeira, Macumba, Umbanda*), but that marginalizes the people themselves. In her poems, there is nothing upon which she can depend other than those unfulfilled wishes.

The Meeting of the Rainbow and the River

Lá fora, no céu cor de iris, um enorme angorô multicolorido se diluía lentamente, enquanto Ponciá Vicêncio, elo e herança de uma memória reencontrada pelos seus, não se perderia jamais, se guardaria nas águas do rio.

—in *Ponciá Vicêncio*

Outside, in a rainbow-colored sky, an enormous multicolored serpent slowly faded, while Ponciá Vicêncio vowed to never lose the link and heritage of a memory re-discovered by her eguns, she would protect it in the waters of the river.

Born in Belo Horizonte, Conceição Evaristo is a writer and a professor, having graduated with her doctorate in Comparative Literature from the Universidade Federal Fluminense in Rio de Janeiro. Her work has been published in several volumes of *Cadernos Negros,* as well as in *Enfim . . . Nós* and *Mulheres Escrevendo.* In addition to the novel under examination here, she has published *Becos da Memória* (novel, 2006), *Poemas da recordação e outros movimentos* (poetry, 2008), and *Insubmissas lágrimas de mulheres* (short stories, 2011). In this her first novel, *Ponciá Vicêncio* (2003), Conceição Evaristo offers the story of a young Afro-Brazilian woman who leaves her family in the country so as to make a life for herself in the city. In uprooting herself, she abandons all that sustains her: not only her nuclear family (which consists of her mother Maria and her brother Luandi José) but also her spirituality, her engagement with both the *nkisis,* primarily Ndanda Lunda, who is associated with the *orixá* Oxum, and with her ancestors. While the desire for economic security compels the migration of both the eponymous protagonist and her brother, it also occasions a disruption of the sustenance of a vibrant spirituality that is characteristic of her community. Only when the family reunites is the spiritual system that guides each member recognized and celebrated. With the inclusion of *Candomblé Bantu* and the honoring of ancestors, Evaristo communicates both continuity and change; though material conditions of life may or may not evolve, the belief systems held by this family continue to serve as a support, even when ignored by the individuals themselves. Evaristo provides a counternarrative to dominant Brazilian tellings of migration, in which the standard trope is the country girl who comes to the city and loses herself, a la Macabéa in Clarice Lispector's *A hora da estrela* (1977). Instead of solitude and isolation, Evaristo emphasizes community and unification of family by infusing her novel with representations of Afro-Brazilian spiritual systems.

Though there are few details specifying the specific location of the account, Evaristo utilizes the recognizable trope of the city versus the country in her novel, evoking the binary of civilization and barbarism. From Domingo Faustino Sarmiento's *Facundo: civilización y barbarie* (1845) to the present day, this pairing is a dominant image of Latin American literature and culture. In that original account, the city is a civilizing space, the inheritor of European values and so that which can combat the supposed primitivism of the countryside. Evaristo upsets this dialectic, revealing that the city and the country are both sites of violence for men and women of African descent in Brazil. Indeed, she immerses her novel in history of the late nineteenth and early twentieth century, referencing the gradual abolition of slavery as well as the enduring impact of poverty and racial discrimination on this population.

She begins her novel with the adult Ponciá recalling her childhood spent in a rural area with her parents and grandfather. Though he dies when she is very young, not yet weaned off of her mother's breast, her grandfather remains a vibrant presence in her life, to the extent that she mimics his movements as soon as she can walk. Her family lives on the same land upon which previous generations worked, and they share their last name with the white family that owned them when they were enslaved, and that continues to own the land itself. She references the systematic repossession of land after it had been distributed to the formerly enslaved after abolition (61–62). For this protagonist and her family, slavery is not a distant memory of the condition of life under which men and women of African ancestry lived until the passage of the Lei Aurea of 1888.[21] Ponciá is one generation from enslavement; her grandparents were slaves who saw several of their own children sold under the Lei do Ventre Livre of 1871 (50).[22] Her grandfather bears the physical marks of slavery, as he has one healthy arm and a stump of the other. The narrator comments that he was born healthy but that he lost his arm in a moment of "revolta" (50), a word that means both "revolt" and "disgust":

Numa noite, o desespero venceu. Vô Vicêncio matou a mulher e tentou acabar com a própria vida. Armado com a mesma foice que lançara contra a mulher, começou a se autoflagelar decepando a mão. Acudido, é impedido de continuar o intento. Estava louco, chorando e rindo.

[One night, desperation won. Vô Vicêncio killed his wife and tried to end his own life. Armed with the same scythe that he used against his wife, he began to cut himself, chopping off his hand. Stopped, he was prevented from realizing his goal. He was crazy, crying and laughing.] (50)

With her simple prose, Evaristo communicates the despair that her protagonist's grandfather feels; there is no one individual moment that triggers his actions, rather, there is a lifetime of violence, betrayals, and indignities. Life and death existed alongside each other on the sugar plantation, as the production of this crop meant assured death for many of the enslaved.[23] His masters have no interest in his sanity, however; more important to them was his ability to be a productive laborer. Because he is incapable of cutting the cane, his value as a laborer is nil, and so he remains on the land, with no purpose, a living ghost as it were.

Her grandfather's descent into madness is marked by the sound of his laughing and crying; this wail is the metonym that comes to symbolize the misery and desolation that the enslaved and their "liberated" descendants feel living on the land. Those who surround him cannot distinguish whether he laughs or cries; for him, there is no difference. The sounds therefore lose their distinct significative power, and come to be a powerful representation of the life of this population. For this man, the wailing of the laugh-cries only ends at his death; despite his visible and audible pain, he remains on Vicêncio land, nowhere else to go.

Though free, Ponciá's father also knew the pain of slavery. As a child, her father was the playmate of the young son of the white family; a page (*pajem*), he was charged with doing whatever his young master (*sinhô-moço*) wanted him to do. They would play together: the latter would ride on her father's back, pretending to survey all of his family's land holdings. On one occasion, he urinates in her father's mouth (14–15). In her distinct narrative style, Evaristo conveys the insidiousness of slavery: disturbing the discourse of the innocence of childhood that arose during the Enlightenment, here she indicts a system that dehumanizes black men, women, and children. The young master knows he is the heir to the family's fortune: for him, games simply simulate the natural order of things. His attendant is an object with which he can do as he wishes: he can be a horse, a latrine, quite literally that which supports him and collects his waste. There is no awareness he merits or deserves human dignity; there would first need to be the recognition of his humanity.

In spite of this sadistic relationship in which he is expected to simply obey his master, her father (who is unnamed in the text) maintained his own humanity; the narrator notes that as a child he would cry when he felt sorrow and laugh when amused (29). This contrasts strongly with his own father, who communicated solely through his wails and through violence. The narrator notes that as a young man, Ponciá's father was very careful around his father: "Tinha medo dos ataques dele. O braço cotoco do homem, ao bater, pesava como se fosse de ferro. Era certeiro na pancada. Atingia-lhe sempre na cabeça, provocando um gosto de sangue na boca [He was afraid of his attacks. The man's stump of an arm, when striking, weighed as if it were made of iron. He was well-aimed in his blows. He would always hit him in the head, causing a burst of blood in his mouth]" (14–15). Incapable of escaping the cycle of violence in which he is trapped, Donciá's grandfather replicated the physical brutality to which he has been subjected.

Though he maintained his ability to express joy and sorrow as a child, Donciá's father became relatively quiet as he grew into adulthood, keeping his feelings to himself (29). Like his ancestors before him, he too worked the land, cutting cane. The narrator implies that the monotony and incessant drudgery of working the cane fields weighed on him; there is nothing to be said in the face of the endless cycle of labor. That which sustained her father and her brother Luandi who worked alongside him in the fields were the songs they sing from their ancestors: "Luandi não entendia as palavras do canto, sabia, porém, que era uma lingua que alguns negros falavam ainda, principalmente os negros. Era uma cantiga alegre. Luandi, além de cantar, acompanhava o ritmo batendo com as palmas da mãos em um atabaque imaginário [Luandi didn't understand the words of the song, however he knew that the language was one that some blacks spoke, principally blacks. It was a happy chant. Luandi, in addition to singing, would accompany the rhythm beating the imaginary *atabaque* (drum) with the palms of his hands]" (89). The endemic poverty that this family faces on a daily basis due to the systematic dispossession of land and the crushing effects of labor conditions that replicate that which their ancestors experienced is mediated by a vibrant spirituality that remains alive for them in spite of the loss of language. Whereas slavery and the subsequent economic conditions articulated the worth of these human beings solely in terms of their labor production, the spiritual systems that these men and women brought with them from Africa to Brazil emphasized their whole beings, their bodies and souls, and so had a restorative effect on these workers, their descendants, at the end of their day. These are not mournful songs in which they lament their circumstances; on the contrary, these are joyful chants that inspire celebration. It is inconsequential that they do not understand the meaning of the words that they sing; rather, they continue to chant and sing and the action of singing and dancing in its totality results in healing. These songs are also not only isolated to the noises that emerge from the mouth but instead are sung with the entire body, so that one's being is completely immersed in the experience. The novel suggests that these songs and dances accompany quotidian activities in traditional African culture: they are sung upon return from hunting or fishing, for example. Though their exterior conditions change, having crossed the Atlantic Ocean, they continue these cultural traditions, passing them down to each subsequent generation.

Throughout the novel, Evaristo juxtaposes the deadening effects of capitalist exploitation of the Afro-Brazilian community with the strategies that they develop in order to combat this economic system and the accompanying cultural values that systematically marginalize it. Ponciá's grandfather, father, brother, husband, and Ponciá herself all lose the capacity to speak Portuguese intelligibly at one point or another in the narrative, an indication of the unremitting pain they endure. She notes: "Os negros eram donos da miséria, da fome, do sofrimento, da revolta suicida [Blacks were the owners of misery, of hunger, of suffering, of disgust]" (82). Though as a child she helps her mother to mold pottery, gathering the clay from the river bed, she longs to escape to the city for greater economic opportunity. Instead, she finds a variation of the misery she left behind in the country. In a 2008 article, Simone Pereira Schmidt comments: "A cidade, onde é desconhecida, suspende de um só golpe seu contato com suas mais profundas raízes. E a personagem mergulha na escuridão de um mundo povoado apenas de lembranças [The city, where she is unknown, ends, in one swoop, contact with her deepest roots. And the character plunges into the darkness of a world populated only by memories]" (24). Though she falls in love and marries in the city, she suffers seven miscarriages, and spends her days staring out the window, trying to make sense of her present circumstances. The protagonist acknowledges that the city itself is not a panacea for her: "A vida escrava continuava até os dias de hoje. Sim, ela era escrava também. Escrava de uma condição de vida que se repetia. Escrava do desespero, da falta de esperança, da impossibilidade de travar novas batalhas, de organizer novos quilombos, de inventar outra e nova vida [Slave life continued until the present day. Yes, she was also a slave. A slave of a condition of life that repeated itself. A slave to desperation, to hopelessness, to the impossibility of waging new battles, of organizing new *quilombos,* of inventing another new life]" (83–84). By the conclusion of the novel, Evaristo makes clear that the missing element for Ponciá is her connection to her family that survives in her spirituality.

Ponciá's decision to leave the country comes suddenly, in a moment of frustration: "Estava cansada de tudo ali. . . . Cansada da luta insana, sem glória, a que todos se entregavam para amanhecer cada dias mais pobres, enquanto alguns conseguiam enriquecer-se a todo o dia. Ela acreditava que poderia traçar outros caminhos, inventar uma vida nova. E avançando sobre o futuro, Ponciá partiu no trem do outro dia, pois tão cedo a máquina não voltaria ao povoado [She was tired of it all. . . . Tired of the insane struggle, without glory, to which they all gave themselves only to wake up more poor, while others made themselves rich every day. She believed she could make other paths, invent a new life. And walking toward her future, Ponciá left on the next day's train, certain that the machine wouldn't return to the village]" (32). The language Evaristo employs here mimics discourse that attracts migrants to the cities searching for work, the train standing in as a symbol for the industrialization efforts that facilitate the movement of low-skilled workers to industrial centers. Living in an exploitative economic system whereby only the owners of land benefit, she instead moves to the city; she quickly comes to understand that the abuse of which she was a victim in the country continues there. Ivette Wilson notes: "[T]he city may be perceived as a site of neo-slavery for Ponciá: she is living in modern times, in an urban (read: 'civilized') environment, nonetheless her conditions replicate (with some variations) the subhuman conditions her ancestors endured since their departure from Africa to the Americas to 'feed' the colonial slavery system" (55). In spite of the challenges she faces, Ponciá works as a domestic, and after several years, is able to purchase a small room on the margins of the city (47). She then returns to the village, intent on reuniting with the mother and brother that she left behind, only to discover that they too have left. In her despair, she finds in her mother's house a clay figure that she molded as a child to look like her grandfather. This object, which she had carried as a child, is the living representation of her deceased grandfather. Returning to her home in the city, clay figure in tow, she grows despondent at the thought of never seeing her family members again. Leaving the clay figure in her rush toward the future underscores her error: the novel suggests that in her haste for progress and modernity, the protagonist turns her back on the traditions that have maintained her family, and indeed, the larger Afro-Brazilian population.

In the clay figure, Evaristo highlights the living presence of the ancestors, the *eguns* or *egunguns*, those spirits who serve as guardian angels to their family members. Though he is deceased, Vô Vicêncio is a living memory for his granddaughter; when he is dying, he mentions that he is leaving an inheritance to Ponciá. She comes to understand that his legacy is that he reminds her from whence she has come, in terms of their land, their people, their customs and traditions. The narrator notes: "Ela beijou respeitosamente a estátua sentindo uma palpável saudade do barro. . . . Era Vô Vicêncio. Apurou os ouvidos e respirou fundo. Não, ela não tinha perdido o contato com os mortos. E era sinal de que encontraria a mãe e o irmão vivos [She kissed the statue respectfully, feeling a palpable longing for clay. It was Vô Vicêncio. She listened and breathed deeply. No, she hadn't lost contact with the spirits. It was a sign she would find her mother and her brother alive]" (75). He gives her hope, then, calling up memories of her childhood, when she used to accompany her mother to the river to fetch the clay they would use to create pottery. For Ponciá, like for many of the female characters in this study, it will come back to the river.

Throughout the narrative, Ponciá recalls her grandfather, sharing the stories of his life; in this way she maintains his memory alive. Though he dies when she is quite young, he nevertheless assists in the decisions she makes. Evaristo compliments the presence of Vô Vicêncio with that of another figure that represents the ancestors, Nêngua Kainda. Alive for most of the narrative, she represents the community's elders, those who still talk an African language that the younger generations no longer comprehend, who understand the words of the return songs sung by the men after working the land. At distinct points in their journeys either to or from the city, her mother Maria, Luandi Josê, and Ponciá herself all speak with Nêngua Kainda, seeking her blessing. Her name itself bears great resemblance to *nengua kende*, the title of one of the priestesses chiefly responsible in a *terreiro* following the traditions of another nation within *Candomblé*, that of *Candomblé Bantu* (also known as *Candomblé Angola*). In fact, both the clay figure that carries the spirit of Vô Vicêncio and Nêngua Kainda reveal to the reader that Evaristo is referring to *Candomblé Bantu*. Similar to those of the Yoruba tradition, these spiritual practices were practiced originally by men and women who spoke the languages of Kikongo and Kimbundu and who originated from the area now known as Cameroon across the continent to Eastern Africa and as far south as Angola and Mozambique. The inclusion of these terms reminds the reader of the diversity of Afro-Brazilian religious practices, as well as of the enslaved population itself.[24] Both the clay figure and Nêngua Kainda serve to offset the legacy of the Vicêncios themselves, the owners of the land upon which their family still works. The living memory of slavery is alive in both the negative and positive senses, then; though there remains the unceasing poverty and economic exploitation, there is also the vibrant spirituality that surrounds the men and women of this community, in the form of their songs and dances, their relationships with the ancestors, which include the elders of the community, and their relationships with nature and the entities that inhabit them, the *orixás* (in Yoruba tradition) or *nkisis* (in Bantu-Angola tradition).

Evaristo opens the novel with Ponciá's memories of walking in the countryside as a little girl and seeing a rainbow. She promptly lies down in the grass and touches herself to make sure that she is still a girl: "Diziam que menina que passasse por debaixo do arco-íris virava menino [They used to say a girl who passed under the rainbow would turn into a boy]" (9). Though as an adult she recalls this moment with bemusement, as a child, Ponciá truly fears turning into a boy: "Depois se apalpava toda. Lá estavam os seinhos, que começavam a crescer. Lá estava o púbis bem plano, sem nenhuma saliência a não ser os pêlos [Afterward she touched everything. There were her breasts that were just beginning to grow. There was her flat pubis with no other protrusions than the hairs]" (9). Evaristo highlights here the identity of a girl-child who is as yet unaware of the social ramifications of that girlhood; that is to say, she does not yet feel the weight of expectations that will ask her to conform to a construction of womanhood that existed in the dominant society. Instead, she revels in her girlhood: "Naquela época Ponciá Vicêncio gostava de ser menina. Gostava de ser ela própria. Gostava de tudo. Gostava. Gostava da roça, do rio que corria entre as pedras, gostava dos pés de pequi, dos pés de coco-de-catarro, das canas e do milharal [In that time Ponciá Vicêncio enjoyed being a girl. She enjoyed being herself. She enjoyed everything. She enjoyed. She enjoyed the country, the river that ran between the rocks, she enjoyed the *pequi* tree, the palm tree, the sugar cane and the cornfields]" (9). As a child, Ponciá enjoys a private relationship with the landscape that surrounds her; she does not see herself as separate from it, or as having dominion over it, but instead sees herself as a part of it. This is in keeping with the African and African diasporic religions that serve as an undercurrent to this novel: for those who live by the precepts of these spiritual systems, the goal of life is to achieve balance between one's self as a human being and all that surrounds you, as well as to discover one's destiny, which is in keeping with God's plan for you.

As an adult woman, she remembers this moment in which she assures her girlhood as the first moment she feels sexual pleasure: "Tocou mais e mais lá dentro e o prazer chegou apesar do espanto e do receio. Lá em cima a cobra celeste, com o seu corpo, curva ameaçadora, pairava sobre ela [She touched more and more there inside and the pleasure came in spite of the awe and fear. On top of her the celestial snake, its threatening curves hovering above her]" (21). Evaristo's juxtaposition of pleasure with childhood innocence normalizes this scene of incipient sexuality: the reader is led to believe that there is nothing wrong or shameful about this exploration of her body. The narrator herself passes no judgment, instead simply relaying the events. More worthy of note is the supposed menace of the rainbow above her, a witness to this moment. Evaristo plays with the reader here: within a Christian context, a serpent near a female in a nature setting recalls the serpent in the garden tempting Eve to taste from the Tree of Knowledge. The serpent within this context is a signifier of temptation and evil. In *Candomblé*, and indeed in many traditional religions of ancient civilizations such as the ancient Egyptian, ancient Greek, Norse, or pre-Columbian Aztec ones, the serpent signifies transformation and the wholeness of life. As the serpent sheds its skin with certain frequency, so too do human beings who grow and evolve, leaving behind old habits and cultivating new ones as they grow closer to their destiny. Ponciá clearly puts a name to this serpent: "Juntava, então, as saias entre as pernas tampando o sexo e, num pulo, com o coração aos saltos, passava por debaixo do angorô [Collecting her skirt between her legs, protecting her sex, with her heart jumping, she leapt, passing underneath the *angorô*]" (9). Angorô is the *nkisi* identified with the rainbow in *Candomblé Bantu*; in the *Candomblé Nagô* tradition, he is identified as Oxumarê. This entity assists in the communication between human beings and the divine intercessors who are the *nkisi* and *orixás*. In this sense, this entity resembles the Biblical rainbow that appears after the floods and that serves as a visual reminder to both God and humanity of His promise to not destroy the world after the floods; it therefore facilitates communication between the Creator and humanity.

The serpent appears twice more in the narrative: when she returns to her village only to discover no one home, she sees the shed skin of a snake in the fireplace. This moment serves as a moment of encouragement for her, though she does not find them in the house: "Encontrariam-se em algum lugar, talvez estivessem até perto dela, esperando que chegasse o tempo de tudo acontecer, para serem novamente os três [They would find each other in some place, perhaps when they were close to her, waiting for the right moment to unfold when they would once again be three]" (81). The snake's skin comes to symbolize home therefore, as it serves to soothe the anxiety that plagues her in the city; after visiting, she returns to the city refortified. At the conclusion of the novel, when she has finally reunited with her mother and her brother, the sacred serpent again appears in the sky. Evaristo therefore utilizes it as to signal to her reader a pivotal moment; as she begins the narrative with the serpent, so does she end it. Life continues, an endless cycle of eternal transformation.

More important than her interaction with her ancestors and Angorô is Ponciá's lifelong relationship with the river. Ponciá's mother Maria recalls that while pregnant, she immersed herself in the river in order to pacify her unborn child, whose cries she heard: "Como aliviar o choro de um rebento ainda guardado, mas tão suplicante, que parecia conhecer as dores infindas do mundo? Caminhou intuitivamente para o rio e à medida que adentrava nas águas, a dor experimentada pela filha se fazia ouvir de uma maneira mais calma [How could she soothe the cries of a child yet within her, pleading, as if she knew of the endless pains of the world? She walked intuitively toward the river and as she entered the waters, the sounds of pain her daughter expressed grew more calm]" (128–29). In this moment, Maria consecrates her unborn child to the river, or more importantly, to the entity associated with the river, Ndanda Lunda, she of sweet waters, fertility, riches and abundance. Though entering the world bearing the angst of humanity, Onciá also is provided with a means by which to ease this responsibility, that is, remaining close to the river, if not literally, then at least through an ongoing relationship with it.

Until she leaves for the city as a young adult, Ponciá remains geographically close to the river. She gathers clay from the riverbed for the pottery that she and her mother mold, clayware that is recognized throughout the region and which is shown at fairs and museums (105–107). On her travels from village to village, Maria recognizes those pieces which she created and those of her daughter. She observes: "Tinha a impressão de que a filha não trabalhava sozinha, algum dom misterioso guiava as mão da menina [She had the impression that her daughter was not working by herself, that a mysterious force was guiding the girl's hands]" (85). Again, the narrator distinguishes Maria and Ponciá by the daughter's spirituality; though they perform the same task, Ponciá perhaps unknowingly infuses her work with sacred force, with *axé*, that is apparent to all who examine her work; like the clay man she identifies with her grandfather, Ponciá leaves her clayware in the village when she travels to the city. Only upon reading her mother's observation about her daughter's interactions with the river and with her clayware does the reader understand that in leaving the countryside she also abandons her relationship with Ndanda Lunda. Her return to the village is the resolution to the anguish and sorrows she suffers in the city.

One may be tempted to read the concluding return to the countryside by Ponciá and her brother Luandi as an admission of failure, that is, as perhaps they never should have left the land of their ancestors. The novel suggests, however, that their despair is caused not from moving away from the land per se, but from leaving behind those spiritual systems that had sustained their ancestors in the face of unimaginable trauma and violence. Ponciá admits as much to herself when she asks: "O que acontecer com os sonhos tão certos de uma vida melhor? Não eram somente sonhos, eram certezas! Certezas que haviam sido esvaziados no momento em que perdera o contato com os seus [What had happened to her clear dreams of a better life? They weren't just dreams, they were truths! Truths that had been emptied out the moment she lost contact with hers]" (33). In acknowledging this loss, she also recognizes the sustaining power of these spiritual systems, which are not remote religious practices but instead mean continued interaction with her ancestors, all of those who have come before her and who continue to guide her and protect her.

The Multiple Representations of Candomblé

Writing within a twenty-year period, Helena Parente Cunha, Sônia Fátima da Conceição, and Conceição Evaristo reflect the multiple relationships that different segments of the Brazilian population have with *Candomblé*. Whereas Parente Cunha writes openly about this religious tradition, including the *orixás* by name as well as a possession scene that occurs in a *terreiro* in Pelourinho, the traditional section of Salvador, neither Conceição nor Evaristo are so explicit. The manner in which each writer features these religious traditions in her writings suggests a different relationship with them; for Helena Parente Cunha, the white Brazilian writer, though there may be a genuine respect for *Candomblé* and for the *orixás*, the religion remains exotic, an expedient tool by which to combat the dominant patriarchal culture in which women are relegated to roles primarily based on their sexuality. Conveniently, she has never returned to this theme in any of her subsequent writings. For Sônia Fátima da Conceição, and Conceição Evaristo, these religions systems are a way of life; they are spiritual traditions that have served as a foundation for their community of men and women of African descent in Brazil. These are not entities one calls by name repeatedly in a text, nor does one represent those moments in which these sacred energies descend to the earth in scenes of possession; instead, there are oblique references that the reader has to uncover and decode, all the while understanding the power of invocation. There is the recognition of the power of the *orixá* and of the act of reading itself, for in doing so, one participates in a tradition that has survived millennia and that transverses time and space, that of prayer to the entities of this sacred system.

⋛ CONCLUSION ⋚

The Response

Reflections in the Mirror

No deberías renunciar al placer de ser tú misma.
—Oshún, in *Casa de juegos*

Chaviano's reminder about never renouncing the pleasure of one's self is an important call to her audience. For women authors across the Americas, the spiritual entity known alternatively as Oshún, or Oxum, is representative not only of pleasure itself, sexual or otherwise, but indeed calls for recognition of all of the aspects of one's self. In her study of this entity, Deidre Badejo highlights that balance is the aim of life, according to the Yorùbá worldview (68). She writes: "Since balance within and between the cosmic and human realms is a primary cosmological objective, a breach or imbalance within or among those realms violates the Yorùbá concept of order. Immorality results from imbalance" (68). We have seen in each of these works each narrative/ poetic voice attempt to restore balance to her life by calling upon spiritual entities associated with African diasporic religions.

In her poem "Ocha," Sandra María Esteves posits that undergoing ceremony in this religious tradition is equivalent to personal liberation. Using the metaphor of a caterpillar's metamorphosis into a butterfly, she writes: "a ritual guided, / pulled forward through a slight crack / like beacon barely sighted over a stormy sea" (*Bluestown Mockingbird Mambo* 86, lines 14–16). In each of these works, the protagonist attempts to make sense of circumstances beyond her control, challenges from both the political and personal realms. Each writer reveals personal uncertainties about being a woman; this is most directly revealed in the characters' personal relationships, as each struggles with her family and with making sense of herself in relation to her family. Who are they if stripped of relationships such as "daughter of" / "wife of" / "mother of"? All of the protagonists of these works reveal their discontent in idealized visions of womanhood that have been created by the Western patriarchal imaginary. Rather than limited binaries dictated by woman's sexual practices (virgin, whore, wife, mother), they search for fuller representations of womanhood. They look to religious systems that allow for a fuller sense of womanhood, ones that celebrate both body and mind, both sacred and secular. These novelists are but a small sample of a number of women writers in the Americas who try to amplify the vision of the Female as they search for wholeness against a patriarchal imaginary.

This study has focused on the varied manifestations of the pursuit for a sense of completeness on the part of the female protagonists of these novels and poems. It is not a coincidence that I have chosen texts that women have authored: for the last several decades, women in the Americas have consciously attempted to map the self in the mode of fiction and poetry. I am in agreement with Gerhild Reisner, who writes: "The strategies of self-figuration manifest themselves in the rewriting of traditional icons of the female....Questioning conventional views of woman and women writers, they often weave into their textual fabric the more or less fantasized perceptions others may have of them" (218). Reisner concludes that by actively incorporating socially constructed images in their works, the artists have the opportunity to systematically challenge them, in what he calls a "mode of defiance" (218).

The study moves from the United States to Cuba to Brazil, where there is a marked shift in terms of the representation of these systems. Whereas the writers of the United States often allude obliquely to these spiritual systems, the writers of Cuba and Brazil include them by name in their works. This highlights a critical difference between the United States on one hand and Brazil and Cuba on the other with regard to the survival of African diasporic religious beliefs, namely, that in the latter two countries, those belief systems exist in the public sphere in a way that they do not in the United States. Tourists can visit Havana and Salvador and find dancers of different racial composition who re-create sacred dances under the guise of folklore. The Virgin of Charity of Cobre (la Santa Caridad de Cobre) and Our Lady of the Appeared Conception (Nossa Senhora de Conceição Aparecida), the syncretized forms of Oshun in Cuba and Brazil, are the patron saints of both countries. In both, even nonpractitioners of these religions are well aware of their cultural import and therefore engage in acts that they may claim to be of superstition but that they perform nevertheless. Every year in Brazil, millions of men and women bring flowers to the ocean on New Year's Eve: some do it simply as a gesture of good luck, others as a means of honoring the *orixá* Iemanjá, the Mother of Salted Waters. This contrast suggests the role of these spiritual systems in the day to day lives of millions across the Americas.

Across cultural traditions, these women writers have incorporated similar mythologies so as to provide for their audience more full images of womanhood. Though they may not all be biologically of African descent, nevertheless each writes within a culture that has benefited from the presence of African peoples. This necessarily prompts a reexamination of the African Diaspora so that it includes those who live in these countries where there have been marked cultural influences and legacies. Several protagonists identify ethnically as belonging to European heritage (Gaia, *a mulher*, Pilar) and yet they continue to seek resolution for their problems in religious systems born of African tradition. That this system is available for them as an inherent component of their cultures underscores that the African Diaspora does not just include those who can claim biological or genetic ties to it. It instead includes everyone whose lives have been touched culturally by the contributions of those of African descent. In Cuba and Brazil, two centers of the slave trade, the influences of enslaved Africans have been neatly incorporated into national culture: *rumba, Regla de Ocha, capoeira, Candomblé Nagó,* and *samba* all have become symbolic of the Nation rather than of marginalized peoples. Both jazz in the first half of the twentieth century and, arguably, hip hop in the last third have become musical forms associated primarily with the United States, each genre having emerged from communities of African descent in urban centers.

All of the writers set their narratives and poems, for the most part, in urban centers (New York, Miami, Havana, Salvador da Bahia); within these settings, their characters labor to achieve balance in their personal lives. Each attempts to reach harmony first by appealing to family members: while they may carry home within themselves (as the protagonists of the U.S. Latina chapter do), they continue to figure themselves within the larger community. It is when they determine that their immediate environments are unhealthy that they strike out. Still, all of them seek out the community that the religion promises, thereby elevating the profile of this system of belief. The novels themselves suggest that the protagonists learn about themselves and become more true versions of themselves after taking part in a religious ceremony or even after learning about the existence of these systems of belief.

These works reveal varied portraits of womanhood; a salient feature of almost each work is the yearning for a restoration of a healthy female sexuality. In the explicit descriptions of Chaviano and Parente Cunha, one finds an answer to Irigaray's challenge to women authors that they must write themselves into the text. These texts, novels and poems alike, reveal an American (in the most ample sense of the world) disillusion with patriarchal static definitions of womanhood, hence the search for alternative definitions. Though this study focuses only on representative authors, there are a number of women who include these entities in works contemporary to those studied here: from the United States, Toni Cade Bambara, Zora Neale Hurston, Toni Morrison, and Gloria Naylor in their novels; from Cuba, Georgina Herrera and Excilia Saldaña in their poetry; from Brazil, Alzira Rufino in her poetry; from Jamaica, Opal Palmer Adisa in her novels; and from England, Helen Oyewemi's novels.

The call-and-response has been a feature of musical forms found throughout Africa and African diasporic religious cultures: a phrase is sung, spoken, or played by one person, and a second answers the call, sometimes repeating the phrasing but more often providing a variation on the first issued phrase. This is a feature in spirituals, the religious ceremonies of *Regla de Ocha* and *Candomblé,* blues, jazz, rumba, samba, salsa, and hip hop, among other musical forms; critics such as Angela Davis, Amiri Baraka, and Houston A. Baker have analyzed the inclusion of these musical forms in African American literature. This form emphasizes the communal in the creation of art, and value is placed not on strict mimesis but on improvisation, on the contributor's individual contribution to that which has been established. The authors included in this study are but a few of the women who have heeded the call of traditional African diasporic religious entities; it is now the audience who must respond.

$$\overset{\backslash}{\diagup} \quad * \quad \overset{\diagup}{\backslash}$$

Notes

Introduction: The Call

1. *Regla de Ocha* means the "Order of Ocha" [*orichas*]; *Lucumí* is an approximation of a Yoruba phrase (*oluku mi*), meaning "my friend" (Thompson 17); *Santería* means "the way of the *santos* [saints]."
2. Nancy Morejón and David Frye, "Cuba and Its Deep Africanity," *Callaloo* 28:4 (2005): 933–51, 938.
3. Dominique Zahan, "Some Reflections on African Spirituality," in *African Spirituality: Forms, Meanings, and Expressions*, ed. Jacob Olupona (New York: Herder and Herder, 2000), 3–25, 4.
4. Zahan 3–4.
5. This is not to imply that patriarchy has not left an imprint on Western Africa or indeed various societies throughout the continent; on the contrary, there are various indicators that highlight abuse of women and children under the guise of traditional African thought. Oyěwùmí's study, subtitled *The Invention of Gender*, examines language in precolonial Western Africa, tracing the alteration of words under colonial influence.
6. In some works under consideration in this study, the authors do not name specifically the presences with whom their characters are communicating, instead preferring to label the metaphysical presence as Spirit. In addition, there are several characters (Celia and Pilar of *Dreaming in Cuban* and Aurelia and Iliana in *Geographies of Home*) that have telepathic abilities. The writers themselves do not attempt to

identify the origin of this skill, nor categorize them into one specific religious tradition; this analysis follows that precedent.

7. The spelling in the title of this study is an approximation of its Yoruba rendering as well as a variation of the name in Spanish.

8. The first book of Fernando Ortiz, known as the Father of Afro-Cuban Studies, bears testimony to the discrimination faced by practitioners of these religions: *Hampa afro-cubana: Los negros brujos (apuntes para un estudio de etnología criminal) / Afro-Cuban Underworld: Black Witches (Notes for a Study of Criminal Ethnology)* (1906). For an overview of this historical moment as well as an analysis of this text, see Jerome Branche, *Colonialism and Race in Luso-Hispanic Literature* (2006). For a discussion of this persecution in Brazil, see Abdias do Nascimento, *Brazil, Mixture or Massacre?* (1979).

9. While the *orishas* mentioned are syncretized with Catholic saints, they do not appear as such in the works analyzed here; when the writers address Oshun/Ochún/Oxum, they use that name and not La Virgen de la Caridad de Cobre (patron saint of Cuba) or Nossa Senhora de Conceição Aparecida (patron saint of Brazil). Consequently, these syncretized identities are not included in this introduction.

10. Solimar Otero studies the migration of Yoruba peoples from Cuba to Nigeria in *Afro-Cuban Diasporas in the Atlantic World* (U of Rochester P, 2010); essays about Brazilian Yorubas who returned to Nigeria can be found in the following edited collections: *Public Memory of Slavery: Victims and Perpetrators in the South Atlantic,* ed. Ana Lucia Araujo (Cambria, 2010); *Cultures of the Lusophone Black Atlantic,* ed. Nancy Priscilla Naro, Roger Sansi-Roca, and David H. Treece (Palgrave Macmillan, 2007); *Transatlantic Dimensions of Ethnicity in the African Diaspora,* ed. Paul H. Lovejoy and David V. Trotman (Continuum, 2003); *Rethinking the African Diaspora: The Making of the Black Atlantic World in the Bight of Benin and Brazil,* ed. Kristin Mann and Edna B. Gay (Frank Cass, 2001).

11. In her study *A Place in the Sun? Women Writers in Twentieth-Century Cuba* (1997), Catherine Davies offers a thorough overview of the status of women in Cuba throughout the twentieth century, beginning in the years immediately following the conclusion of the Spanish-American War of 1898, in which Spain lost Cuba to the United States.

12. Here I follow the denomination that William Luis establishes in his study *Dance between Two Cultures* (1997), when he distinguishes

between Puerto Rican authors of the Island and those of the mainland by adding "American" to the latter. Though it is a designation that has not received popular support, perhaps because it is redundant (to be Puerto Rican is to be American), nevertheless it is useful to distinguish those writers who were either born or raised primarily in the United States from those who were born or raised primarily on the Island. In the context of this study, Sandra Maria Esteves was born and raised in the Bronx, New York.

Chapter 1. Diasporic Revelation

1. Cuban exiles who migrated to the United States in the immediate aftermath of the Revolution of 1959 brought these religious practices with them to such cities as New York and Miami; in the former, they found African Americans interested in learning about ways of life derived from West Africa. For a review of the growth of *orisha* worship within the African American communities in the 1960s and 1970s, see Hucks 2008.

2. Cubans were greatly responsible for introducing these entities to the U.S. public sphere not only in terms of religious practice itself but also through cultural production. Desi Arnaz did so most famously with his song "Babalu" in *I Love Lucy*; many still do not know that the song is a reference to the entity associated with the causing and healing of smallpox. Known as Babalú-Ayé in Cuban *Regla de Ocha* (and syncretized as Saint Lazarus), he is known as Obaluaiye in traditional Yoruba religion. See Thompson 61–67.

3. In an essay about her writing process, Lorde comments on the stifling nature of the literary scene of the late 1970s, saying that creativity was being silenced by the "tacit insistence upon some unilateral definition of what 'Blackness' is or requires" (263). More pointedly, she adds: "I consider myself to have been a victim of this silencing in the Black literary community for years, and I am certainly not the only one. For instance, there is no question about the *quality* of my work at this point. Then why do you think my last book, *The Black Unicorn*, has not been reviewed, or even mentioned, in any Black newspaper or Black magazine within the thirteen months since it appeared?" (263)

4. Initially a passionate supporter of the Revolution, Heberto Padilla (1932–2000) grew disenchanted with the government mandate that

all aspects of Cuban society, including the production of art, would demonstrate support of the Revolution. In 1968, his collection *Fuera del juego* was awarded the Julian del Casal Poetry Prize by Casa de las Americas, the state publishing house, despite the inclusion of poems that revealed his dissent. In 1971, he was placed under house arrest; he was released only upon issuing a statement renouncing his work and was later paraded in front of the Unión de Escritores y Artistas de Cuba (UNEAC), and forced not only to confess his "crime" of opposition to the regime but also to identify fellow writers also guilty of counterrevolutionary propaganda. His plight became a *cause célèbre* for leftist intellectuals throughout the world, as Susan Sontag, Jean-Paul Sartre, Simone de Beauvoir, Mario Vargas Llosa, Alberto Moravia, and Heinrich Boll, among others, signed a petition showing their support.

5. The Yoruba and the Fon are ethnic groups who have historically lived in West Africa in Nigeria, the Republic of Benin (formerly known as Dahomey), and Togo; "Yoruba" and "Fon" also refer to the languages that are spoken there. The Yoruba "[are] black Africa's largest population, creators of one of the premier cultures of the world" (Thompson xv). These were two of the predominant cultures transported to the Americas in the Middle Passage, as evidenced by the popularity of the religions, art, and philosophies that inform the lives of hundreds of millions in the countries of the Western Hemisphere.

6. In a letter to Mary Daly, Lorde criticizes Daly for only including mythologies of Western Europe in her text *Gyn/Ecology: The Metaethics of Radical Feminism* (1979), ostensibly one that addressed all myths that had contributed to the development of patriarchy. See Lorde, "An Open Letter to Mary Daly."

7. Though Lorde self-identified as a black woman, this assertion does not mean solely African American (see Provost); in fact, Lorde's definition of black is more complex than simple reduction of race. In her interview with Adrienne Rich, Lorde put forth that we should embrace that which is black within us, which she defines as the following: "the terror, to the chaos which is Black which is creative which is female which is dark which is rejected which is messy which is . . . sinister, smelly, erotic, confused, upsetting" (101). Black, then, does not necessarily have a relationship with race or ethnicity but instead with those qualities that are often rejected in preference of comfort and order.

8. See Keating, Provost, and Wallerstein for their investigations of these themes in *The Black Unicorn* and *Zami*.

9. Thompson writes: "In Abomey, these deities are called *vodun* (mysteries)" (166).

10. This is taken from her interview with Adrienne Rich, in which she explains the black mother that she advocates should be recovered by men and women alike of all backgrounds (100).

11. The moniker "Nuyorican" refers to New York Puerto Ricans, often the children of Puerto Rican migrants who had moved to New York City in the 1930s, 1940s, and 1950s, seeking employment in the aftermath of industrialization efforts of Operation Bootstrap on the island. Accused of having assimilated to the culture of the United States by their island counterparts, they were called "Nuyorican" so as to distinguish them from "authentic" Puerto Ricans, that is, those who had remained on the island. Originally used as a pejorative, it was quickly claimed during the 1960s and 1970s as a source of pride.

12. For an overview of the political doctrines of these groups, see Enck-Wanzer and Foner.

13. See "Young Lords Party 13-Point Program and Platform."

14. The Young Lords Party was founded in Chicago in the mid-1960s; the New York City chapter was founded in 1969.

15. Janet Pérez notes: "Much of the characteristic nature of Nuyorican writing derives from relationships with the culture of poverty, experiences of discrimination or racism, and notes of anger, protest, and the search for identity. Political ideology is often an implicit or explicit ingredient, as are curses, obscenities, and bilingualism" (486). In her article, Edna Acosta Belén uses two of Estéves's poems, "Here" (which is widely anthologized) and "Not neither," to demonstrate the dichotomies featured in much Nuyorican writing of this era. She writes: "The most prevalent dualities in Puerto Rican literature include: 1) the fragmentation of identity produced by marginalization and oscillation between the two cultural and linguistic contexts (boricua vs. spic; Spanish vs. English; white people vs. people of color)" (993). Alberto Sandoval notes that this group of writers force Puerto Rican nationalist writers on the island to confront their strict conceptions of Puerto Ricanness (321).

16. *Bomba* refers to the traditional folkloric music of Puerto Rico that is of African origin; it has survived along the northeastern coast of the island, and is associated especially with the town of Loíza Aldea.

17. Yvonne Daniel studies what she calls "embodied knowledge" by looking at the role of dance in the rituals of *Santería, Candomblé,* and *Vodou;* she demonstrates how practitioners of these religions reference whole areas of knowledge, including "history, philosophy, religion, physiology, psychology, botany, and mathematics in addition to music and dance" (5). Though the practice of these religions may have been lost by a great majority of the populations formed in the Western Hemisphere by enslaved Africans and their descendants, there nevertheless remains an epistemology that is rooted not solely through cognitive analysis but in combination with the body, reflecting the holistic philosophies of many traditional African cultures.

18. The *griot* (masculine) / *griotte* (feminine) is a West African storyteller who preserves the tales, legends, and history of his/her community; critics of African American literature and culture often use this figure in a metaphorical setting. See Hale.

19. Though this nomenclature is no longer used, it was prevalent at the time.

20. Reinaldo L. Román offers a history of the persecution of these religions in his study *Governing Spirits: Religion, Miracles, and Spectacles in Cuba and Puerto Rico, 1898–1956* (2007).

21. In their study *Creole Religions of the Caribbean: An Introduction from Vodou and Santería to Obeah and Espiritismo* (2003/2011), Margarite Fernández Olmos and Lizabeth Paravisini-Gebert write that these entities appear in what they identify as "Santerismo," a practice that blends the entities of *Regla de Ocha* or *Santería* with Caribbean Spiritism (*Espiritismo*). Spiritism is the practice associated with Frenchman Allan Kardec, the pseudonym of Hippolyte Léon Denizard Rivail (1804–1869) in which mediums communicate with spirits for moral guidance. Spiritism had a substantial impact throughout nineteenth-century Europe and the Americas. See Fernández Olmos and Paravisini-Gebert.

22. "Albizu" is a reference to Dr. Pedro Albizu Campos (1891/1893–1965), founder of the Puerto Rican Nationalist Party and leader most often identified with the Puerto Rican independence movement of the twentieth century. "Betances" refers to Dr. Ramón Emeterio Betances (1827–1898), organizer of the Grito de Lares (1868), a revolt against Spanish imperial rule, and therefore a leader of Puerto Rican independence. "Burgos" refers to Julia de Burgos (1914–1953), considered by

many to be Puerto Rico's finest poet and a supporter of Puerto Rican independence.

23. "Yerba Buena," literally "Good herb," is not normally translated in common parlance; it refers to mint, which is often used medicinally.

24. "Bruja Buena" literally "Witch's Weed," refers to a grass that is resistant to eradication, hence it seems to have magical capacities; symbolically it is a term of Puerto Rican nationalism, a reference to the nation's resistance after centuries of colonization, first by the Spanish and later by the United States. In 1976, Juan Antonio Corretjer (1908–1985), poet and nationalist, published a collection of this name dedicated to the Taíno, the indigenous population of the island prior to the arrival of the Europeans.

25. Esteves identifies it as a rumba in the poem itself.

26. The translations of this poem are mine.

27. The poet's use of Spanish is sparing in this poem, as she uses it for the title and to refer to the head priest of the house (that is, the gathering of priests). Initiates will call this man their "Padrino" (2), or Godfather; he is also the "Babalorisha" (17), "Father Possessing Orisha," again, the head of the house. If the house is headed by a woman, she is the Madrina to her initiates, the Iyalorisha.

28. Courtney George argues that playing the fiddle situates Indigo in the history of slave spirituals; with the assistance of the spirits of enslaved African laborers, with whom she develops a relationship through her playing, Indigo achieves both personal and communal liberation. See George.

29. For an overview of the African Diaspora in Shange's work, see Valdés (2009).

30. A word about nomenclature: when using the word *colored*, Shange does not simply mean those who had lived solely in the United States but instead all who were enslaved throughout the Americas.

31. In a recent study, Catherine E. McKinley provides a historical overview of the role of indigo within the slave trade, as well as the development of the crop since then, and its importance within West African cultures. See McKinley.

32. "Afrika" recalls the Republic of New Afrika, a social movement founded in 1968 in Detroit with the aim of promulgating independence for African Americans; promoting and protecting the integrity of this community; and stimulating economic self-sufficiency. Founders

claimed the southern states of South Carolina, Georgia, Alabama, Mississippi, and Louisiana as the site of a newly independent black republic, and demanded reparations from the United States government to the amount of $400 billion for labor done by enslaved Africans. For an overview of the demand for reparations, including a contextualization of this movement, see Allen; for an analysis of its development in Mississippi, see Cunnigen.

33. Josephine Baker (1906–1975) was an African American artist (actress, dancer, and entertainer) who left the United States for France in 1925 and caused a sensation for her dancing, often done in the nude. In her most iconic role, she danced in a skirt of artificial bananas in the Folies Bergères. She was active both in the French Resistance during World War II and the civil rights movement in the United States, and was later honored by France with the Croix de Guerre, bestowed to those individuals who show heroism in combat with enemy forces.

34. Sassafras and Mitch live in the New World Found Collective, which may be a fictionalized version of the Oyotunji African Village, founded in 1970 by Oseijeman Adefunmi in South Carolina, it purports to have replicated on American soil a true Yoruba village. See Tracey Hucks's article on the history of African American participation in the predominantly Cuban religion in the United States (2008) as well as her study on Adefunmi (2012).

35. The narrator comments that the defining quality of this character is love: "Still, Sassafrass was so full of love she couldn't call anybody anything without bringing good vibes from a whole lot of spirits to everything she touched" (76).

Chapter 2. The Search for Home

1. In her article "From Cuban *Santería* to African Yorùbá: Evolutions in African American Òrìṣà History, 1959–1970," Tracey E. Hucks writes that as a result of the Cuban Revolution, tens of thousands of Cuban exiles arrived in New York City, some of whom were practitioners of this religion.

2. I use this term to emphasize that the Caribbean extends beyond the physical borders of the landmasses found in the Caribbean Sea, instead extending throughout the world to include certain cities within the United States, Canada, and Europe. This term suggests

that the Diasporic Caribbean is a place where the peoples and the values of the Caribbean not only exist but thrive. Andrea O'Reilly Herrera uses a similar term, "Caribbean bred" to indicate those born outside of the Caribbean but raised with the sensibility of the region. See O'Reilly Herrera.

3. Eliana Rivero writes: "[T]his book became paradigmatic of what it was to create fiction that, through evocative language, linked the two worlds of Cuban immigrant and island families and projected their exilic memories and their social and political hopes on both sides of the Florida Strait" (117).

4. For the most part, males are silent in the novel: both Jorge (born 1897) and Ivanito, Felicia's son (born 1967), are supporting characters.

5. Ominously, Papito, or "Father," is the only character whose proper name is not disclosed, intimating an all-knowing figure, the patriarch, the center of his family's life.

6. Christine Ayorinde details this period in *Afro-Cuban Religiosity, Revolution, and National Identity* (2004), in which she examines Afro-Cuban religions as expressions of *cubanidad*. Also, Jerome Branche provides a detailed overview of the demonization of these belief systems in *Colonialism and Race in Luso-Hispanic Literature* (2006).

7. The novelist suggests that blue has potential healing powers by noting that Jorge, Celia's husband, receives cobalt treatments for stomach cancer when he arrives in New York (33). Blue also links husband and wife, as Celia envisions Jorge on the night of his death emerging from the horizon line and walking toward her on the ocean: "His blue eyes are like lasers in the night. The beams bounce off his fingernails, five hard blue shields. They scan the beach, illuminating shells and sleeping gulls, the focus on her. The porch turns blue, ultraviolet. His hands, too, are blue" (5). For Celia, blue is a peaceful color; Jorge's goodbye is not one filled with spite and anger but rather one of serenity, as this separated couple unites one last time.

8. "Bienvenida" means "welcome"; Pérez underscores the convivial nature of this spiritual system, which does not discriminate, by naming the matriarch of the family in this way.

9. This spiritual system goes unnamed in the novel; critics have labeled it "vudú dominicano" (Alcaide Ramírez); "ancestral spiritual practices" (Méndez); and "prácticas espirituales feminocéntricas" (Palmer). Dominican spirituality grounded in African belief systems continues

to be widely disparaged within the Dominican and Dominican American communities, often labeled pejoratively as *brujería*. Pérez's choice to integrate these practices without naming them reflects lived experience; nevertheless, this spiritual system is marked by communication with spirits and telepathy in the novel.

10. Bridget Kevane examines the representation of Seventh Day Adventism in *Profane and Sacred: Latino/a American Writers Reveal the Interplay of the Secular and the Religious* (2008).

11. Suárez's study is the first to analyze the cultural production of the island as a whole, which underscores the similar histories and other commonalities these neighboring countries share.

12. She speaks of walking alongside the river (68); patrolling the river as an auxiliary policewoman (132–33). She is at the river when her father communicates with her.

13. Pilar notes: "When I was a kid, Mom slept in air thin and nervous as a magnetic field, attracting small disturbances. She tossed and turned all night, as if she were wrestling ghosts in her dreams. Sometimes she'd wake up crying, clutching her stomach and moaning from deep inside a place I couldn't understand" (221).

14. A *babalawo* is a priest of Orula, the *orisha* of divination; he is the highest oracle of the religion.

15. For a brief overview of the history of the inclusion of the Afro-Cuban in Cuban nationalist discourse, see de la Fuente.

16. This emphasis on nature recalls the gifts that Bienvenida gives to Aurelia: "*A fistful of earth to which we return to nourish those who follow.* . . . Settled in the dirt was an earthen jug corked to contain water. *To remind you that in our blood we carry the power of the sea.* Also in the sack was a clear piece of glass reflecting rainbow colors. *Because beauty exists in the most unlikely places.* Deeper still lay a stone with features resembling Bienvenida's face and mysteriously radiating heat; a wishbone, clean and smooth; a scroll of bark; an owl's feather. *To quell your fear of darkness and teach your spirit it can soar*" (134–35; italics in the original). Bienvenida's gifts emphasize the natural and the relationship humans must have with their surroundings.

17. In the *Lucumí* religion, as in *Vodou* and *Candomblé*, the gender of the practitioner does not influence the identity of his/her guiding entity. That is, a man could be ruled by Oshun or Yemanyá as much as a woman could be guided by Obatalá or Changó, as in this case.

18. Upon first seeing Iliana, Marina comments that she looks "just like a model" (36). Her friend Ed suggests that she wear contact lenses, which leads Iliana to take greater care in her appearance.

Chapter 3. Love, Revolution, Survival

All of the translations of Morejón's poetry are by Kathleen Weaver, whose collaboration with Morejón resulted in the publication of the bilingual collection *Where the Islands Sleeps Like a Wing* (1985); this volume introduced Morejón to many in the United States. The translation of Daína Chaviano's novel is my own.

1. Though Lorde associates this with women, she claims in an interview that both men and woman can lay claim to this form of knowledge that privileges feeling as a legitimate epistemology: See Lorde's interview with Adrienne Rich.

2. These statistics are taken from Louis A. Pérez, *Cuba: Between Reform and Revolution* (1995), 358–59.

3. When asked in a 1996 interview if her parents were religious, Morejón responds: "No, para nada. Mi padre, todo lo contrario, era un comunista. Yo me formé alejada de la religión por completo. Me criaron con el tabú natural que había en esa época en relación con la santería y esas cosas [Absolutely not. My father was the complete opposite, he was a Communist. I was raised completely away from religion. I was raised with the natural taboo of that time with reference to *Santería* and those things]" (Maloof and Morejón 48; my translation).

4. For a more in-depth examination of the development of *Negrismo*, see Cuervo Hewitt (2009) and Badiane (2010).

5. Antonio Machado (1875–1939) was a member of the *Generación del '98*; in the aftermath of the loss of the last colonies of the Spanish Empire in the Spanish-American War of 1898, Spain was plunged into an existential crisis: how would it define itself if it was no longer an imperial power? Spanish writers, artists, and poets of the time recalled previous epochs of greatness, accusing the contemporary political leaders of stagnation and ignorance. Machado is one of the most well-known members of this group; his poetry is marked by melancholy and introspection, as he lauds the Spanish countryside and his fellow countrymen and women.

6. The Catholic saints West names are saints with which Elegguá has been

syncretically identified; however, there is no overt reference to these beings within the poem itself.

7. This is also indicative of a critical difference between the practice of Christianity and these African diasporic religions: unlike in Brazil, where priestesses live together in the sanctified space known as the *terreiro,* in Cuba and the United States, there are few formal settings such as churches or temples in which practitioners gather. Instead, priests and priestesses build altars to their ancestors and their *orichas* within their homes, thereby converting their personal living area into a hallowed space.

8. In the original collection, this entity's name appears without an accent on the final vowel; however this accentuation is standard and so I have included it in my analysis.

9. In "Race, Poetry, and Revolution in the Works of Nancy Morejón," William Luis describes the significance of these years for Afro-Cuban writers and scholars, when the civil rights movement of the United States inspired visits from prominent African American activists such as Alice Walker, Eldridge Cleaver, and Angela Davis. Cuba's involvement with the wars for independence in Angola and Mozambique also brought heightened awareness of the long-standing relationship between the island and the African continent.

10. The most complete examination of the economics of slavery in Cuba is Fernando Ortiz's *Contrapunteo cubano del tabaco y el azúcar* (1940), in which he analyzes the effect of these two crops on the development of Cuban society. Including both of these crops, then, Morejón presents the master as an allegorical figure representing those who are in power.

11. Though the poetic voice mentions the tobacco fields, we learn at the end that the land is also the site of sugar cultivation, hence the presence of cauldrons, used to boil the sap.

12. In offering this reading, I follow the example of Beatriz Calvo Peña, who argues that Chaviano is writing on at least three levels in her first novel *El hombre, la hembra y el hambre.* She identifies a literal reading, an allegorical reading, and an extraliterary reading. See Calvo Peña.

13. Mount Parnassus is also home of Dionysus, god of wine, winemaking, and revelry; under the regime, the university has lost this attribute as well, as diversion of decades past gives way to public assemblies of criticism and self-criticism where students admit their faults (124).

14. "Total, lo único que vas a lograr es pudrirte en un calabozo sin que nadie se entere [In the end, the only thing you'll accomplish is rotting in a cell without anyone's notice]" (112).

15. The first publication of Fernando Ortiz provides a vivid demonstration of contemporary perceptions of the Afro-Cuban population. Later known as the Father of Afro-Cuban Studies, Ortiz's *Hampa afrocubana. Los negros brujos (apuntes para un estudio de etnología criminal)* was published in 1906. Following contemporary Positivist theories of the age, he set out to document the sources of criminal behavior in the Cuban capital; he identified Afro-Cuban priests, their beliefs, and their way of life as primitive and backward, and advocated the elimination of these creeds as necessary for the progress of the country. See Cuervo Hewitt (2009) and Branche.

16. Upon learning her name, Eri immediately notes this, calling her "La Madre Tierra [Mother Earth]" (43).

17. It is in later renderings that Eros is identified as the son of Aphrodite, goddess of love.

18. Alicia E. Vadillo makes a similar argument when she writes that the novel: "reproduce algunas leyendas religiosas siguiendo sus patrones fundamentales; en otros casos, altera las valencias de los signos y combina textos de diferentes naturalezas; y finalmente, en terceros casos, tomando elementos aislados de la tradición, rellena los espacios vacíos para dar lugar a un nuevo texto [reproduces several religious legends following their fundamental patterns; in other cases, changes the combination of the symbols used and combines texts from different sources; and finally, in third case, taking isolated elements from the tradition, fills empty spaces so as to create a new text]" (185–86).

19. Julia Cuervo Hewitt, Alicia E. Vadillo, and Eugenio Matibag are the only three writers to dedicate monograph-length studies to the topic. See Vadillo, Cuervo Hewitt (1988), and Matibag.

20. Within Cuban literature, the inclusion of figures from a variety of Afro-Cuban religious systems is more notable in poetry and short story than in narrative.

21. For an overview of the *mulata* as a critical cultural trope in Cuban popular culture, see Vera Kutzinski, Claudette M. Williams, and Richard L. Jackson.

22. "Gaia pudo contemplar su perfil, de ojos rasgados y nariz morisca [Gaia could study her profile, her almond-shaped eyes and Moorish

nose]" (12); "una mujer alta, de piernas insuperables [a tall woman, legs a mile long]" (14); "El cabello caía abundante sobre sus pechos cobrizos [Her lush hair fell upon her copper-colored breasts]" (83); "y su piel acanelada y tersa brillaba como miel [And her smooth and cinnamon-colored skin shone like honey]" (83).

23. Chaviano only reveals at the end of the novel that Gaia may have been interacting with these spiritual entities at key moments; in the middle of the work she discovers Oshún's identity and only at the conclusion does she learn about Eri's identity as an *oricha*.

24. For more on Western culture's views of sex and sexuality in the last three centuries, see Foucault. Also, with Gaia's reference to the cycle of pleasure and pain, that is, the pain that she feels when she transgresses her own limits of pleasure, Chaviano is referencing a twentieth-century discussion of Freud's pleasure principle. For an overview of Luce Irigaray's rereading of this concept, see Gallop.

25. During the Special Period, the government rationed meat, milk, cheese, among other basic foodstuffs. Seafood could only be found on the black market, and even then, in limited quantities.

26. Due to food shortages beginning during the Special Period and continuing until today, many Cubans either go without eating or eat very little. The protagonist's revelry at her meal reflects a general disbelief in the face of abundance.

27. In her study *The Technology of Orgasm: "Hysteria," the Vibrator, and Women's Sexual Satisfaction* (1999), Rachel P. Maines offers a history of the effort to combat hysteria from ancient times until the Industrial Age, and how the invention of the vibrator in Europe in the late nineteenth century provided an alleviation of this "illness." Symptoms of this ailment included: "anxiety, sleeplessness, irritability, nervousness, erotic fantasy, sensations of heaviness in the abdomen, lower pelvic edema, and vaginal lubrication" (8).

28. For an assessment of the Enlightenment's role in the birth of the modern age and its emphasis on reason, see Dupré.

29. With the arrival of Europeans and enslaved Africans as laborers, both Catholicism and African religions were established as systems of belief on the island. Well into the nineteenth century, however, there were greater numbers of Africans and their descendants than their European counterparts. For a historical overview of the African presence in Cuba, see Andrews.

30. Gaia identifies her heritage: "Allí estaba ella, biznieta de asturianos y franceses, obedeciendo los mandatos de los dioses africanos [There she was, the great-granddaughter of Asturians and Frenchmen, obeying the mandates of African gods]" (159).

31. "¿Habría penetrado, sin darse cuenta, en el espíritu de una metrópolis plagada de brujos que tal vez hubieran creado un espacio donde existía lo prohibido? [Had she, without realizing it, penetrated the spirit of a metropolis plagued by witches that perhaps had created a space where the prohibited existed?]" (48).

32. "¿Habrían emigrado al trópico los vampiros, ansiosos de un sustento más ardiente que la sangre europea? [Had vampires emigrated to the tropics, anxious to find a foodsource more hearty than European blood?]" (123).

33. "Fantaseó con la idea de que viajaba por el subconsciente de una ciudad cuyo acceso sólo era posible por la gracia de un guía que se ofreciera a mostrarlo, como hiciera Virgilio con el bardo florentino [She fantasized with the idea of traveling through the subconscious of a city whose only access was possible through the grace of a guide that offered to show it to her, as if she were Virgil with the Florentine bard]" (135).

34. In her article "La Habana real y la Habana imaginada," Araceli San Martín-Moreno argues that Havana becomes a symbol of Cuban identity for exiled writers. She observes that it acts as the following: "el símbolo de una identidad esquizofrénica que vacila siempre entre la aceptación del discurso oficial o la invención de un discurso propio que, a su pesar, sólo puede construir con fragmentos [the symbol of a schizophrenic identity that always vacillates between acceptance of official discourse or the invention of its own discourse that, to its own lament, one can only construct with fragments]" (221). While at no point does Chaviano reveal an acceptance of official discourse in this novel, she does exhibit an ambivalence in her depiction of the *Lucumí* religion.

35. For an overview of depictions of explicit sexuality in Latin American women's writing, see Marting. For an introduction to the Cuban erotic poetry written by women, see Fernández Olmos. For a critical anthology of such writing, see Fernández Olmos and Paravasini-Gebert.

36. In this way she follows the exhortation of Hélène Cixous in "The

Laugh of the Medusa"; there she encourages women to inscribe themselves in their writing, thereby liberating other women to do the same. She writes: "Write your self. Your body must be heard. Only then will the immense resources of the unconscious spring forth" (880).

37. "y a ella siempre le habían gustado los hombres altos; de esos que la obligaban a doblar el cuello hasta casi fracturarse una vértebra, como si estuviera frente a un altar donde hay que elevar la mirada para ver a Cristo en su lejana cruz [she had always liked tall men; those that forced her to bend her neck until practically fracturing her vertebra, as if she were standing in front of an altar where you would have to raise your look in order to see Christ on his distant cross]" (18).

38. With the Painter she notes: "Se desbocaba siempre, pero él volvía a sujetar sus bridas [She always used to run away, but he held his reins]" (25). With Erinle: "Se vio obligada a lamer y a chupar, mientras era cabalgada como una yegua a la que tiraban de los cabellos, a modo de bridas [She was obligated to lick and suck while being ridden like a pony, bareback]" (175).

Chapter 4. Sacrifice and Salvation

The translation of the novel, by Fred P. Ellison and Naomi Lindstrom, was published as *Woman between Mirrors* (Austin: University of Texas Press, 1989); the translations provided here are my own. The translation of *Ponciá Vicêncio* by Paloma Martinez-Cruz was published in 2007 (Austin: Host, 2007); the translations here are also my own.

1. There have been great efforts on the part of the Brazilian populace to come to terms with this period of their history with the election of President Rousseff in 2011, including the establishment of a truth commission; for a brief overview, see Coelho.

2. In the course of the novel, the protagonist's racial identification changes: while there are no explicit mentions of her racial identity at the beginning of the narrative, by its conclusion she speaks of dark skin and curly hair. However, within a Brazilian context, the recognition of African ancestry however oblique does not necessarily mean an assertion of an Afro-Brazilian identity.

3. For two excellent studies about the writers of Quilombhoje, see Duke

and Oliveira; for a survey of Brazilian literary history featuring Afro-Brazilian writers, see Valdés (2012).

4. I am following the stylistic conventions Parente Cunha establishes in her novel, using italics to distinguish the voice of "*a mulher*" from "eu."

5. For a study of the role of Iemanjá and Xangô in the text, see Sáenz de Tejada 1998.

6. In this interview with Elizbieta Szoka, Parente Cunha leaves open the possibility that this novel is in part autobiographical: like the protagonist, she had an "unbelievably special nursemaid . . . [who was] a granddaughter or great-granddaughter of slaves" (42); she describes her father as "very strict, very severe . . . [who] wouldn't let [her] walk on the beach or go to parties" (43); and she describes having a complicated relationship with her body which was only resolved upon entering a spiritual path (49).

7. Lindstrom recognizes the role of Afro-Brazilian culture in the refashioning of the protagonist's identity (145), but does not explore this line of thought due to the scope of her study.

8. For a fascinating discussion of the physical space where the protagonist lives and its function in the text, see Somerlate Barbosa.

9. The protagonist's family life reflects a traditional mold of life in many Latin American countries. Women of all classes and races throughout the region are taught to obey the men in their lives and to be silent, accessories to their fathers, brothers, husbands, and sons.

10. Jacob Kehinde Olupona writes of the Yoruba creation myth, in which Osun forces the male deities to reveal the accords they had reached in secret, without consulting the female ones. He writes: "The power of the myth lies precisely in making the male principles retrace their steps and communicate with female principles for the overall good of the world" (viii).

11. For a fascinating account of this process in Latin America, see George Reid Andrews, *Afro-Latin America, 1800–2000* (2004).

12. In his *Brazilian Narrative Traditions in a Comparative Context*, Earl E. Fitz writes that Parente Cunha writes firmly in the tradition of Clarice Lispector by "allowing the act of masturbation to function subversively as a sign of female empowerment and self-realization" (146).

13. In the *Dicionário de cultos afro-brasileiros*, Oxum is characterized as a

"deusa-menina, faceira [goddess-girl, charming]" (213). Here, then, "eu" once again recalls her guiding entity.

14. These critics include Cristina Sáenz de Tejada in her book-length study; Elizabeth Ann Stoebner; and Joanne Gass.

15. There is a growing body of critical study regarding the representation of madness in literature, though it remains primarily concerned with works from the Western canon. Among representative works are Liliane Feder's *Madness in Literature* (Princeton: Princeton University Press, 1983); *Dionysius in Literature: Essays on Literary Madness* (Madison, WI: Popular Press, 1994) edited by Branimir M. Rieger; *Revels in Madness: Insanity in Medicine and Literature* by Allen Thiher (Ann Arbor: University of Michigan Press, 2004); and *Madness in Post-1945 British and American Fiction* (London: Palgrave, 2010) by Paul Crawford, Charley Baker, Ronald Carter, Brian Brown, and Maurice Lipsedge.

16. For the now-canonical study of this topic, see Michel Foucault's *Folie et déraison: Histoire de la folie à l'âge classique* (1961), translated as *Madness and Civilization: A History of Insanity in the Age of Reason* (1964 abridged/ 2006).

17. I use Carolyn Richardson Durham's translations of these poems, as she was the translator that worked with Miriam Alves to produce *Enfim . . . Nós*.

18. Of all the African diasporic religions to survive the Middle Passage, *Candomblé Nagô* practiced in Salvador da Bahia resembles most closely traditional Yoruba religion found in Nigeria. This is undoubtedly due to the continued transport of enslaved Africans well into the nineteenth century in the face of the official end of this trade in Brazil in 1831.

19. The *quilombos* were communities created by escaped enslaved Africans and their descendants in colonial Brazil, the most famous one being Palmares, created in 1605 and destroyed by the Portuguese almost nine decades later in 1694. In Afro-Brazilian literature and culture they signify resistance to and defiance of the hegemonic culture that continues to marginalize them. The writing collective based out of São Paulo known as Quilombhoje, for example, know their writings as the means by which they challenge the dominant culture's insistence of racial democracy. For a history of *quilombos* and slave resistance, see Kim D. Butler, João José Reis, and Stuart Schwartz; for a review of

the use of the *quilombo* in Brazilian literature, see Niyi Afolabi, Márcio Barbosa, and Esmeralda Ribeiro, eds., *A Mente Afro-Brasileira: Crítica Literária e Cultural Afro-Brasileira Contemporânea (The Afro-Brazilian Mind: Contemporary Afro-Brazilian Literary and Cultural Criticism)* (2007).

20. In *Enfim* . . . , the translator repeats "sacrifique" in the English translation; in any case, this is the imperative form of *sacrificar,* and so I have chosen to modify the poem by including this translation.

21. The narrator notes: "Há tempos e tempos, quando os negros ganharam aquelas terras, pensaram que estivessem ganhando a verdadeira alforria. Engano. Em muito pouca coisa a situação de antes diferia da do momento. . . . Todos, ainda, sob o jugo de um poder que, como Deus, se fazia eterno [For years and years, when the blacks gained those lands, they believed they were gaining true emancipation. Lie. There was little difference between the current situation and the past. . . . Still, they were all under the yoke of a power that, like God, had become eternal]" (47–48). All English translations are my own.

22. The Free Womb laws were a series of laws enacted across Spanish America beginning in the early part of the nineteenth century in those territories seeking independence from Spain; they were meant to ensure the continuance of slavery under the guise of liberalism. Passed in Brazil in 1871, the Lei do Ventre Livre (or Lei Rio Branco after the politician who led its passage) freed children born to enslaved mothers; the masters of these women could require that the children work until the age of twenty-one, whereupon they were freed, or they could turn the children over to the government. See Reid Andrews, *Afro-Latin America, 1800–2000.*

23. For a history of slavery and abolition in Brazil, see Kim D. Butler, Edison Carneiro, Kátia M. DeQueirós Mattoso, Stuart Schwartz, and Emilia Viotta da Costa.

24. In *Afro-Latin America, 1800–2000,* George Reid Andrews writes: "Though there were tendencies for slaves from given regions of Africa to be concentrated in certain parts of the colonies, nowhere in the New World were local African populations ethnically homogeneous. In Rio de Janeiro, directly connected by transatlantic trade routes to Congo and Angola, and probably the largest urban concentration of Bantu-speaking slaves anywhere in the Americas, a sizeable

minority—approximately one quarter—of the city's Africans were from Mozambique, and another 5 to 7 percent were from West Africa. The Bahian capital of Salvador, a long-standing trading partner of West Africa, was the reverse: three-quarters West African and one-quarter Congo and Angolan" (20). The name of Ponciá's brother, Luandi, recalls the capital of Angola, Luanda.

≥ * ≤

Works Cited

Acosta-Belén, Edna. "Beyond Island Boundaries: Ethnicity, Gender, and Cultural Revitalization in Nuyorican Literature." *Callaloo* 15:4 (1992): 979–98.

Afolabi, Niyi, Márcio Barbosa, and Esmeralda Ribeiro, eds. *A Mente Afro-Brasileira: Crítica Literária e Cultural Afro-Brasileira Contemporânea / The Afro-Brazilian Mind: Contemporary Afro-Brazilian Literary and Cultural Criticism.* Trenton, NJ: Africa World Press, 2007.

Alcaide Ramírez, Dolores. "'I'm Hispanic, not Black': Raza, locura y violencia en *Geographies of Home* de Loida Maritza Pérez." *Ciberletras* 14 (2005): n.p.

Alcantud Ramón, María Dolores. "Nancy Morejón: poeta vital, mujer comprometida con la realidad." Interview. Web. May 14, 2000.

Algarín, Miguel, and Miguel Piñero, eds. *Nuyorican Poetry: An Anthology of Puerto Rican Words and Feelings.* New York: Morrow, 1975.

Algarín, Miguel. "Nuyorican Literature." *MELUS Journal* 8:2 (1981): 89–92.

Allen, Robert. "Past Due: The African American Quest for Reparations." *African Americans in the U.S. Economy.* Ed. Cecilia Conrad. Lanham, MD: Rowman and Littlefield, 2005. 319–26.

Alves, Miriam, and Maria Helena Lima, eds. *Women Righting: Afro-Brazilian Women's Short Fiction / Mulheres Escrevendo: Uma Antologia Bilingüe de Escritoras Afro-Brasileiras Contemporâneas.* London: Mango, 2005.

———, and Carolyn Richardson Durham, eds. *Enfim . . . Nós / Finally . . . Us. Escritoras Negras Brasileiras Contemporâneas / Contemporary Black*

Brazilian Women Writers. Boulder: Three Continents and Lynne Rienner Publishers, 1994.

Andrews, George Reid. *Afro-Latin America, 1800–2000*. New York: Oxford UP, 2004.

Anzaldúa, Gloria. *Borderlands / La frontera: The New Mestiza*. San Francisco: Aunt Lute, 1987.

Ayorinde, Christine. *Afro-Cuban Religiosity, Revolution, and National Identity*. Gainesville: UP of Florida, 2004.

Ayuso, Mónica G. "Toward the Canonization of Loida Maritza Pérez's *Geographies of Home*." *PALARA: Publication of Afro-Latin American Research Association* 8 (2004): 20–26.

Bádéjo, Deidre L. "African Feminism: Mythical and Social Power of Women of African Descent." *Research in African Literatures* 29:2 (1998): 94–111.

———. *Òsun Sèègesi: The Elegant Deity of Wealth, Power, and Femininity*. Trenton, NJ: Africa World Press, 1996.

Badiane, Mamadou. *The Changing Face of Afro-Caribbean Cultural Identity: Negrismo and Négritude*. New York: Lexington, 2010.

Ball, M. Charlene. "Old Magic and New Fury: The Theaphany of Afrekete in Audre Lorde's 'Tar Beach.'" *NWSA Journal* 13:1 (2001): 61–85.

Barbosa, Márcio. "From the Private Space to the Quilombo: Quilombhoje as a Brazilian Cultural Movement." *The Afro-Brazilian Mind: Contemporary Afro-Brazilian Literary and Cultural Criticism / A Mente Afro-Brasileira: Crítica Literaria e Cultural Afro-Brasileira Contemporânea*. Ed. Niyi Afolabi, Márcio Barbosa, and Esmeralda Ribeiro. Trenton, NJ: Africa World Press, 2007. 67–74.

Beard, Laura J. "The Mirrored Self: Helena Parente Cunha's *Mulher no Espelho*." *College Literature* 22:1 (Feb 1995): 103–18.

Behar, Ruth, and Lucía Suárez. "Two Conversations with Nancy Morejón." *Michigan Quarterly Review* 33:3 "Bridges to Cuba Vol. 1" (1994): 625–35.

Bellegarde-Smith, Patrick. *Fragments of Bone: Neo-African Religions in a New World*. Chicago: U of Chicago P, 2005.

Branche, Jerome. *Colonialism and Race in Luso-Hispanic Literature*. Columbia: U of Missouri P, 2006.

Butler, Kim D. *Freedoms Given, Freedoms Won: Afro-Brazilians in Post-Abolition São Paulo and Salvador*. New Brunswick, NJ: Rutgers UP, 1998.

Cacciatore, Olga. *Dicionário dos cultos afro-brasileiros*. 3rd ed. Rio de Janeiro: Forense Universitaria, 1977.

Calvo Peña, Beatriz. "Entre la memoria y el deseo: Daína Chaviano y la creación de *puentes de encuentro* cubanos." *Guayaba Sweet: literatura cubana en los Estados Unidos*. Cádiz, Spain: Aduana Vieja, 2003. 331–49.

Campbell, Kirsten. *Jacques Lacan and Feminist Epistemology*. New York: Routledge, 2004.

Carneiro, Edison. *Antologia do Negro Brasileiro*. 1950. Rio de Janeiro: Agir, 2005.

Chancy, Myriam J. A. *From Sugar to Revolution: Women's Visions of Haiti, Cuba, and the Dominican Republic*. Waterloo, Ont.: Wilfrid Laurier UP, 2012.

Chaves Tesser, Carmen. "Post-Structuralist Theory Mirrored in Helena Parente Cunha's *Woman between Mirrors*." *Hispania* 74:3 (Sept. 1991): 594–97.

Chaviano, Daína. *Casa de juegos*. Barcelona: Planeta, 1999.

Chinosole. "Audre Lorde and Matrilineal Diaspora: 'Moving history beyond nightmare into structures for the future . . . '" *Wild Women in the Whirlwind: Afra-American Culture and the Contemporary Literary Renaissance*. Ed. Joanne M. Braxton and Andrée Nicola McLaughlin. New Brunswick, NJ: Rutgers UP, 1990. 379–94.

Cixous, Hélène. "The Laugh of the Medusa." 1975. *Feminisms: An Anthology of Literary Theory and Criticism*. Ed. Robyn R. Warhol and Diane Price Herndl. New Brunswick, NJ: Rutgers UP, 1997. 347–62.

Clarke, Cheryl. *"After Mecca": Women Poets and the Black Arts Movement*. New Brunswick, NJ: Rutgers UP, 2005.

Coelho, Paulo, Filho. "Truth Commission in Brazil: Individualizing Amnesty, Revealing the Truth." *The Yale Review of International Studies* (2012): n.p.

Cole, Sally. "Ruth Landes in Brazil: Writing, Race, and Gender in 1930s American Anthropology." Introduction. *The City of Women*. By Ruth Landes. Albuquerque: U of New Mexico P, 1994. vii–xxxiv.

Collins, Patricia Hill. *Black Feminist Thought. Knowledge, Consciousness, and the Politics of Empowerment*. 2nd ed. New York: Routledge, 2000.

Cuervo Hewitt, Julia. *Voices out of Africa in Twentieth-Century Spanish Caribbean Literature*. Lewisburg, PA: Bucknell UP, 2009.

———. *Aché: presencia africana. Tradiciones yoruba-lucumí en la narrativa cubana*. New York: Peter Lang, 1988.

Cunnigen, Donald. "Bringing the Revolution Down Home: The Republic of New Africa in Mississippi." *Sociological Spectrum* 19:1 (1999): 63–92.

Daniel, Yvonne. *Dancing Wisdom: Embodied Knowledge in Haitian Vodoun, Cuban Yoruba, and Bahian Candomblé*. Chicago: U of Illinois P, 2005.

Davies, Carole Boyce. *Black Women, Writing and Identity: Migrations of the Subject*. New York and London: Routledge, 1994.

Davies, Catherine. *A Place in the Sun? Women Writers in Twentieth-Century Cuba*. London: Zed, 1998.

Dayan, Joan. "Erzulie: A Woman's History of Haiti." *Research in African Literatures*. 24:2 (1994): 5–31.

DeCosta-Willis, Miriam. "Sandra María Esteves's Nuyorican Poetics: The Signifying Difference." *Afro-Hispanic Review* 23:2 (2004): 3–12.

———. "An Aesthetic of Women's Art in Nancy Morejón's 'Ana Mendieta.'" *Daughters of the Diaspora: Afra-Hispanic Writers*. Ed. Miriam DeCosta-Willis. Miami: Ian Randle, 2003. 240–48.

———. "Meditations on History: The Middle Passage in the Afro-Hispanic Literary Imagination." *Afro-Hispanic Review* 22:1 (2003): 3–12.

———. "Orishas Circling Her House: Race as (Con)Text in Morejón's Poetic Discourse." *Singular like a Bird: The Art of Nancy Morejón*. Ed. Miriam DeCosta-Willis. Washington, DC: Howard UP, 1999. 277–96.

Degler, Carl N. *Neither Black nor White: Slavery and Race Relations in Brazil and the United States*. 1971. New York: Macmillan, 1986.

De la Fuente, Alejandro. *A Nation for All: Race, Inequality, and Politics in Twentieth Century Cuba*. Chapel Hill: U of North Carolina P, 2000.

De Queiros Mattoso, Kátia M. *To Be a Slave in Brazil, 1550–1888*. Trans. Arthur Goldhammer. New Brunswick, NJ: Rutgers UP, 1987.

———. *Ser Escravo no Brasil*. São Paulo: Brasiliense, 1982.

De Veaux, Alexis. *Warrior Poet: A Biography of Audre Lorde*. New York: Norton, 2004.

Dias, Ângela Maria. "Longe do Paraiso: *Jazz*, de Toni Morrison, e *Ponciá Vicêncio*, de Conceição Evaristo." *Estudos de Literatura Brasileira Contemporânea* 32 (2008): 173–85.

Di Iorio Sandín, Lyn. *Killing Spanish: Literary Essays on Ambivalent U.S. Latino/a Identity*. New York: Palgrave, 2004.

Duke, Dawn. *Literary Passion and Ideological Commitment: Toward a Legacy of Afro-Cuban and Afro-Brazilian Women Writers*. Lewisburg, PA: Bucknell UP, 2008.

Dupré, Louis. *The Enlightenment and the Intellectual Foundations of Modern Culture*. New Haven: Yale UP, 2004.

Eakin, Marshall. *Brazil: The Once and Future Country*. New York: St. Martin's Griffin, 1997.

Elder, Arlene. "*Sassafrass, Cypress, and Indigo*: Ntozake Shange's Neo-Slave/Blues Narrative." *African American Review* 26:1 (1992): 99–107.

Enck-Wanzer, Darrel. *The Young Lords: A Reader*. New York: New York UP, 2010.

Esteves, Sandra Maria. *Bluestown Mockingbird Mambo*. Houston: Arte Público, 1990.

———. *Tropical Rains: A Bilingual Downpour*. The Bronx: African Caribbean Poetry Theater, 1984.

———. *Yerbabuena*. Greenfield, NY: Greenfield Review Press, 1980.

Evans, Mari, ed. *Black Women Writers 1950–1980*. Garden City, NY: Anchor Doubleday, 1984.

Evaristo, Conceição. *Ponciá Vicencio*. Trans. Paloma Martínez-Cruz. Austin: Host, 2007.

———. *Ponciá Vicêncio*. Belo Horizonte: Mazza Edições, 2003.

Feracho, Leslie. "Arrivals and Farewells: The Dynamics of Cuban Homespace through African Mythology in Two Eleggua Poems by Nancy Morejón." *Hispania* 83:1 (2000) 51–58.

Ferreira-Pinto, Cristina. *Gender, Discourse, and Desire in Twentieth-Century Brazilian Women's Literature*. West Lafayette, IN: Purdue UP, 2004.

Fernández Olmos, Margarite. "El erotismo revolucionario de las poetas cubanas." *Explicación de textos literarios*. 24:1/2 (1995): 137–48.

———, Margarite and Lizabeth Paravisini-Gebert. *Creole Religions of the Caribbean: An Introduction from Vodou and Santería to Obeah and Espiritismo*. 2nd ed. New York: New York UP, 2011.

———. *El placer de la palabra: literatura erótica femenina de América Latina*. Barcelona: Planeta, 1991.

Fitz, Earl E. *Brazilian Narrative Traditions in a Comparative Context*. New York: MLA, 2005.

Flores, Juan. *From Bomba to Hip Hop: Puerto Rican Culture and Latino Identity*. New York: Columbia UP, 2000.

———. "Memorias (En lenguas) rotas / Broken English Memories" *Revista de Crítica Literaria Latinoamericana* 23:45 (1997): 341–50.

———. *Divided Borders: Essays on Puerto Rican Identity*. Houston: Arte Público Press, 1992.

Foner, Philip S., ed. *The Black Panthers Speak*. New York, Da Capo, 2002.

Foucault, Michel. *The History of Sexuality: An Introduction.* Vol. 1. 1978. Trans. Robert Hurley. New York: Vintage-Random House, 1990.

Fox, Patricia D. *Being and Blackness in Latin America: Uprootedness and Improvisation.* Gainesville: UP of Florida, 2006.

Gallop, Jane. "Impertinent Questions: Irigaray, Sade, Lacan." *SubStance* 9:1 (1980): 57–67.

Gass, Joanne. "Where Am I? Who Am I? The Problem of Location and Recognition in Helena Parente Cunha's *Woman between Mirrors.*" *Studies in Twentieth and Twenty-First Century Literature* 29:1 (Winter 2005): 63–78.

Gates, Henry Louis Jr. *The Signifying Monkey: A Theory of Afro-American Literary Criticism.* New York: Oxford UP, 1989.

Gebara, Ivone, and Maria Clara Lucchetti Bingemer. *As incômodas filhas de Eva na Igreja da América Latina.* São Paulo: Edições Paulinas, 1989.

———. *A Mulher Faz Teologia.* Rio de Janeiro: Editora Vozes, 1986.

George, Courtney. "The Woman's Note: Reclaiming African American Musical History and Community in Ntozake Shange's *Sassafrass, Cypress, and Indigo.*" *Interdisciplinary Humanities* 23:2 (1996): 27–38.

Godsland, Shelley. *Writing Reflection, Reflecting on Writing. Female Identity and Lacan's Mirror in Helena Parente Cunha and Sylvia Molloy.* Valladolid: Universitas Castellae, 2006.

Grosz, Elizabeth. *Jacques Lacan: A Feminist Introduction.* New York: Routledge, 1990.

Gutiérrez, Maricela A. "Nancy Morejón's Avenging Resistance in 'Black Woman' and 'I Love My Master': Examples of a Black Slave Woman's Path to Freedom." *Singular like a Bird: The Art of Nancy Morejón.* Ed. Miriam DeCosta-Willis. Washington, DC: Howard UP, 1999. 209–19.

Hale, Thomas J. *Griots and Griottes: Masters of Words and Music.* Bloomington: Indiana UP, 1998.

Hall, Stuart. "Cultural Identity and Diaspora." *Identity: Community, Culture, Difference.* Ed. Jonathan Rutherford. London: Lawrence and Wishart, 1990. 222–37.

Hampton, Janet Jones. "The Subversion of the Concept of 'Home' in Loida Maritza Pérez's *Geographies of Home.*" *PALARA: Publication of Afro-Latin American Research Association* 9 (2005): 34–41.

Hanchard, Michael. *Orpheus and Power: The Movimento Negro of Rio de Janeiro and São Paulo, Brazil, 1945–1988*. Princeton: Princeton UP, 1994.

Hardin, Michael. "Dissolving the Reader/Author Binary: Sylvia Molloy's *Certificate of Absence*, Helena Parente Cunha's *Woman between Mirrors*, and Jeanette Winterson's *Written on the Body*." *International Fiction Review* 29:1–2 (2002): 84–96.

Howe, Linda S. *Transgression and Conformity: Cuban Writers and Artists after the Revolution*. Madison: U of Wisconsin P, 2004.

———. "Nancy Morejón's Womanism." *Singular like a Bird: The Art of Nancy Morejón*. Ed. Miriam DeCosta-Willis. Washington, DC: Howard UP, 1999. 153–68.

Hucks, Tracey E. *Yoruba Traditions and African American Religious Nationalism*. Albuquerque: U of New Mexico P, 2012.

———. "From Cuban Santería to African Yorùbá: Evolutions in African American Òrìṣà History, 1959–1970." *Òrìṣà Devotion as World Religion: The Globalization of Yorùbá Religious Culture*. Ed. Jacob Kẹhinde Olupona and Terry Rey. Madison: U of Wisconsin P, 2008. 337–54.

Hull, Gloria T. "Living on the Line: Audre Lorde and *Our Dead Behind Us*." *Changing Our Own Words: Essays on Criticism, Theory, and Writing by Black Women*. Ed. Cheryl A. Wall. New Brunswick, NJ: Rutgers UP, 1989. 150–72.

Isfahani-Hammond, Alexandra. *White Negritude: Race, Writing, and Brazilian Cultural Identity*. New York: Palgrave, 2008.

Jackson, Richard L. *The Black Image in Latin American Literature*. Albuquerque: U of New Mexico P, 1976.

Jennings, LaVinia Delois. *Toni Morrison and the Idea of Africa*. New York: Cambridge UP, 2008.

Keating, AnnLouise. "'Our Shattered Myths Whole': The Black Goddess and Audre Lorde's Revision of Patriarchal Myth." *Frontiers: A Journal of Women Studies* 13:1 (1992): 20–33.

Kevane, Bridget. *Profane and Sacred: Latino/a American Writers Reveal the Interplay of the Secular and the Religious*. New York: Rowman and Littlefield, 2008.

Kristeva, Julia. *Powers of Horror: An Essay on Abjection*. Trans. Leon S. Roudiez. New York: Columbia UP, 1982.

Kutzinski, Vera. *Sugar's Secrets: Race and the Erotics of Cuban Nationalism*. Charlottesville: U of Virginia P, 1993.

Landes, Ruth. *The City of Women*. 2nd ed. Albuquerque: U of New Mexico P, 1994.

Leonard, Suzanne. "Dreaming as Cultural Work in *Donald Duk* and *Dreaming in Cuban*." *MELUS* 29:2 (2004) 181–203.

Lindstrom, Naomi. "Narrative Experiment and Social Statement: Helena Parente Cunha." *Luso-Brazilian Review* 33:1 (1991): 141–50.

Lockhart, Melissa Fitch. "Erotic Subversions in Helena Parente Cunha's 'Mulher no Espelho.'" *Chasqui: Revista de literatura latinoamericana* 27:1 (1998): 3–10.

Lombardi, Carlos. *Os Orixás*. São Paulo: Editora Três, 1991.

Lopes, Nei. *Enciclopédia brasileira da diáspora africana*. São Paulo: Selo Negro, 2004.

Lorde, Audre. *Undersong: Chosen Poems Old and New*. New York: Norton, 1992.

———. "Uses of the Erotic: The Erotic as Power." *Sister Outsider*. New York: Norton, 1984. 53–59.

———. "An Open Letter to Mary Daly." *Sister Outsider: Essays and Speeches*. New York: Crossing Press, 1984. 66–71.

———. "An Interview: Audre Lorde and Adrienne Rich." *Sister Outsider: Essays and Speeches*. New York: Norton, 1984. 81–109.

———. "My Words Will Be There." *Black Women Writers 1950–1980*. Ed. Mari Evans. Garden City, NY: Anchor Doubleday, 1984. 261–68.

———. *The Black Unicorn*. New York: Norton, 1978.

Luis, William. "Race, Poetry, and Revolution in the Works of Nancy Morejón." *Singular like a Bird: The Art of Nancy Morejón*. Ed. Miriam DeCosta-Willis. Washington, DC: Howard UP, 1999. 45–67.

———. *Dance between Two Cultures: Latino Caribbean Literature Written in the United States*. Nashville: Vanderbilt UP, 1997.

Machado Sáez, Elena, and Raphael Dalleo. *The Latino/a Canon and the Emergence of Post-Sixties Literature*. New York: Palgrave Macmillan, 2007.

Maines, Rachel P. *The Technology of Orgasm: "Hysteria," the Vibrator, and Women's Sexual Satisfaction*. Baltimore: Johns Hopkins UP, 1999.

Maloof, Judy, and Nancy Morejón. "Nancy Morejón." *Hispamérica* 25:73 (1996): 47–58.

Martin, Joan. "The Unicorn is Black: Audre Lorde in Retrospect." *Black Women Writers 1950–1980*. Ed. Mari Evans. Garden City, NY: Anchor Doubleday, 1984. 277–91.

Marting, Diane E. *The Sexual Woman in Latin American Literature: Dangerous Desires.* Gainesville: UP of Florida, 1993.

Mason, John. *Orin Òrìṣà: Songs for Selected Heads.* Brooklyn: Yoruba Theological Archminstry, 1997.

Matibag, Eugenio. *Afro-Cuban Religious Experience: Cultural Reflections in Narrative.* Gainesville: UP of Florida, 1996.

McKinley, Catherine E. *Indigo: In Search of the Color that Seduced the World.* New York: Bloomsbury, 2011.

Méndez, Susan Carol. "Geographies of spirit: Locating an Afro-Latina/o Diasporic Space in United States Latina/o Literary Studies." PhD diss. University of California-Riverside, 2005.

Méndez-Rodenas, Adriana, "Engendering the Nation: The Mother/Daughter Plot in Cuban-American Fiction." *Cuban-American Literature and Art: Negotiating Identities.* Ed. Isabel Alvarez Borland and Lynette M. F. Bosch. Albany: State U of New York P, 2009. 47–60.

Miller, Mary Grace. "Transculture, Terror, and the Language of 'Love' in Nancy Morejón's 'Amo a Mi Amo.' *Chasqui: revista de literatura latinoamericana* 32:2 (2003): 3–16.

Morejón, Nancy. *Where the Island Sleeps Like a Wing.* Trans. Kathleen Weaver. San Francisco: Black Scholar Press, 1985.

———, and David Frye. "Cuba and Its Deep Africanity." *Callaloo* 28:4 (2005): 933–51.

Morris, Ann R., and Margaret M. Dunn, "'The Bloodstream of Our Inheritance': Female Identity and the Caribbean Mothers'-Land," *Motherlands: Black Women's Writing from Africa, the Caribbean and South Asia.* Ed. Susheila Nasta. New Brunswick, NJ: Rutgers UP, 1992. 219–37.

Morris, Margaret Kissam. "Audre Lorde: Textual Authority and the Embodied Self." *Frontiers: A Journal of Women's Studies.* 23:1 (2002): 168–87.

Morrison, Toni. "Rootedness: The Ancestor as Foundation." 1984. *Toni Morrison: What Moves at the Margins: Selected Nonfiction.* Ed. Carolyn C. Denard. Jackson, MS: UP of Mississippi, 2008. 56–64.

Munn, Mark. *The Mother of the Gods, Athens and the Tyranny of Asia: A Study of Sovereignty in Ancient Religion.* Berkeley: University of California Press, 2006.

Mujcinovic, Fatima. "Multiple Articulations of Exile in US Latina

Literature: Confronting Exile Absence and Trauma." *Speech and Silence: Ethnic Women Writers*. Spec. issue of *MELUS* 28:4 (2003): 167–86.

Murphy, Joseph M. and Mei-Mei Sanford, eds. *Òsun across the Waters: A Yoruba Goddess in Africa and the Americas*. Bloomington: Indiana UP, 2001.

Nascimento, Abdias do. *Brazil, Mixture or Massacre? Essays in the Genocide of a Black People*. 1979. Dover, MA: Majority Press, 1989.

Olajubu, Oyeronke. *Women in the Yoruba Sphere*. Albany: State U of New York P, 2003.

Oliveira, Emanuelle. *Writing Identity: The Politics of Contemporary Afro-Brazilian Literature*. West Lafayette, IN: Purdue UP, 2008.

Olupona, Jacob Kehinde. Foreword. *Women in the Yoruba Sphere*. Oyeronke Olajubu. Albany: State U of New York P, 2003. vii–x.

———, and Terry Rey, eds. *Òrìṣà Devotion as World Religion: The Globalization of Yorùbá Religious Culture*. Madison: U of Wisconsin P, 2008.

Ongiri, Amy Abugo. *Spectacular Blackness: The Cultural Politics of the Black Power Movement and the Search for a Black Aesthetic*. Charlottesville: U of Virgina P, 2010.

O'Reilly Herrera, Andrea. "Women and the Revolution in Cristina García's 'Dreaming in Cuban.'" *Modern Language Studies* 27:3/4 (1997): 69–91.

Oyěwùmí, Oyèrónké. *The Invention of Women: Making an African Sense of Western Gender Discourses*. Minneapolis: U of Minnesota P, 1997.

Palmer, Cynthia L. "Discursos espirituales contrahegemónicos y resistencia femenina en *Geographies of Home* de Loida Maritza Perez." *ALPHA: Revista de Artes, Letras y Filosofia* 23 (2006): 283–90. *MLA International Bibliography*. Web. Jan. 17, 2011. n.p.

Parente Cunha, Helena. "A Mulher partida: a busca do verdadeiro rosto na miragem dos espelhos." *Entre Resistir e Identificar-se: Para uma teoria da prática da narrativa brasileira de autoria feminina*. Ed. Peggy Sharpe. Florianópolis: Editora Mulheres; Goiania: Editora da UFG: 1997. 107–37.

———. *Mulher no Espelho*. 1983. Rio de Janeiro: Tempo Brasileiro, 2003.

Pereira Schmidt, Simone. "Casa, Canela, Bala e Favela." *Revista Estudos Feministas* 17:3 (2009): 799–817.

———. "De volta pra casa ou o caminho sem volta em duas narrativas do Brasil." *Estudos de Literatura Brasileira Contemporânea* 32 (2008): 21–30.

Pérez, Emma. *The Decolonial Imaginary: Writing Chicanas into History*. Bloomington: Indiana UP, 2008.

Pérez, Janet. "The Island, the Mainland and Beyond: Literary Space in Puerto Rican Women's Poetry." *Presencia y ausencia de la mujer en las letras hispánicas.* Spec. issue of *Revista Canadiense de Estudios Hispánicos* 14:3 (1990): 473–94.

Pérez, Louis A. Jr. *Cuba: Between Reform and Revolution.* New York: Oxford UP, 1995.

Provost, Kara, and Audre Lorde. "Afrekete: The Trickster in the Work of Audre Lorde." *Maskers and Tricksters.* Spec. Issue of *MELUS* 20:4 (1995): 45–59.

Reis, João José. *Slave Rebellion in Brazil: The 1835 Muslim Uprising in Bahia.* Baltimore: The Johns Hopkins UP, 1995.

———. *Rebelião Escrava no Brasil: A história do levante dos Malês em 1835.* São Paulo: Brasiliense, 1986.

Reisner, Gerhild. "Introduction: Restlessness and Identity, Writing and Self." *Daughters of Restlessness: Women's Literature at the End of the Millennium.* Ed. Sabine Coelsch-Foster, Hannah Wallinger, and Gerhild Reisner. Heidelberg: Universitätsverlag C. Winter, 1998. 217–25.

Rivero, Eliana. "Writing in Cuban, Living as Other: Cuban American Women Writers Getting It Right." *Cuban-American Literature and Art: Negotiating Identities.* Ed. Isabel Alvarez Borland and Lynette M. F. Bosch. Albany: State U of New York P, 2009. 109–25.

Román, Reinaldo L. *Governing Spirits: Religion, Miracles, and Spectacles in Cuba and Puerto Rico, 1898–1956.* Chapel Hill: U of North Carolina P, 2007.

Romero, Channette. *Activism and the American Novel: Religion and Resistance in Fiction by Women of Color.* Charlottesville: U of Virginia P, 2012.

Rowell, Charles H, and Audre Lorde. "Above the Wind: An Interview with Audre Lorde." *Gay, Lesbian, Bisexual, Transgender: Literature and Culture.* Special Issue of *Callaloo* 23:1 (2000): 52–63.

Rudolph, Amanda M. "Images of African Traditional Religions and Christianity in *Joe Turner's Come and Gone* and *The Piano Lesson.*" *Journal of Black Studies* 33: 5 (2003), 562–75.

Sáenz de Tejada, Cristina. "Representaciones de la negritude brasileña en *Mulher no Espelho* y *As Mulheres de Tijucopapo.*" *Afro-Hispanic Review* 16:1 (Spring 1997): 47–52.

———. *La (re)construcción de la identidad femenina en la narrative autobiográfica latinoamericana, 1975–1985.* New York: Peter Lang, 1998.

Safi-Eddine, Khadija. "*Woman between Mirrors*: Writing the Self." *Modern Language Studies* 24:2 (Spring 1994): 48–56.

Sánchez González, Lisa. *Boricua Literature: A Literary History of the Puerto Rican Diaspora*. New York: New York UP, 2001.

Sandoval, Alberto. "Mira, que vienen los nuyoricans!: El temor de la otredad en la literatura nacionalista puertorriqueña." *Revista de Crítica Literaria Latinoamericana* 23:45 (1997): 307–25.

San Martín-Moreno, Araceli, and José Luis Muñoz de Baena Simón. "La Habana real y la Habana imaginada." *Aves de paso: autores latinoamericanos entre exilio y transculturación*. Madrid: Frankfurt: Iberoamericana-Vervuert, 2005. 219–25.

Schwartz, Stuart. *Slaves, Peasants, and Rebels: Reconsidering Brazilian Slavery*. Champaign: U of Illinois P, 1997.

Shange, Ntozake. *Sassafrass, Cypress & Indigo*. New York: St. Martin's, 1982.

Skidmore, Thomas. *Black into White: Race and Nationality in Brazilian Thought*. New York: Oxford UP, 1974.

Smethurst, James Edward. *The Black Arts Movement: Literary Nationalism in the 1960s and 1970s*. Chapel Hill and London: U of North Carolina P, 2005.

Somerlate Barbosa, Maria José. "*Espaçamento* como registro cultural na obra de Helena Parente Cunha." *Entre Resistir e Identificar-se: Para uma teoria da prática da narrativa brasileira de autoria femenina*. Ed. Peggy Sharpe. Florianópolis: Editora Mulheres; Goiania: Editora da UFG, 1997. 139–52.

Stefanko, Jaqueline. "New Ways of Telling: Latinas' Narratives of Exile and Return." *Frontiers: A Journal of Women's Studies* 17:2 (1996): 50–69.

Stevens, Evelyn P. "*Marianismo*: The Other Face of *Machismo* in Latin America." *Female and Male in Latin America*. Ed. Ann Pescatelo. Pittsburgh: U of Pittsburgh P, 1973.

Stoebner, Elizabeth Ann. "At the Crossroads of Feminism and Postmodernism: Negotiating the Space of Self and Other in Two Latin American Women's Novels. MA thesis. University of Texas at Austin, 1989.

Suárez, Lucía M. *The Tears of Hispaniola: Haitian and Dominican Diaspora Memory*. Gainesville: UP of Florida, 2006.

Szoka, Elizbieta. *Fourteen Female Voices from Brazil: Interviews and Works*. Austin: Host, 2002.

Thompson, Robert Farris. *Flash of the Spirit: African and Afro-American Art and Philosophy*. New York: Vintage, 1984.

Tillis, Antonio D., ed. *Critical Perspectives on Afro-Latin American Literature*. New York and London: Routledge, 2012.

Tirado Bramen, Carrie. "Translating Exile: The Metamorphosis of the Ordinary in Dominican Short Fiction." *Latin American Literary Review* 26:51 (1998) 63–78.

Tishken, Joel, Tóyìn Fálolá, and Akíntúndé Akínyemí, eds. *Şàngó in Africa and the African Diaspora*. Bloomington and Indianapolis: Indiana UP, 2009.

Torres-Saillant, Silvio. "La literatura dominicana en los Estados Unidos y la periferia del margen." *Cuadernos de Poética* VII:21 (1993): 7–26.

Vadillo, Alicia E. *Santería y vudú; sexualidad y homoerotismo. Caminos que se cruzan sobre literatura cubana contemporánea*. Madrid: Biblioteca Nueva, 2001.

Valdés, Vanessa K. "Afro-Brazilian Literature, from the Periphery to the Center." *The Future Is Now: A New Look at African Diaspora Studies*. Ed. Vanessa K. Valdés. Newcastle upon Tyne: Cambridge Scholars Publishers, 2012. 107–30.

———. "'there is no incongruence here': Hispanic Notes in the Works of Ntozake Shange." *CLA Journal* 53:2 (2009): 131–44.

———. "The Voice of Oxum: *Mulher no Espelho* (1983)." *PALARA* 13 (Fall 2009): 102–12.

Vernant, Jean Pierre. *El universo, los dioses, los hombres: El relato de los mitos griegos*. Trans. Joaquín Jordá. Barcelona: Anagrama, 2000.

Viotti da Costa, Emilia. *The Brazilian Empire: Myths and Histories*. 1985. Chapel Hill: U of North Carolina P, 2000.

Wallerstein, Nicholas. "Audre Lorde and the Poetics of African Spirituality in *The Black Unicorn*." *MAWA Review* 14:2 (1999): 65–75.

Washington, Theresa N. *Our Mothers, Our Powers, Our Texts: Manifestations of Àjé in Africana Literature*. Bloomington: Indiana UP, 2005.

Weir-Soley, Donna Aza. *Eroticism, Spirituality, and Resistance in Black Women's Writings*. Gainesville: UP of Florida, 2009.

West, Alan. *Tropics of History: Cuba Imagined*. Westport, CT: Bergin and Garvey, 1997.

Williams, Claudette M. *Charcoal and Cinnamon: The Politics of Culture in Spanish Caribbean Literature*. Gainesville: UP of Florida, 2000.

Williams, Lorna V. "The Revolutionary Feminism of Nancy Morejón."

Singular like a Bird: The Art of Nancy Morejón. Ed. Miriam DeCosta-Willis. Washington, DC: Howard UP, 1999. 131–52.

Wilson, Ivette. "Resisting Silence / Silence as Resistance: (Re) Affirming Brazil's African Heritage in Conceição Evaristo's *Ponciá Vicêncio.*" *PALARA: Publication of the Afro-Latin American Research Association* 14 (2010): 54–71.

Young Lords Internet Resource. "Young Lords Party 13-Point Program and Platform." Web. Dec. 4, 2010.

Zahan, Dominique. "Some Reflections on African Spirituality." *African Spirituality: Forms, Meanings, and Expressions.* Ed. Jacob Olupona. New York: Herder and Herder, 2000. 3–25.

Index